The
Anthology
of
American
POETRY

The Anthology of American POETRY

Colonial to Contemporary

HILARY RUSSELL

Wayside Publishing

Consultants:
Richard Lederer
St. Paul's School
David Smith
Milton Academy

ISBN 1-877653-49-7

Contents

part two

Modern American Poetry

Contents   xi

Foreword

An African American saying tells us, "If somebody asks where you goin', tell 'em where you been." We learn who we are and where we are going by discovering who we were and whence we came—and there is no better way to make that connection than through the reading of poems, especially the poems of one's own country. This anthology embraces the saga of poetry in the United States, from the Puritan poet Anne Bradstreet to poets who are creating their poems as they ride the earth with us today.

This is a big book—generous in the number of poets who live in these pages and generous in the number of their poems. With its inclusive selection of men and women of majority and minority and urban and rural backgrounds, these pages travel a ribbon of poetic highway from California to the New York island, from the northern lakes to the Gulf Stream waters, capturing the vastness and variety of people and land in the United States. The span of more than three centuries, the diversity of the poets represented, and the many registers of their music reveal how America gradually found a voice to sing of itself.

The editor, a long-time English teacher, knows that poems do not exist in vacuums. They feed on life, and life feeds on them. On the one hand, a poem is shaped by a unique set of circumstances that is a human life. On the other, a writer lives in a particular political and social context, and literature represents a continuing dialogue between that individual and his or her world. The editor's concise period introductions offer a sense of the intellectual and emotional climates in which the poets live, while the brief biographies catch and crystallize the particular lives that glow from the center of those compact and indestructible diamonds we call poems.

The editor also knows that poetry is more than just a unit in a language arts curriculum and that poetry is something that happens more than one class period a day over an assigned length of time. He knows that poetry is more than a collection of hidden literary devices waiting to be uncovered in an academic treasure hunt. He knows that poetry is more than a sampling of pronouncements by I'll-tell-you-so critics. He knows that questions and exercises can be helpful not so much to test a reader's knowledge of facts but to deepen initial responses and encourage a student to read, think, feel, discuss, and write with an open mind and heart.

Most important, this book reveals that poetry and people are images of each other. The most human of all languages, poetry is the way it is because we are the way we are. In this collection you will come to know some of the greatest poets who have ever used the English language. At the same time, you will discover some things about yourself that you did not know you knew.

Richard Lederer

xiii

Preface

This chronological anthology reveals the gradual development of American poetry from its beginnings in the seventeenth century until the present. Part I, "The Beginnings of American Poetry," illustrates how between 1650 and 1850 our poetry moved toward but never fully realized an authentic American voice. Part II, "Modern American Poetry," after recognizing Walt Whitman and Emily Dickinson as the first truly original and great American poets, shows how the poets of the first half of the twentieth century built an American poetic tradition of revolt and experimentation tempered by an enduring connection to its European roots. Taking the reader from the mid-twentieth century to the present, Part III, "Recent American Poetry," demonstrates that while contemporary poets have continued to experiment with new ways of making poems, the poetic principles of our early modern poets continue to influence American poetry.

Through commentary, questions, and biographical sketches, this book traces recurring themes and forms of American poetry. As well as noting the impact of the European poetic tradition, *The Longman Anthology of American Poetry* describes the influences of oriental poetry, of various American dialects, or our history and culture, and of our land itself—the ground from which our songs, poems, and music have sprung.

More important than realizing historical continuities, however, is understanding each poem's mixture of emotion, image, idea, and music. The questions and commentary will help readers understand how poems make meaning and also how poets make poems. Toward this second purpose readers will sometimes be asked to write a poem that imitates the style of a given poet. We will consider American poetry from the outside, the social and historical forces that influenced it, and from the inside, the craft that has shaped it.

Acknowledgments

I want to thank Berkshire School for giving me the time to write this book. Also I am grateful to my colleagues Arthur Chase, Liz Clifford, Joe McCarthy, Norman Merrill, Sue Montgomery, and John Toffey, who have made valuable suggestions about both focus and content. As well, the following teachers have generously offered ideas for poets and poems to be included: Carol Clark, Crystal Springs Upland School; Laura Conklin, St. Paul's School; William DeVoti, Housatonic Valley Regional High School; Douglas Frickey, Milton Academy; Anne Gerbner and Meg Goldner, Germantown Friends Academy; John Groff, Ethel Walker School; Frank Henry, Deerfield Academy; Rex McGuinn, Phillips Exeter Academy, Tom Scattergood, Germantown Academy; and Barry Sternlieb, Pittsfield, Massachusetts, public schools. For defining words and composing footnotes I have relied primarily upon *The American Heritage Dictionary, The Random House Dictionary,* Skeat's *Etymological Dictionary, The Columbia Encyclopedia,* and *The Encyclopedia Americana.*

Throughout this project David Smith of Milton Academy has offered valuable ideas and insights about the lives and the work of poets and about approaches to particular poems. At the same time, Richard Lederer of St. Paul's School, Concord, New Hampshire, has edited keenly and has enthusiastically supported the concept of devoting an entire text to American poetry. Gifted and experienced teachers as well as lovers of poetry, they have been enormously helpful in aiming the book at the abilities and interests of students.

Hilary Russell

The
Anthology
of
American
POETRY

The Beginnings of American Poetry

On top of a bookshelf in our town library rests a bronze bust of Henry Wadsworth Longfellow. So high is the bookshelf and so small the room that we have to strain our necks to see the poet's long, apparently wind-blown beard, hooked nose, and broad brow. Large, darkly framed portraits of William Cullen Bryant, Ralph Waldo Emerson, and Longfellow hang on three of the walls. And on the fourth is a frame containing individual portraits of Bryant, Emerson, and Longfellow, as well as John Greenleaf Whittier, Oliver Wendell Holmes, and James Russell Lowell. Inscribed on the yellowed mat beneath this row of six hand-painted prints that stare out through their small oval windows are the words "Our Poets."

Romantic vitality, humor, and optimism characterize many of the poems that won these New England men their popular reputations. Most of these poets employed American dialects, subjects, or settings—important steps in the evolution of a truly American poetry.

Our Poets, the bust, and the three large prints used to be in the library's main room, as were similar prints and busts in prominent rooms of libraries and schools across the country. But since World War II the reputations of all these poets, with the exception of Ralph Waldo Emerson's, have declined. Emerson endures because, while other American poets of his day wrote poems celebrating American life, Emerson, influenced by Hindu scripture and other Eastern works, defined and celebrated the spirit that connects all life. In a sense, Emerson's thought is the ultimate extension of America's democratic dream of equality. Now more than a century after his death, as we realize more than ever the need for international cooperation to solve global problems, Emerson's concept of an Over-Soul or a Universal Oneness remains instructive to modern man.

Poetry existed in America long before "Our Poets" and their white forebears arrived, for Native Americans used the evocative power of poetic language in healing, making war, hunting, and most aspects of life. Many of these ancient chants, prayers, and songs have been preserved and have influenced the work of modern poets. But since this text treats the development of American poetry from its European origins, we will consider Anne Bradstreet, who arrived in the Massachusetts Bay Colony in 1630, as the first American poet. Although her work is not distinguished by craft, Bradstreet presents an inspiring portrait of a person undaunted by the hardships of frontier life and devoted to her family and her God. Edward Taylor, who came to Boston from England in 1668 and became a minister in Westfield, Massachusetts, wrote tightly and ingeniously crafted verse in forms clearly influenced by English poets. Taylor's poems, like Bradstreet's, reflect courage and powerful religious devotion. In the eighteenth century, Phillis Wheatley, who was brought to America from Africa as a slave, emerged as another symbol of the poet's determination to write in the face of adversity. Living in the Age of Reason, which is also called the Enlightenment or the neoclassic age, Wheatley wrote poems like "To His Excellency General Washington" that reflect the optimism of the period.

As we trace the development of American poetry from eighteenth-century neoclassicism to nineteenth-century romanticism, Philip Freneau becomes particularly valuable, for his poems exemplify both movements. For instance, "On the Uniformity and Perfection of Nature" reflects the neoclassic idea that nature is organized rationally and, therefore, can be comprehended entirely through the rational process. Unlike Bradstreet and Taylor, Freneau does not depend upon God's mercy. Instead, he believes that "All, nature made, in reason's sight / Is order all, and ALL is right." The God in this poem, after creating a rationally ordered world where there is no natural evil, has stepped aside to let man use his reason to perpetuate goodness. In contrast, Freneau's poems like "The Wild Honey Suckle" and "The Indian Burying Ground" contain two clearly romantic elements: the idealization of nature and the wisdom of the noble savage. Called "the poet of the American Revolution," Freneau embraces both the romantic idealism of a new nation in a virgin land and the firm belief in the power of reason to shape a good and just society.

Bryant and Longfellow also wrote about the Native American, thus exploring the romantic idea that people who lived closest to nature understood nature's secrets better than people living in towns and cities. The influence of Romanticism—a movement that valued the heart and the soul over the mind, intuition and imagination over reason, dream and fantasy over reality, idealism over realism, the natural over the artificial, and the country over the city—is evident in the work of Our Poets as well as in the gloomy, hypnotically musical, dreamlike poems of Edgar Allan Poe. Poe's "The Raven" and "Annabel Lee," for instance, remind us that romanticism has a dark side as well as a bright.

So after reading the colonial poets Anne Bradstreet and Edward Taylor and the eighteenth-century poet Phillis Wheatley, we will see how Philip Freneau provides a transition from eighteenth-century neoclassicism to the nineteenth-century romanticism of Bryant, Emerson, Poe, Longfellow, Whittier, Holmes, and others. We will also note a consistent European influence, broken only by Emerson's Eastern-influenced idea of the Over-Soul, the spirit flowing through all creation. In the second part of this book we will read poems that use this idea to create an American poetry, as Emerson put it, "of insight and not of tradition."

ANNE BRADSTREET
1612–1672

Picture her in 1630 when she was eighteen—already a wife of two years, a survivor of a smallpox epidemic, and a pilgrim, courageous but most certainly weak from her voyage to a rough and wild world where in every house, it was said, at least one person had died. Isn't it likely that, longing for the comfort and civility of Old England, this gentlewoman from a cultivated family would have shrunk from the New England wilderness? Forty-two years later she wrote, "I found a new world and new manners, at which my heart rose."

She had made the famous voyage to Massachusetts in the *Lady Arabella* with John Winthop; her father, Thomas Dudley; her mother; and her husband, Simon Bradstreet. All three men served as governor of Massachusetts; Anne became the gracious wife of an influential citizen, a mother of eight children, a frontier farm wife in Ipswich and North Andover, and this continent's first English-speaking poet.

Although Puritan New England approved of the writing of poetry on edifying topics, women were not encouraged toward intellectual pursuit. Since her father had been a magistrate in the court that excommunicated the heretic Anne Hutchinson, Anne Bradstreet must have been well aware of the danger of appearing to neglect her responsibilities of church, family, and community.

The poems that follow not only portray Anne Bradstreet's religious faith but also record what must have been common feelings of a first-generation New England colonist—a strong belief in God, the fear of sudden death, gratitude for a husband's safe return from sea, and the simple pleasures of nature.

The Author to Her Book

Anne Bradstreet wrote "The Author to Her Book" after her brother-in-law took her manuscript to England and, without the poet's permission, had it published in 1650 under the title of *The Tenth Muse, Lately Sprung Up in America*. The second edition, which appears to contain the poet's corrections, was printed six years after Bradstreet's death. This second edition adds six new poems to the book, including "The

5

Author to Her Book" and "Contemplations." The other poems that follow here were added in still later editions. It is interesting to note, therefore, that the poet may well have considered these last poems too light or too personal for publication.

> Thou ill-form'd offspring of my feeble brain,
> Who after birth did'st by my side remain,
> Till snatcht from thence by friends, less wise then true
> Who thee abroad, expos'd to publick view,
> 5   Made thee in raggs, halting to th' press to trudge,
> Where errors were not lessened (all may judg).
> At thy return my blushing was not small,
> My rambling brat (in print) should mother call,
> I cast thee by as one unfit for light,
> 10   Thy Visage was so irksome in my sight;
> Yet being mine own, at length affection would
> Thy blemishes amend, if so I could;
> I wash'd thy face, but more defects I saw,
> And rubbing off a spot, still made a flaw.
> 15   I stretcht thy joints to make thee even feet,
> Yet still thou run'st more hobling then is meet;
> In better dress to trim thee was my mind,
> But nought save home-spun Cloth, i' th' house I find.
> In this array, 'mongst Vulgars mayst thou roam,
> 20   In Criticks hands, beware thou dost not come;
> And take thy way where yet thou art not known,
> If for thy Father askt, say, thou hadst none:
> And for thy Mother, she alas is poor,
> Which caus'd her thus to send thee out of door.

COMMENTARY AND QUESTIONS

1. What is the central metaphor in "The Author to Her Book"? Note specifically how Bradstreet extends this metaphor throughout the poem. We call an elaborately extended metaphor a *conceit*, a technique popular in the seventeenth century.

2. What is the tone of this poem? Explain how certain phrases help create this tone.

from *Contemplations*

1

> Sometime now past in the Autumnal Tide,
> When *Phœbus*[1] wanted but one hour to bed,
> The trees all richly clad, yet void of pride,
> Were glided o're by his rich golden head.
> 5   Their leaves & fruits seem'd painted, but was true

[1] **Phoebus:** Apollo, the Greek God of the sun.

Of green, of red, or yellow, mixed hew,
Rapt were my sences at this delectable view.

9

I heard the merry grashopper then sing,
The black clad Cricket, bear a second part,
10   They kept one tune, and plaid on the same string,
Seeming to glory in their little Art.
Shall Creatures abject, thus their voices raise?
And in their kind resound their makers praise:
Whilst I as mute, can warble forth no higher layes.[2]

21

15   Under the cooling shadow of a stately Elm
Close sate I by a goodly Rivers side,
Where gliding streams the Rocks did overwhelm;
A lonely place, with pleasures dignifi'd.
I once that lov'd the shady woods so well,
20   Now thought the rivers did the trees excel,
And if the sun would ever shine, there would I dwell.

26

While musing thus with contemplation fed,
And thousand fancies buzzing in my brain,
The sweet-tongu'd Philomel[3] percht ore my head,
25   And chanted forth a most melodious strain
Which rapt me so with wonder and delight,
I judg'd my hearing better then my sight,
And wisht me wings with her a while to take my flight.

---

[2] **layes:** ballads.
[3] **Philomel:** A nightingale, a songbird often the subject of poems; native to England, not to North America.

COMMENTARY AND QUESTIONS

1. How specific are Bradstreet's references to nature in "Contemplation"? That is, does she name certain plants, animals, bodies of water, hills, or valleys?

2. Does the poet effectively show you the sounds and sights in the poem?

3. Comment on her technique by quoting specific phrases and discuss how these phrases affect the reader. You will want to come back to this poem later, when you have read nature poems by other American poets.

Upon Some Distemper of Body

In anguish of my heart repleat with woes,
And wasting pains, which best my body knows,
In tossing slumbers on my wakeful bed,
Bedrencht with tears that flow'd from mournful head.
5 Till nature had exhausted all her store,
Then eyes lay dry, disabled to weep more;
And looking up unto his Throne on high,
Who sendeth help to those in misery;
He chac'd away those clouds, and let me see
10 My Anchor cast i'th' vale[1] with safety.
He eas'd my Soul of woe, my flesh of pain,
And brought me to the shore from troubled Main.

[1] **vale:** valley.

COMMENTARY AND QUESTIONS

1. Discuss why Bradstreet chose to capitalize *Throne*, *Anchor*, and *Main*.

2. What is the subject of this poem? Describe the speaker's attitude toward God.

Before the Birth of One of Her Children

All things within this fading world hath end,
Adversity doth still our joyes attend;
No tyes so strong, no friends so dear and sweet,
But with death's parting blow is sure to meet.
5 The sentence past is most irrovocable,
A common thing, yet oh inevitable;
How soon, my Dear, death may my steps attend,
How soon't may be thy Lot to lose thy friend,
We both are ignorant, yet love bids me
10 These farewell lines to recommend to thee,
That when that knot's untyd that made us one,
I may seem thine, who in effect am none.
And if I see not half my dayes that's due,
What nature would, God grant to yours and you;
15 The many faults that well you know I have,
Let be interr'd in my oblivious grave;
If any worth or virtue were in me,
Let that live freshly in thy memory
And when thou feel'st no grief, as I no harms,
20 Yet love thy dead, who long lay in thine arms:

And when thy loss shall be repaid with gains
Look to my little babes, my dear remains.
And if thou love thy self, or loved'st me
These O protect from step Dame's injury.
25   And if chance to thine eyes shall bring this verse,
With some sad sighs honour my absent Hearse;
And kiss this paper for thy love's dear sake,
Who with salt tears this last Farewel did take.

COMMENTARY AND QUESTIONS

1. The speaker in the poem is Anne Bradstreet. Whom is she addressing?

2. Why do you think the poet wrote this poem?

3. Referring to specific lines, what does this poem tell us about Anne Bradstreet's relationship with her husband, God, and her unborn child?

To My Dear and Loving Husband

If ever two were one, then surely we.
If ever man were loved by wife, then thee;
If ever wife was happy in a man,
Compare with me ye women if you can.
5   I prize thy love more than whole mines of gold,
Or all the riches that the East[1] doth hold.
My love is such that rivers cannot quench,
Nor ought but love from thee give recompense.
Thy love is such I can no way repay;
10   The heavens reward thee manifold, I pray.
Then while we live, in love let's so persever,
That when we live no more we may live ever.

[1] **East:** the Orient.

COMMENTARY AND QUESTIONS

1. Describe and discuss the husband–wife relationship portrayed in the poem.

REVIEW

1. Write down your first impressions of Anne Bradstreet's poems. Which poem do you like best? Least? As specifically as possible, explain the reasons for your likes and dislikes.

2. Given the poet's experience as described in the biography, does the subject matter of these poems seem predictable? How, if at all, do the subjects of these poems help us to understand the poet?

3. Note the poet's technique—meter, stanzas, rhyme scheme, other sound devices, figurative language, the voice of the speaker, and so forth. Which devices does she use the most? Does she use them well? Discuss.

4. Anne Bradstreet has been called an extremely conventional poet whose rhymes and meter tend to be heavy-handed and uninteresting, whose images are predictable, and whose themes are simple. Discuss your opinion of her poetry.

EDWARD TAYLOR
1642–1729

The town of Westfield, Massachusetts, lies one hundred miles west of Boston, not far west of Springfield, and just east of the Berkshire hills. This was wild country in the winter of 1671, when this twenty-nine-year-old, not-yet-ordained minister journeyed there on horseback from Boston—so wild in fact that native American uprisings prevented Edward Taylor from being ordained to the ministry until 1679. Although Taylor, who had just graduated from Harvard, must have felt isolated when he first arrived in Westfield, he remained there for the rest of his life, serving as the town's minister and physician. During those fifty-eight years Taylor married Elizabeth Fitch in 1674, after her death married Ruth Wyllys in 1692, kept a small farm, and fathered thirteen children.

Like Anne Bradstreet, Edward Taylor had emigrated to the Massachusetts Bay Colony from England. Shortly after arriving, he entered Harvard College as a sophomore and soon distinguished himself as a scholar. After his graduation Taylor was offered a position at the college. Instead, he chose to become the minister in the frontier town of Westfield. Although this severe life might well have sapped his poetic energies, Taylor, in fact, wrote a large volume of poems, drawing inspiration primarily from both his great religious faith and the trials of daily life.

Taylor's poems, unpublished until 1939, were given to the Yale University library in 1883 by the poet's great-grandson. Thus, after 210 years of obscurity, Edward Taylor was read and almost immediately praised for his poetic craft and particularly for his mastery of the style characterized by English metaphysical poets such as John Donne and George Herbert.

Upon a Spider Catching a Fly

Thou sorrow, venom Elfe:
　Is this thy play,
To spin a web out of thyselfe
　To Catch a Fly?
5　　For why?

I saw a pettish[1] wasp
　Fall foule therein:
Whom yet thy whorle pins[2] did not clasp
　Lest he should fling
10　　His sting.

But as afraid, remote
　Didst stand hereat,
And with thy little fingers stroke
　And gently tap
15　　His back.

Thus gently him didst treate
　Lest he should pet,[3]
And in a froppish, aspish heate[4]
　Should greatly fret
20　　Thy net.

Whereas the silly Fly,
　Caught by its leg,
Thou by the throate took'st hastily,
　And 'hinde the head
25　　Bite Dead.

This goes to pot, that not
　Nature doth call.
Strive not above what strength hath got,
　Lest in the brawle
30　　Thou fall.

This Frey seems thus to us:
　Hells Spider gets
His intrails spun to whip Cords thus,
　And wove to nets,
35　　And sets.

---

[1] **pettish**: peevish.
[2] **pins**: pins in a spinning wheel's flywheel.
[3] **pet**: become bad-tempered.
[4] **heate**: anger, like that of a poisonous snake, an asp.

To tangle Adams race
   In's stratagems
To their Destructions, Spoil'd, made base
   By venom things,
40   Damn'd Sins.

But mighty, Gracious Lord,
   Communicate
Thy Grace to breake the Cord; afford
   Us Glorys Gate
45   And State.

We'l Nightingaile sing like,
   When pearcht on high
In Glories Cage, thy glory, bright:
   [Yea,] thankfully,
50   For joy.

COMMENTARY AND QUESTIONS

1. Explain the central metaphor.

2. What lessons does the poet take from the spider's treatment of the fly and then of the wasp?

3. How does the poet hope to escape Satan's "nets"?

Huswifery

Make me, O Lord, thy Spinning Wheele[1] compleat;
   Thy Holy Worde my Distaff make for mee.
Make mine Affections thy Swift Flyers neate,
   And make my Soule thy holy Spoole to bee.
5   My Conversation make to be thy Reele,
   And reele the yarn theron spun of thy Wheele.

Make my thy Loome then, knit therein this Twine:
   And make thy Holy Spirit, Lord, winde quills:
Then weave the Web thyselfe. The yarn is fine.
10   Thine Ordinances make my Fulling Mills.
   Then dy the same in Heavenly Colours Choice,
   All pinkt with Varnish't Flowers of Paradise.

---

[1] **Spinning Wheele:** The raw wool or flax is held on a *distaff*, spun into yarn, or *twine* by the *wheele* and its *flyers*, then wound on the the *reele*. This twine is wound on to a *quill*, or spindle, to be woven. Next, it is cleaned and finished by *fulling mills*. Finally it is dyed and decorated, or *pinkt*.

Then cloath therewith mine Understanding, Will,
Affections, Judgment, Conscience, Memory;
15 My Words and Actions, that their shine may fill
My ways with glory and thee glorify.
Then mine apparell shall display before yee
That I am Cloathd in holy robes for glory.

COMMENTARY AND QUESTIONS

1. The elaborately developed metaphor in "Huswifery" is an excellent example of a *conceit*. Explain the metaphor and examine how Taylor extends it.

2. How does this conceit compare to the one in Bradstreet's "The Author to Her Book"? Which poem exhibits the greater craft?

REVIEW

1. What immediate similarities do you see between the poems of Anne Bradstreet and those of Edward Taylor? Which poet do you like better? Why?

2. Compose a conceit (a strikingly original extended metaphor) of eight to twelve lines, rhymed and metered in the form of Bradstreet's "To My Dear and Loving Husband."

PHILLIS WHEATLEY
1753–1784

In 1761 Susannah Wheatley, desiring to employ a domestic servant, boarded a slave ship in Boston harbor and purchased a frail child of eight. As the child became stronger and healthier, it soon became evident that she possessed uncommon curiosity and intelligence. Through the fond tutelage of Mrs. Wheatley's daughter Mary, the child, in just sixteen months, learned to read the Bible fluently. Soon she read the poetry of English poets John Milton (1608–1674) and Alexander Pope (1688–1744), mastered Latin well enough to read Latin literature, made use of the best libraries in Boston, and met the most distinguished people in the city. By the time she was thirteen, Phillis Wheatley had begun to write poetry; and six years later, in 1773, her book *Poems on Various Subjects, Religious and Moral* was printed in London, where it was well received. In the same year the poet sailed with Nathaniel, Mary's twin brother, to England, where she met the Earl of Dartmouth, the Countess of Huntington, and other well-regarded English men and women. When she heard, however, that Mr. Wheatley had become ill, Phillis returned to America, canceling plans to be presented at the court of George III.

After the deaths of Susannah Wheatley in 1774 and Mr. Wheatley four years later, Phillis Wheatley married John Peters, a free African American. When the British occupied Boston, the couple fled to Wilmington, Massachusetts, where the young wife bore the first two of her three children. John Peters, unsuccessful in several businesses, was unable to raise his family from poverty. Phillis died in 1784 at age thirty; two of her three children had already died, and the third expired hours after her mother. Despite the poverty and the depression that Phillis Wheatley Peters must have felt during the last six years of her life, the poet continued to write. When friends found her in a cold apartment with her last living child, both seriously ill and uncared for, she was still writing and planning to publish poetry. In fact, she had prepared a second manuscript, which has unfortunately been lost.

That Phillis Wheatley, who as a child had been taken from her home in Africa, brought to America, and enslaved, wrote the bulk of her surviving poems before her twentieth birthday testifies not only to her early talent but also to the endurance of the human mind and spirit.

On Being Brought from Africa to America[1]

'Twas mercy brought me from my *Pagan* land,
Taught my benighted soul to understand
That there's a God, that there's a *Saviour* too:
Once I redemption neither sought nor knew.
5 Some view our sable race with scornful eye,
"Their colour is a diabolic die."
Remember, *Christians*, *Negroes*, black as *Cain*,
May be refin'd, and join th' angelic train.

---

[1] **"On Being Brought from Africa to America"**: One of Phillis Wheatley's earliest poems, it may have been written when the poet was thirteen years old.

COMMENTARY AND QUESTIONS

1. Paraphrase the first four lines, paying attention to *benighted* and *redemption*.

2. What is the poet's attitude toward her "land" and her race? Discuss this attitude in relation to both Wheatley's life and to African Americans today.

To His Excellency General Washington

Celestial choir! enthron'd in realms of light,
    Columbia's[1] scenes of glorious toils I write.
While freedom's cause her anxious breast alarms,
She flashes dreadful in refulgent arms.
5 See mother earth her offspring's fate bemoan,
And nations gaze at scenes before unknown!
See the bright beams of heaven's revolving light
Involved in sorrows and the veil of night!
    The goddess comes, she moves divinely fair,
10 Olive and laurel binds her golden hair:
Wherever shines this native of the skies,
Unnumber'd charms and recent graces rise.
    Muse! bow propitious while my pen relates

---

[1] **Columbia's:** the United States personified as a goddess.

How pour her armies through a thousand gates,
15 As when Eolus[2] heaven's fair face deforms,
Enwrapp'd in tempest and a night of storms;
Astonish'd ocean feels the wild uproar,
The refluent surges beat the sounding shore;
Or thick as leaves in Autumn's golden reign,
20 Such, and so many, moves the warrior's train.
In bright array they seek the work of war,
Where high unfurl'd the ensign waves in air.
Shall I to Washington their praise recite?
Enough thou know'st them in the fields of fight.
25 Thee, first in peace and honours,—we demand
The grace and glory of thy martial band.
Fam'd for thy valour, for thy virtues more,
Hear every tongue thy guardian aid implore!
    One century scarce perform'd its destined round,
30 When Gallic[3] powers Columbia's fury found;
And so may you, whoever dares disgrace
The land of freedom's heaven-defended race!
Fix'd are the eyes of nations on the scales,
For in their hopes Columbia's arm prevails.
35 Anon[4] Britannia[5] droops the pensive head,
While round increase the rising hills of dead.
Ah! cruel blindness to Columbia's state!
Lament thy thirst of boundless power too late.
    Proceed, great chief, with virtue on thy side,
40 Thy ev'ry action let the goddess guide.
A crown, a mansion, and a throne that shine,
With gold unfading, WASHINGTON! be thine.

[2] **Eolus:** Aeolus, the Greek god of the wind.
[3] **Gallic:** French, referring to the French and Indian War (1754–1763).
[4] **Anon:** soon.
[5] **Britannia:** England.

COMMENTARY AND QUESTIONS

1. Identify three figures of speech in "To His Excellency General Washington." How do they extend the poem's meaning?

2. Who is the "goddess"?

3. From your knowledge of American history, do you believe this poem expresses views of Washington and the American cause that were common during the American Revolution?

REVIEW

1. One notices the influence of the great English poet Alexander Pope (1688–1744) in Phillis Wheatley's employment of *heroic couplets*, rhyming pairs of iambic pentameter lines with a pause coming at the end of the first line and a heavier pause at the end of the second. The following are two heroic couplets from Pope's long poem called *An Essay on Criticism*:

   > True ease from writing comes from art, not chance,
   > As those move easiest who have learned to dance.
   > 'Tis not enough no harshness gives offense,
   > The sound must seem an echo to the sense.

   Identify a few of Phillis Wheatley's heroic couplets that come closest to fulfilling the requirements Alexander Pope sets down in the previous lines.

2. Although Phillis Wheatley wrote remarkably well as a young person, her work has been criticized for not employing language in interesting, original ways and for offering simple themes that hold little interest after the first reading. What do you think of these criticisms?

3. How does Wheatley's poetry compare in depth and complexity to the work of Edwards and Bradstreet?

4. Write a poem that employs four or more heroic couplets.

PHILIP FRENEAU
1752–1832

Called the poet of the American Revolution and the father of American poetry, Philip Freneau wrote a large body of poems that were published widely during his lifetime. Many of these poems attacked the British, and others glorified American war heroes and their victorious battles. Although he became famous for his poems about the Revolutionary War and for his often bitter and satirical attacks on his political enemies, Freneau also wrote popular light verse and serious poems about nature and the relationship between God and man.

Born into an affluent family, Freneau divided his boyhood between New York City, where he was born, and his family's plantation in New Jersey. At fifteen he entered Princeton University (then called the College of New Jersey) as a sophomore. A classmate of James Madison, Freneau became interested in poetry, politics, political writing, and American independence. Well read in classical and English literature, Freneau understood as a young man that America must win cultural and political independence from Europe. As you read the following poems, note that Freneau did in fact succeed in writing poems that draw powerfully from the American experience.

During his long life, Freneau worked briefly as a teacher, then later as a ship's captain, a journalist, a U.S. government official, and a farmer. During the first years of the Revolution he wrote patriotic poems and essays. From 1776 to 1778 he lived in St. Croix, and then returned to New Jersey to find that his family land had been ravaged by the war. First joining the local militia, Freneau then became a privateer; he was wounded, captured, became ill, and was then imprisoned on a British hospital ship before being released. For the rest of the war he published articles and editorials attacking the British. After the war, he again went to sea, where he survived and wrote about a hurricane that destroyed many ships in the West Indies.

Marrying Eleanor Forman in 1789, Freneau began writing and editing papers that supported the agrarian, democratic ideals of Thomas Jefferson against Hamilton's Federalists. When his Philadelphia paper, the *National Gazette*, closed in 1793, Freneau worked briefly on two other newspapers and then retired to his family plantation in New Jersey. In the last years of his life Freneau lost his house in a fire,

19

suffered financial reverses, was forced to take odd jobs, and was largely forgotten by the public. He died in December 1832, at the age of eighty, having lost his way in a blizzard.

The Wild Honey Suckle

1   Fair flower, that dost so comely grow,
     Hid in this silent, dull retreat,
     Untouched thy honied blossoms blow,
     Unseen thy little branches greet:
5   No roving foot shall crush thee here,
       No busy hand provoke a tear.

     By Nature's self in white arrayed,
     She bade thee shun the vulgar eye,
     And planted here the guardian shade,
10   And sent soft waters murmuring by;
      Thus quietly thy summer goes,
      Thy days declining to repose.

     Smit[1] with those charms, that must decay,
     I grieve to see your future doom;
15   They died—nor were those flowers more gay,
     The flowers that did in Eden bloom;
      Unpitying frosts, and Autumn's power
      Shall leave no vestige of this flower.

     From morning suns and evening dews
20   At first thy little being came:
     If nothing once, you nothing lose,
     For when you die you are the same;
      The space between, is but an hour,
      The frail duration of a flower.

[1] **Smit:** from to smite; to move deeply (smitten with love); also, to strike.

COMMENTARY AND QUESTIONS

1. "The Wild Honey Suckle" is the first poem in this anthology that could be called a "nature poem," although Anne Bradstreet praises nature in "Contemplations." Compare the role of nature in the two poems.

2. What does "The Wild Honey Suckle" help us to understand about America in the late eighteenth century?

3. How does the poem qualify as an early romantic poem? See the introduction to Part 1 for a discussion of romanticism.

The Indian Burying Ground

In spite of all the learned have said,
I still my old opinion keep;
The *posture*, that *we* give the dead,
Points out the soul's eternal sleep.

5 Not so the ancients of these lands—
The Indian, when from life released,
Again is seated with his friends,
And shares again the joyous feast.[1]

His imaged birds, and painted bowl,
10 And venison, for a journey dressed,
Bespeak the nature of the soul,
ACTIVITY, that knows no rest.

His bow, for action ready bent,
And arrows, with a head of stone,
15 Can only mean that life is spent,
And not the old ideas gone.

Thou, stranger, that shalt come this way,
No fraud upon the dead commit—
Observe the swelling turf, and say
20 They do not *lie*, but here they *sit*.

Here still a lofty rock remains,
On which the curious eye may trace
(Now wasted, half, by wearing rains)
The fancies of a ruder race.[2]

25 Here still an aged elm aspires,
Beneath whose far-projecting shade
(And which the shepherd still admires)
The children of the forest played!

There oft a restless Indian queen
30 (Pale *Shebah*,[3] with her braided hair)
And many a barbarous form is seen
To chide the man that lingers there.

---

[1] **Again . . . feast:** Freneau provided this note: "The North American Indians bury their dead in a sitting posture; decorating the corpse with wampum, the images of birds, quadropeds, &c: And (if that of a warrior) with bows, arrows, tomhawks and other military weapons."

[2] **ruder race:** more primitive.

[3] ***Shebah:*** a biblical allusion to the queen of Sheba, a wise and beautiful woman who paid a visit to Solomon.

By midnight moons, o'er moistening dews,
In habit for the chase arrayed,
35   The hunter still the deer pursues,
The hunter and the deer, a shade!

And long shall timorous fancy see
The painted chief, and pointed spear,
And Reason's self shall bow the knee
40   To shadows and delusions here.

COMMENTARY AND QUESTIONS

1. "The Indian Burying Ground," written in 1788, is the first poem we have seen that considers a Native American point of view, and it is also the first to indulge in fancy—imagination for its own sake. What historical events had taken place that might have encouraged Freneau to write a fanciful poem that romanticizes the Native American?

On the Uniformity and Perfection of Nature

On one fix'd point all nature moves,
Nor deviates from the track she loves;
Her system, drawn from reason's source,
She scorns to change her wonted[1] course.

5   Could she descend from that great plan
To work unusual things for man,
To suit the insect of an hour—
This would betray a want of power,

10   Unsettled in its first design
And erring, when it did combine
The parts that form the vast machine,
The figures sketch'd on nature's scene.

Perfections of the great first cause
15   Submit to no contracted laws,
But all-sufficient, all-supreme,
Include no trivial views in them.

Who looks through nature with an eye
That would the scheme of heaven descry,
20   Observes her constant, still the same,
In all her laws, through all her frame.

[1] **wonted:** wanted.

No imperfection can be found
In all that is, above, around,—
All, nature made, in reason's sight
25 Is order all, and *all is right.*

COMMENTARY AND QUESTION

1. "On the Uniformity and Perfection of Nature" explains the central idea of deism, the eighteenth-century Neoclassic belief that God ordered the universe rationally and then left it to run on its own. Man, therefore, was to rely on his intellect to solve his problems rather than on the Almighty. Compare and contrast the ideas in this poem with those in "The Wild Honey Suckle" and "The Indian Burying Ground." Does there appear to be any serious contradictions? Explain in detail.

REVIEW

1. Discuss Freneau's prosody—that is, the way he structures meter, rhyme, stanzas, and other sound devices such as assonance, consonance, and alliteration. Do you recognize any similarities between his poems and those by earlier poets we have read?

2. Explain how Freneau's poetry contains both neoclassic and romantic qualities. See the introduction to Part 1 for discussions of these two movements.

WILLIAM CULLEN BRYANT
1794–1878

William Cullen Bryant grew up in Cummington, a rural town on the eastern slopes of the Berkshire hills of western Massachusetts, not far from Westfield, where Edward Taylor had lived. Like every poet we have seen thus far, Bryant had the advantage of being exposed to books at an early age. His father, a physician, whose library numbered seven hundred volumes, arranged for his precocious son to study Latin and Greek privately, before entering nearby Williams College in 1810. Bryant left Williams after a year with the intention of attending Yale, but because of financial difficulties his father encouraged the seventeen-years-old Bryant to work in a law office. Bryant took his father's advice, and was admitted to the bar in 1815. He continued his law practice, first in Plainfield, Massachusetts, and then in Great Barrington. Despite the demands of practicing law, Bryant wrote most of his most famous poems between 1817 and 1825.

In 1817 the *North American Review* published "Thanatopsis," the first poem of Bryant's to earn critical attention. Although this early success is impressive, it is even more noteworthy that Bryant first drafted the poem in 1811, when he was seventeen years old. The 1821 publication of *Poems*, Bryant's first book, won the poet further acclaim. In that year Bryant married Frances Fairchild and read the Phi Beta Kappa poem at the Harvard College commencement. By then an established literary figure, Bryant left his Great Barrington law practice in 1825, moved to New York City, and began his fifty-year editorship of the *Evening Post*. Although at first he resisted making the commitment required by his new position, Bryant eventually became a devoted and highly respected newspaper editor.

The *Evening Post* did deplete Bryant's creative energies, but he continued to write poetry throughout his life. In 1832 he published another volume called *Poems*; in 1842, *The Fountain and Other Poems*; and in 1844, *White-footed Doe, and Other Poems*. His translations of the *Iliad* in 1870 and the *Odyssey* in 1872 were widely admired. Traveling extensively in Europe and America during these years, Bryant also wrote correspondences, which were published in the *Evening Post* and later collected as *Letters of a Traveller* in 1850.

William Cullen Bryant wrote from an intimate understanding of and fondness for physical place, particularly the landscape and seasons of the western hills of Massa-chusetts, where he spent the first thirty-one years of his life. In this sense his subjects—unlike Bradstreet's and Taylor's and more powerfully than Freneau's—spring from American soil.

Thanatopsis[1]

To him who in the love of Nature holds
Communion with her visible forms, she speaks
A various language; for his gayer hours
She has a voice of gladness, and a smile
5   And eloquence of beauty, and she glides
Into his darker musings, with a mild
And healing sympathy, that steals away
Their sharpness, ere he is aware. When thoughts
Of the last bitter hour come like a blight
10 Over thy spirit, and sad images
Of the stern agony, and shroud, and pall,
And breathless darkness, and the narrow house,
Make thee to shudder, and grow sick at heart;—
Go forth, under the open sky, and list[2]
15 To Nature's teachings, while from all around—
Earth and her waters, and the depths of air—
Comes a still voice—Yet a few days, and thee
The all-beholding sun shall see no more
In all his course; nor yet in the cold ground,
20 Where thy pale form was laid, with many tears,
Nor in the embrace of ocean, shall exist
Thy image. Earth, that nourished thee, shall claim
Thy growth, to be resolved to earth again,
And, lost each human trace, surrendering up
25 Thine individual being, shalt thou go
To mix for ever with the elements,
To be a brother to the insensible rock
And to the sluggish clod, which the rude swain
Turns with his share,[3] and treads upon. The oak
30 Shall send his roots abroad, and pierce thy mould.

Yet not to thine eternal resting-place
Shalt thou retire alone, nor couldst thou wish
Couch more magnificent. Thou shalt lie down
With patriarchs of the infant world—with kings,

[1] **"Thanatopsis":** a meditation on death.
[2] **list:** listen.
[3] **share:** plowshare.

35   The powerful of the earth—the wise, the good,
       Fair forms, and hoary seers of ages past,
       All in one mighty sepulchre. The hills
       Rock-ribbed and ancient as the sun,—the vales
       Stretching in pensive quietness between;
40   The venerable woods—rivers that move
       In majesty, and the complaining brooks
       That make the meadows green; and, poured round all,
       Old Ocean's gray and melancholy waste,—
       Are but the solemn decorations all
45   Of the great tomb of man. The golden sun,
       The planets, all the infinite host of heaven,
       Are shining on the sad abodes of death,
       Through the still lapse of ages. All that tread
       The globe are but a handful to the tribes
50   That slumber in its bosom.—Take the wings
       Of morning, pierce the Barcan[4] wilderness,
       Or lose thyself in the continuous woods
       Where rolls the Oregon, and hears no sound,
       Save his own dashings—yet the dead are there:
55   And millions in those solitudes, since first
       The flight of years began, have laid them down
       In their last sleep—the dead reign there alone.
       So shalt thou rest, and what if thou withdraw
       In silence from the living, and no friend
60   Take note of thy departure? All that breathe
       Will share thy destiny. The gay will laugh
       When thou art gone, the solemn brood of care
       Plod on, and each one as before will chase
       His favorite phantom; yet all these shall leave
64   Their mirth and their employments, and shall come
       And make their bed with thee. As the long train
       Of ages glide away, the sons of men,
       The youth in life's green spring, and he who goes
       In the full strength of years, matron and maid,
70   The speechless babe, and the gray-headed man—
       Shall one by one be gathered to thy side,
       By those, who in their turn shall follow them.

         So live, that when thy summons comes to join
       The innumerable caravan, which moves
75   To that mysterious realm, where each shall take
       His chamber in the silent halls of death,
       Thou go not, like the quarry-slave at night,

---

[4] **Barcan:** a desertic area of North Africa

Scourged to his dungeon, but, sustained and soothed
By an unfaltering trust, approach thy grave,
80 Like one who wraps the drapery of his couch
About him, and lies down to pleasant dreams.

COMMENTARY AND QUESTIONS

1. What is the main idea in the first section of "Thanatopsis"? What lines express this idea most vividly? What is the main idea of the second section? To our modern taste this stanza in particular, and the poem in general, may appear unnecessarily long. After reading "Thanatopsis" aloud and listening for the poem's voice (the tone in which its narrator speaks), consider the advantage of Bryant's choice to express these ideas expansively rather than concisely.

2. Discuss a passage that you find particularly effective. Tell why you like particular phrases and words.

3. "Thanatopsis," like Phillis Wheatley's "To His Excellency General Washington," is an unrhymed poem with sections of unequal length. Bryant wrote "Thanatopsis" in *blank verse* (unrhymed iambic pentameter), a popular English form often used for long narrative poems because it provides a metrical structure while not calling attention to itself. You may recall that William Shakespeare employed blank verse in his plays. As you read the poem, were you aware of the meter? Find lines where the iambic rhythm is heavy and, therefore, obvious. Identify places where the poet breaks the strict iambic pattern with extra syllables, misplaced stresses, or punctuation marks. How do these breaks affect the poem's meaning?

To a Waterfowl

Whither,[1] midst falling dew,
While glow the heavens with the last steps of day,
Far, through their rosy depths, dost thou pursue
    Thy solitary way?

5   Vainly the fowler's[2] eye
Might mark thy distant flight to do thee wrong,
As, darkly seen against the crimson sky,
    Thy figure floats along.

    Seek'st thou the plashy brink[3]
10 Of weedy lake, or marge[4] of river wide,
Or where the rocking billows[5] rise and sink
    On the chafed ocean-side?

[1] **Whither:** to what specified place? Where?
[2] **fowler:** a hunter of ducks and geese.
[3] **plashy brink:** the puddles and small pools of a marsh that borders a lake.
[4] **marge:** the margin of the river, shoreline.
[5] **billows:** waves.

There is a Power whose care
Teaches thy way along that pathless coast
15 The desert and illimitable air—
     Lone wandering, but not lost.

All day thy wings have fanned,
At that far height, the cold, thin atmosphere,
Yet stoop[6] not, weary to the welcome land,
20   Though the dark night is near.

And soon that toil shall end;
Soon shalt thou find a summer home, and rest,
And scream among thy fellows; reeds shall bend,
     Soon, o'er thy sheltered nest.

25   Thou'rt gone, the abyss of heaven
Hath swallowed up thy form; yet, on my heart
Deeply has sunk the lesson thou hast given,
     And shall not soon depart.

He who, from zone to zone,
30 Guides through the boundless sky thy certain flight,
In the long way that I must tread alone,
     Will lead my steps aright.

[6] **stoop:** dive, descend from a height.

COMMENTARY AND QUESTIONS

1. "To a Waterfowl" was inspired when, while walking between Cummington and Plainfield, Bryant observed at sunset a lone waterfowl. In this poem, as in those by Bradstreet and Taylor, Bryant connects the natural world to the supernatural. Note the last stanza and contrast Bryant's depiction of God and nature to the two earlier poets' treatment of these subjects.

An Indian at the Burial-Place of His Fathers

It is the spot I came to seek—
    My father's ancient burial-place,
Ere from these vales, ashamed and weak,
    Withdrew our wasted race.
5 It is the spot—I know it well—
  Of which our old traditions tell.

For here the upland bank sends out
   A ridge toward the river-side;
I know the shaggy hills about,
10   The meadows smooth and wide,
The plains, that, toward the southern sky,
Fenced east and west by mountains lie.

A white man, gazing on the scene,
   Would say a lovely spot was here,
15 And praise the lawns, so fresh and green,
   Between the hills so sheer.
I like it not—I would the plain
Lay in its tall old groves again.

The sheep are on the slopes around,
20   The cattle in the meadows feed,
And laborers turn the crumbling ground,
   Or drop the yellow seed,
And prancing steeds, in trappings gay,
Whirl the bright chariot o'er the way.

25 Methinks it were a nobler sight
   To see these vales in woods arrayed,
Their summits in the golden light,
   Their trunks in grateful shade,
And herds of deer that bounding go
30 O'er hills and prostrate trees[1] below.

And then to mark the lord of all,
   The forest hero, trained to wars,
Quivered and plumed, and lithe and tall,
   And seamed with glorious scars,
35 Walk forth, amid his reign, to dare
The wolf, and grapple with the bear.

This bank, in which the dead were laid,
   Was sacred when its soil was ours;
Hither[2] the silent Indian maid
40   Brought wreaths of beads and flowers,
And the gray chief and gifted seer
Worshipped the god of thunders here.

---

[1] **prostrate trees:** fallen trees.
[2] **Hither:** here.

But now the wheat is green and high
   On clods that hid the warrior's breast,
45 And scattered in the furrows lie
   The weapons of his rest;
And there, in the loose sand, is thrown
Of his large arm the mouldering bone.

Ah, little thought the strong and brave
50   Who bore their lifeless chieftain forth—
      Or the young wife that weeping gave
   Her first-born to the earth,
That the pale race, who waste us now,
Among their bones should guide the plough.

55 They waste us—ay—like April snow
   In the warm noon, we shrink away;
And fast they follow, as we go
   Toward the setting day—
Till they shall fill the land, and we
60 Are driven in the Western sea.

But I behold a fearful sign,
   To which the white men's eyes are blind;
Their race may vanish hence, like mine,
   And leave no trace behind,
65 Save ruins o'er the region spread,
And the white stones above the dead.

Before these fields were shorn and tilled,
   Full to the brim our rivers flowed;
The melody of waters filled
70   The fresh and boundless wood;
And torrents dashed and rivulets played,
And fountains spouted in the shade.

Those grateful sounds are heard no more,
   The springs are silent in the sun;
75 The rivers, by the blackened shore,
   With lessening current run;
The realm our tribes are crushed to get
May be a barren desert yet.

COMMENTARY AND QUESTIONS

1. What attitudes toward Native Americans does Bryant's "An Indian at the Burial-Place of His Fathers" share with Freneau's "The Indian Burying Ground"? To what extent are the last two lines of Bryant's poem prophetic?

"I broke the spell that held me long"

I broke the spell that held me long,
The dear, dear witchery of song.
I said, the poet's idle lore
Shall waste my prime of years no more,
5 For Poetry, though heavenly born,
Consorts with poverty and scorn.

I broke the spell—nor deemed its power
Could fetter me another hour.
Ah, thoughtless! how could I forget
10 Its causes were around me yet?
For wheresoe'er I looked, the while,
Was Nature's everlasting smile.

Still came and lingered on my sight
Of flowers and streams the bloom and light,
15 And glory of the stars and sun;—
And these and poetry are one.
They, ere the world had held me long,
Recalled me to the love of song.

COMMENTARY AND QUESTIONS

1. What does Bryant mean by *song*?

2. Why was he unable to give up *song*? Explain his logic.

3. What does this poem tell us about Bryant's idea of nature? Reread this poem when you reach the poetry of Ralph Waldo Emerson.

To Cole,[1] the Painter, Departing for Europe

Thine eyes shall see the light of distant skies;
    Yet, COLE! thy heart shall bear to Europe's strand
    A living image of our own bright land,
Such as upon thy glorious canvas lies;
5 Lone lakes—savannas where the bison roves—
    Rocks rich with summer garlands—solemn streams—
    Skies, where the desert eagle wheels and screams—
Spring bloom and autumn blaze of boundless groves.
Fair scenes shall greet thee where thou goest—fair,
10 But different—everywhere the trace of men,
    Paths, homes, graves, ruins, from the lowest glen

[1] *Cole:* Thomas Cole (1801–1848), an American landscape painter.

To where life shrinks from the fierce Alpine air.
  Gaze on them, till the tears shall dim thy sight,
  But keep that earlier, wilder image bright.

COMMENTARY AND QUESTIONS

1. In "To Cole, the Painter, Departing for Europe," what does Bryant tell us about the relationship between an artist and his native land?

2. Compare the theme of this poem to the theme of "I broke the spell that held me long."

REVIEW

1. Using specific examples, discuss the romantic characteristics of Bryant's poetry. See the introduction to Part 1 for a discussion of romanticism.

2. Identify the American characteristics of Bryant's poetry. Be specific.

3. How, if at all, is Bryant's poetry more American than that of the earlier poets we have studied?

4. Discuss Bryant's craft compared to that of one or two of the other poets we have read.

RALPH WALDO EMERSON
1803–1882

The publication in 1836 of Ralph Waldo Emerson's essay "Nature" announced the United States' cultural independence from Europe. Here Emerson asked,

> Should not we have a poetry and philosophy of insight and not of tradition, and a religion by revelation to us, and not the history of theirs? . . . There are new lands, new men, new thoughts. Let us demand our own works and laws and worship.

How exciting it must have been for thoughtful young Americans to read these words. With the revolution and the War of 1812 behind it, the country now sought to be completely self-reliant; and Ralph Waldo Emerson articulated this impulse in his essays, lectures, and poems.

Emerson's father, who was pastor of the First Church of Boston, died leaving his wife with six children under ten years old. At the time of his father's death, eight-year-old Emerson lived in Boston, where he attended Boston Latin School. For one year he also attended a school in Concord, the small town northwest of Boston where he was eventually to settle. Later he attended Harvard College. Though not a distinguished student in college, he was named class poet and also began keeping the journal that he maintained for more than half a century.

After graduation from Harvard in 1821, Emerson taught school for four years. He then attended divinity school and began preaching in 1826. Coming from a long line of New England preachers, Emerson must have felt that he was destined for the ministry. In 1829 he was invited to become the pastor of the Second Church of Boston, and in that same year he married Ellen Tucker, whose death seventeen months later devastated him.

Emerson severed his formal relations with the church in 1832 because he could not believe in certain of its teachings. Given his family background, this must have been a difficult act, amounting to Emerson's declaration of moral independence. In the same year he furthered his independence by sailing to Europe, where he met some of the major English literary figures of the day, including the essayist Thomas Carlyle and the great romantic poets William Wordsworth and Samual Taylor Coleridge.

33

After returning from Europe, Emerson began to give the lectures that eventually were to make him famous. In 1835 he married Lydia Jackson and bought the house in Concord that he would own for forty-seven years. A year later he published his influential essay "Nature," and in 1837 he delivered his address, "The American Scholar," which announced, "First in time and first in importance of the influences upon the mind is that of nature." This assertion, together with others like the passage quoted earlier from "Nature," helped American writers to look for inspiration here at home, rather than in Europe. With other lectures—like "The Divinity School Address" of 1838 and essays like "Self-Reliance," "The Over-Soul," and "The Poet"— Emerson stressed the importance of nature as a reflection of the unifying spirit that resides in all beings.

Many have called Emerson's thought transcendentalism—a doctrine maintaining that reality is spiritual rather than physical and can be understood through intuition rather than rational thought. Although Emerson never fully embraced the term, he did support his transcendentalist friends such as Margaret Fuller, Bronson Alcott, George Ripley, and Jones Very. It is ironic that Henry David Thoreau—the other great transcendental writer, who was also a friend and fellow townsman of Emerson—did not call himself a transcendentalist either. Neither writer wanted to be part of a movement, yet today people call Emerson and Thoreau transcendentalists. As Emerson wrote in his journal, "It [the intent of Emerson's teachings] did not go from any wish in me to bring men to me, but to themselves. I delight in driving them from me."

At the time of his death in 1882, Emerson was an internationally famous man of letters whose ideas and belief in the power of the human spirit had laid the foundation for the great American writing that was to come.

Thought

Influenced by his readings of Hindu scriptures, Emerson believed that a single unifying spirit flowed through all things. Although he usually referred to this spirit as the Over-Soul, he also called it the Unity, the Supreme Critic, the One, the Supreme Mind, the Deity, the Seer, the Spirit, the Omniscience, God, and many other names. Emerson said that we can perceive Over-Soul in two ways: directly through intuition and indirectly through observing Nature, which reflects the Over-Soul.

To Emerson, Nature, which he defined as all natural and man-made objects, was an illusion. The real world was the world of the spirit, which radiates through the illusory world of nature. Thus people whose life is in accord with the Over-Soul perceive the Spirit in a river or in a landscape, whereas people who are out of touch with the Over-Soul see only water, grass, trees, sky, and topography. Emerson believed that most of us are too caught up with the details of life to take the time to see the beauty and spirituality around us and to listen for the messages the Over-Soul sends us through our faculty of intuition.

I am not poor, but I am proud,
   Of one inalienable right,
Above the envy of the crowd,—
   Thought's holy light.

5 Better it is than gems or gold,
   And oh! it cannot die,
But thought will glow when the sun grows cold,
   And mix with Deity.

COMMENTARY AND QUESTIONS

1. What do you think of these ideas? Have you heard them in similar forms before? If so, where? Why do you think Emerson's views were popular with young Americans in the mid-nineteenth century? Can you see traces of Emerson's thought in the poetry of Bryant? Where? Explain?

2. What does Emerson mean when he says that thought will "mix with Deity"? How does this idea relate to the Over-Soul?

Self-Reliance

Henceforth, please God, forever I forego
The yoke of men's opinions. I will be
Light-hearted as a bird, and live with God.
I find him in the bottom of my heart,
5 I hear continually his voice therein.

          *   *   *

The little needle always knows the North,
The little bird remembereth his note,
And this wise Seer within me never errs.
I never taught it what it teaches me;
10 I only follow, when I act aright.

COMMENTARY AND QUESTIONS

1. "Self-Reliance" describes that virtue that allows us to follow our own beliefs, instincts, and intuitions, rather than to follow blindly the opinions of others. Only through self-reliance, taught Emerson, can we stay in touch with the Over-Soul. How does "Self-Reliance" develop Emerson's idea of the Over-Soul? Carefully note lines 6–10.

2. Note that Emerson thinks of self-reliance as following, not initiating. How do you conceive of self-reliance?

The Rhodora[1]

On Being Asked, Whence Is the Flower?

In May, when sea-winds pierced our solitudes,
I found the fresh Rhodora in the woods,
Spreading its leafless blooms in a damp nook,
To please the desert and the sluggish brook.
5 The purple petals, fallen in the pool,
Made the black water with their beauty gay;
Here might the red-bird come his plumes to cool,
And court the flower that cheapens his array.
Rhodora! if the sages ask thee why
10 This charm is wasted on the earth and sky,
Tell them, dear, that if eyes were made for seeing,
Then Beauty is its own excuse for being:
Why thou wert[2] there, O rival of the rose!
I never thought to ask, I never knew:
15 But, in my simple ignorance, suppose
The self-same Power that brought me there brought you.

[1] **Rhodora:** a shrub with rose-purple flowers.
[2] **wert:** were.

COMMENTARY AND QUESTIONS

1. Compare the last lines of "The Rhodora" to the last lines of Bryant's "To a Waterfowl." What do the similarities between the two poems suggest about the American romantic attitude toward nature?

The Snow-Storm

Announced by all the trumpets of the sky,
Arrives the snow, and, driving o'er the fields,
Seems nowhere to alight: the whited air
Hides hills and woods, the river, and the heaven,
5 And veils the farm-house at the garden's end.
The sled and traveller stopped, the courier's feet
Delayed, all friends shut out, the housemates sit
Around the radiant fireplace, enclosed
In a tumultuous privacy of storm.

10 Come see the north wind's masonry.
    Out of an unseen quarry evermore
    Furnished with tile, the fierce artificer
    Curves his white bastions with projected roof
    Round every windward stake, or tree, or door.
15 Speeding, the myriad-handed, his wild work
    So fanciful, so savage, nought[1] cares he
    For number or proportion. Mockingly,
    On coop or kennel he hangs Parian[2] wreaths;
    A swan-like form invests[3] the hidden thorn;
20 Fills up the farmer's lane from wall to wall,

    Maugre[4] the farmer's sighs; and at the gate
    A tapering turret overtops the work.
    And when his hours are numbered, and the world
    Is all his own, retiring, as he were not,
25 Leaves, when the sun appears, astonished Art
    To mimic in slow structures, stone by stone,
    Built in an age, the mad wind's night-work,
    The frolic architecture of the snow.

[1] **nought:** nothing.
[2] **Parian:** compares the snow to pure white marble from the Greek island of Paros.
[3] **invests:** adorns.
[4] **Maugre:** in spite of.

COMMENTARY AND QUESTIONS

1. What appears to be Emerson's intention for "The Snow-Storm"? How, if at all, is this poem unlike the other Emerson poems included here? Where does the poem bear the mark of Emerson's thought and style?

2. Paraphrase the last sentence of "The Snow-Storm," lines 23–28. Are the lines effective? Why or why not?

3. Do you detect the presence of the Over-Soul in "The Snow-Storm"? If so, where?

The Apology

    Think me not unkind and rude
        That I walk alone in grove and glen;
    I go to the god of the wood
        To fetch his word to men.

5   Tax not my sloth that I
        Fold my arms beside the brook;
    Each cloud that floated in the sky
        Writes a letter in my book.

    Chide me not, laborious band,
10   For the idle flowers I brought;
    Every aster in my hand
      Goes home loaded with a thought.

    There was never mystery
      But 't is figured in the flowers;
15   Was never secret history
      But birds tell it in the bowers.

    One harvest from thy field
      Homeward brought the oxen strong;
    A second crop thine acres yield
20   Which I gather in a song.

COMMENTARY AND QUESTIONS

1. In "The Apology," who or what is the "laborious band" in line 9?

2. Paraphrase stanza 5 of "The Apology," being sure to explain the "second crop" of line 19.

3. What is Emerson's apology? To whom and how seriously does he make it?

4. What does the poem tell us of the relationship between the physical world Emerson called Nature and the spiritual world?

Brahma[1]

    If the red slayer think he slays,
      Or if the slain think he is slain,
    They know not well the subtle ways
      I keep, and pass, and turn again.
5   Far or forgot to me is near;
      Shadow and sunlight are the same;
    The vanished gods to me appear;
      And one to me are shame and fame.

    They reckon ill who leave me out;
10   When me they fly, I am the wings;
    I am the doubter and the doubt,
      And I the hymn the Brahmin sings.

    The strong gods pine for my abode,
      And pine in vain the sacred Seven;[2]
15   But thou, meek lover of the good!
      Find me, and turn thy back on heaven.

[1] **Brahma:** a Hindu God.
[2] **sacred Seven:** Hindu saints.

COMMENTARY AND QUESTIONS

1. "Brahma" reflects the influence of Hindu thought on Emerson. The speaker embraces all being and transcends our ideas of time, space, and conventional morality. Who or what is the speaker in this poem? How does this speaker express ideas of time, space, and morality?

2. In a paragraph, explain the theme of "Brahma."

REVIEW

1. Cite your favorite line or brief passage from Emerson's poetry and tell why you like the line or passage.

2. Using the poems and the commentary preceding "Thought," define Emerson's doctrine.

HENRY WADSWORTH LONGFELLOW
1807–1882

Perhaps the most popular American poet of his time, Henry Wadsworth Longfellow published more than thirty books—the best remembered being *Evangeline* (1847), *The Song of Hiawatha* (1855), *The Courtship of Miles Standish and Other Poems* (1858), and *Tales of A Wayside Inn* (1863). In the years immediately preceding his death, his birthday was celebrated in public schools, and in 1884 his bust was placed in the Poets' Corner of Westminster Abbey.

Born in Portland, Maine, Longfellow attended Portland Academy and entered the class of 1825 at Bowdoin College, where he was a classmate of Nathaniel Hawthorne. During his years at Bowdoin, Longfellow wrote and published poetry. After graduation he studied from 1826 to 1829 in France, Spain, Italy, and Germany before assuming a professorship of modern languages at his alma mater. In 1835 and 1836 Longfellow studied in Germany and Scandinavia in preparation for a professorship at Harvard College. On this second trip to Europe his young wife of four years died suddenly.

As a professor of modern languages at Harvard from 1836 to 1854, Longfellow published his poems frequently, traveled widely, and made many close friends in Europe and America. In 1843 he married Fanny Appleton; the couple had six children and enjoyed eighteen happy years before Fanny died tragically in 1861. Longfellow made his last visit to Europe from 1868 to 1869 and continued to publish his poems up to his death in 1882.

Like the earlier poet Philip Freneau and his friend John Greenleaf Whittier, Longfellow wrote patriotic poems about recent and historical events. And like James Fenimore Cooper, in the "Song of Hiawatha" Longfellow developed the Native American as a literary subject in more depth than had Freneau and Bryant. More important, however, Longfellow used his broad knowledge of European languages and literatures to experiment with poetic forms, a step that helped set the stage for experimentation in American poetry.

40

from *The Song of Hiawatha*

Hiawatha and Mudjekeewis

Out of childhood into manhood
Now had grown my Hiawatha,
Skilled in all the craft of hunters,
Learned in all the lore of old men,
5   In all youthful sports and pastimes,
In all manly arts and labors.
    Swift of foot was Hiawatha;
He could shoot an arrow from him,
And run forward with such fleetness,
10   That the arrow fell behind him!
Strong of arm was Hiawatha;
He could shoot ten arrows upward,
Shoot them with such strength and swiftness,
That the tenth had left the bow-string
15   Ere the first to earth had fallen!
    He had mittens, Minjekahwun,
Magic mittens made of deer-skin;
When upon his hands he wore them,
He could smite the rocks asunder,
20   He could grind them into powder.
He had moccasins enchanted,
Magic moccasins of deer-skin;
When he bound them round his ankles,
When upon his feet he tied them,
25   At each stride a mile he measured!
    Much he questioned old Nokomis[1]
Of his father Mudjekeewis;
Learned from her the fatal secret
Of the beauty of his mother,
30   Of the falsehood of his father;
And his heart was hot within him,
Like a living coal his heart was.
    Then he said to old Nokomis,
"I will go to Mudjekeewis,
35   See how fares it with my father,
At the doorways of the West-Wind,
At the portals of the Sunset!"
    From his lodge went Hiawatha,
Dressed for travel, armed for hunting;
40   Dressed in deer-skin shirt and leggings,

---

[1] **Nokomis:** Hiawatha's grandmother, "daughter of the Moon."

Richly wrought with quills and wampum;
On his head his eagle-feathers,
Round his waist his belt of wampum,
In his hand his bow of ash-wood,
45 Strung with sinews of the reindeer;
In his quiver oaken arrows,
Tipped with jasper,[2] winged with feathers;
With his mittens, Minjekahwun,
With his moccasins enchanted.
50   Warning said the old Nokomis,
"Go not forth, O Hiawatha!
To the kingdom of the West-Wind,
To the realms of Mudjekeewis,
Lest he harm you with his magic,
55 Lest he kill you with his cunning!"
    But the fearless Hiawatha
Heeded not her woman's warning;
Forth he strode into the forest,
At each stride a mile he measured;
60 Lurid seemed the sky above him,
Lurid seemed the earth beneath him,
Hot and close the air around him,
Filled with smoke and fiery vapors,
As of burning woods and prairies,
65 For his heart was hot within him,
Like a living coal his heart was.
    So he journeyed westward, westward,
Left the fleetest deer behind him,
Left the antelope and bison;
70 Crossed the rushing Esconaba,
Crossed the mighty Mississippi,
Passed the Mountains of the Prairie,
Passed the land of Crows and Foxes,
Passed the dwellings of the Blackfeet,
75 Came unto the Rocky Mountains,
To the kingdom of the West-Wind,
Where upon the gusty summits
Sat the ancient Mudjekeewis,
Ruler of the winds of heaven.
80   Filled with awe was Hiawatha
At the aspect of his father.
On the air about him wildly
Tossed and streamed his cloudy tresses,
Gleamed like drifting snow his tresses,

[2] **jasper:** a variety of quartz, reddish, brown, or yellow.

85 Glared like Ishkoodah, the comet,
    Like the star with fiery tresses.
        Filled with joy was Mudjekeewis
    When he looked on Hiawatha,
    Saw his youth rise up before him
90 In the face of Hiawatha,
    Saw the beauty of Wenonah
    From the grave rise up before him.
        "Welcome!" said he, "Hiawatha,
    To the kingdom of the West-Wind!
95 Long have I been waiting for you!
    Youth is lovely, age is lonely,
    Youth is fiery, age is frosty;
    You bring back the days departed,
    You bring back my youth of passion,
100 And the beautiful Wenonah!"
        Many days they talked together,
    Questioned, listened, waited, answered;
    Much the mighty Mudjekeewis
    Boasted of his ancient prowess,
105 Of his perilous adventures,
    His indomitable courage,
    His invulnerable body.
        Patiently sat Hiawatha,
    Listening to his father's boasting;
110 With a smile he sat and listened,
    Uttered neither threat nor menace,
    Neither word nor look betrayed him,
    But his heart was hot within him,
    Like a living coal his heart was.
115   Then he said, "O Mudjekeewis,
    Is there nothing that can harm you?
    Nothing that you are afraid of?"
    And the mighty Mudjekeewis,
    Grand and gracious in his boasting,
120 Answered, saying, "There is nothing,
    Nothing but the black rock yonder,
    Nothing but the fatal Wawbeek?"
        And he looked at Hiawatha
    With a wise look and benignant,
125 With a countenance paternal,
    Looked with pride upon the beauty
    Of his tall and graceful figure,
    Saying, "O my Hiawatha!
    Is there anything can harm you?
130 Anything you are afraid of?"

But the wary Hiawatha
Paused awhile, as if uncertain,
Held his peace, as if resolving,
And then answered, "There is nothing,
135   Nothing but the bulrush yonder,
Nothing but the great Apukwa!"
And as Mudjekeewis, rising,
Stretched his hand to pluck the bulrush,
Hiawatha cried in terror,
140   Cried in well-dissembled terror,
"Kago! kago! do not touch it!"
"Ah, kaween!" said Mudjekeewis,
"No indeed, I will not touch it!"
Then they talked of other matters;
145   First of Hiawatha's brothers,
First of Wabun, of the East-Wind,
Of the South-Wind, Shawondasee,
Of the North, Kabibonokka;
Then of Hiawatha's mother,
150   Of the beautiful Wenonah,
Of her birth upon the meadow,
Of her death, as old Nokomis
Had remembered and related.
And he cried, "O Mudjekeewis,
155   It was you who killed Wenonah,
Took her young life and her beauty,
Broke the Lily of the Prairie,
Trampled it beneath your footsteps;
You confess it! you confess it!"
160   And the mighty Mudjekeewis
Tossed upon the wind his tresses,
Bowed his hoary head in anguish,
With a silent nod assented.
Then up started Hiawatha,
165   And with threatening look and gesture
Laid his hand upon the black rock,
On the fatal Wawbeek laid it,
With his mittens, Minjekahwun,
Rent the jutting crag asunder,
170   Smote and crushed it into fragments,
Hurled them madly at his father,
The remorseful Mudjekeewis,
For his heart was hot within him,
Like a living coal his heart was.
175   But the ruler of the West-Wind
Blew the fragments backward from him,

With the breathing of his nostrils,
With the tempest of his anger,
Blew them back at his assailant;
180 Seized the bulrush, the Apukwa,
Dragged it with its roots and fibres
From the margin of the meadow,
From its ooze, the giant bulrush;
Long and loud laughed Hiawatha!
185   Then began the deadly conflict,
Hand to hand among the mountains;
From his eyry screamed the eagle,
The Keneu, the great war-eagle
Sat upon the crags around them,
190 Wheeling flapped his wings above them.
    Like a tall tree in the tempest
Bent and lashed the giant bulrush;
And in masses huge and heavy
Crashing fell the fatal Wawbeek;
195 Till the earth shook with the tumult
And confusion of the battle,
And the air was full of shoutings,
And the thunder of the mountains,
Starting, answered, "Baim-wawa!"
200   Back retreated Mudjekeewis,
Rushing westward o'er the moutains,
Stumbling westward down the mountains,
Three whole days retreated fighting,
Still pursued by Hiawatha
205 To the doorways of the West-Wind,
To the portals of the Sunset.
To the earth's remotest border,
Where into the empty spaces
Sinks the sun, as a flamingo
210 Drops into her nest at nightfall,
In the melancholy marshes.
    "Hold!" at length cried Mudjekeewis,
"Hold, my son, my Hiawatha!
'T is impossible to kill me,
215 For you cannot kill the immortal.
I have put you to this trial,
But to know and prove your courage;
Now receive the prize of valor!
    "Go back to your home and people,
220 Live among them, toil among them,
Cleanse the earth from all that harms it,
Clear the fishing-grounds and rivers,

Slay all monsters and magicians,
All the Wendigoes, the giants,
225 All the serpents, the Kenabeeks,
As I slew the Mishe-Mokwa,
Slew the Great Bear of the mountains.
    "And at last when Death draws near you,
When the awful eyes of Pauguk
230 Glare upon you in the darkness,
I will share my kingdom with you . . ."

COMMENTARY AND QUESTIONS

1. Compare the story of Hiawatha and Mudjekeewis, Hiawatha's immortal father, to similar stories from Greek and Roman mythology. Does the story's plot—the departure from home, Nokomis's warnings, the journey, the characters' cunning, the fight, the solution—bring to mind similar narratives? Explain fully.

2. Does Hiawatha remind you of any other heroes from film, television, or literature? Explain.

3. The meter of "Hiawatha" was inspired by Longfellow's reading of German poetry. Scan the poem's meter. What kinds of metrical feet occur? How is the effect of this rhythm different from the effect of iambic rhythm, the predominant rhythm in English poetry? Is the poem's meter appropriate to the subject matter? What other poems have we read that depart from a primarily iambic pattern? What conclusions can you draw?

4. What do you think was Longfellow's intention in writing "Hiawatha"?

Chaucer[1]

An old man in a lodge within a park;
    The chamber walls depicted all around
    With portraitures of huntsman, hawk, and hound.
    And the hurt deer. He listeneth to the lark,
5 Whose song comes with the sunshine through the dark
    Of painted glass in leaden lattice bound;
    He listeneth and he laugheth at the sound,
    Then writeth in a book like any clerk.
He is the poet of the dawn, who wrote
10   The Canterbury Tales, and his old age
    Made beautiful with song; and as I read
I hear the crowing cock, I hear the note
    Of lark and linnet,[2] and from every page
    Rise odors of ploughed field or flowery mead.

---

[1] **Chaucer:** Geoffrey Chaucer (1340–1400), the first great English poet and the author of the *Canterbury Tales*, which depicted characters from all levels of his society.
[2] **linnet:** a small songbird.

COMMENTARY AND QUESTIONS

1. In what traditional form is this poem written?

2. What do you think Longfellow means in line 9 by "poet of the dawn"?

3. The last lines claim that Chaucer brings to life the sounds, sights, and even the odors of his time. What poem or poems have you read in this book that evoke three senses?

Aftermath[1]

When the Summer fields are mown,
When the birds are fledged and flown,
   And the dry leaves strew the path;
With the falling of the snow,
5 With the cawing of the crow,
Once again the fields we mow
   And gather in the aftermath.

Not the sweet, new grass with flowers
Is this harvesting of ours;
10   Not the upland clover bloom;
But the rowen[2] mixed with weeds,
Tangled tufts from marsh and meads,
Where the poppy drops its seeds
   In the silence and the gloom.

[1] **aftermath:** a period of time following a disastrous event.
[2] **rowen:** the second crop (of hay, for instance) of a season.

COMMENTARY AND QUESTIONS

1. Note the poem's rhyme scheme and discuss its effectiveness.

2. Describe and discuss the tone of "Aftermath."

REVIEW

1. Reread Bryant's and Freneau's poems about Native Americans. Can you identify interesting similarities and differences between these poems and "Hiawatha"? How accurately do you think these poems represent the experience of Native Americans? How, if at all, does "Hiawatha" represent another stage in the evolution of American poetry?

2. Longfellow was the most popular poet of his day. Judging from the selections in this book and from other Longfellow poems you may have read, what do you think was the source of his popularity? Do you find his work meaningful and moving? Discuss.

3. Write a poem of at least ten lines in the rhythm of "Hiawatha."

JOHN GREENLEAF WHITTIER
1807–1892

John Greenleaf Whittier wrote many of his best poems about rural New England—evoking the homely yet moving details of daily life. He was in fact the first popular American poet to describe convincingly, if often sentimentally, the lives of Americans living in small towns and on farms. Although other writers of his day viewed American scenes through history books or through windows of studys, Whittier employed his recollections of his own rural boyhood as the subjects of his poems.

Born in Haverhill, Massachusetts, Whittier attended local schools for his primary education and spent two short periods at the Haverhill Academy. At nineteen he placed his first poem in the *Haverhill Gazette,* and the next year he became *Gazette's* editor, the first of many editorial positions he would hold. Born a Quaker, Whittier became an active abolitionist, published his first antislavery article in 1833, and in that same year won a seat in the Massachusetts State Legistature. Later he ran for Congress, opposed the Mexican war, and helped establish the Republican party.

Despite his active political involvement in Pennsylvania, New York, and Massachusetts, Whittier continued to write poetry. His poems appeared frequently in the *Atlantic Monthly* and other magazines, eventually achieving a popularity close to that of Longfellow's work. Before his death he edited a seven-volume set of his collected works. In 1876 Whittier retired to Danvers, Massachusetts, where he spent the last years of his life.

Skipper Ireson's Ride

Of all the rides since the birth of time,
Told in story or sung in rhyme,—
On Apuleius's Golden Ass,[1]
Or one-eyed Calendar's[2] horse of brass,

[1] **Golden Ass:** a Roman satire that depicts man as an ass.
[2] **Calender:** a character from the *Arabian Knights.*

5   Witch astride of a human back,
Islam's prophet[3] on Al-Borák,—
The strangest ride that ever was sped
Was Ireson's, out from Marblehead!
   Old Floyd Ireson, for his hard heart,
10   Tarred and feathered and carried in a cart
      By the women of Marblehead!

Body of turkey, head of owl,
Wings a-droop like a rained-on fowl,
Feathered and ruffled in every part,
15   Skipper Ireson stood in the cart.
Scores of women, old and young,
Strong of muscle, and glib of tongue,
Pushed and pulled up the rocky lane,
Shouting and singing the shrill refrain:
20   "Here's Flud Oirson, fur his horrd horrt,
     Torr'd an' futherr'd an' corr'd in a corrt
      By the women o' Morble'ead!"

Wrinkled scolds with hands on hips,
Girls in bloom of cheek and lips,
25   Wild-eyed, free-limbed, such as chase
Bacchus[4] round some antique vase,
Brief of skirt, with ankles bare,
Loose of kerchief and loose of hair,
With conch-shells blowing and fish-horns' twang,
30   Over and over the Mænads[5] sang:
     "Here's Flud Oirson, fur his horrd horrt,
     Torr'd an' futherr'd an' corr'd in a corrt
      By the women o' Morble'ead!"

Small pity for him!—He sailed away
35   From a leaking ship in Chaleur Bay,[6]—
Sailed away from a sinking wreck,
With his own town's-people on her deck!
"Lay by! lay by!" they called to him.
Back he answered, "Sink or swim!
40   Brag of your catch of fish again!"
And off he sailed through the fog and rain!
   Old Floyd Ireson, for his hard heart,
     Tarred and feathered and carried in a cart
      By the women of Marblehead!

[3] **Islam's prophet:** Mohammed, who was taken to heaven by a creature named Al-Borák.
[4] **Bacchus:** the Greek god of wine.
[5] **Maenads:** women belonging to Bacchus's cult.
[6] **Chaleur Bay:** located in the Gulf of Saint Lawrence.

45 Fathoms deep in dark Chaleur
   That wreck shall lie forevermore.
   Mother and sister, wife and maid,
   Looked from the rocks of Marblehead
   Over the moaning and rainy sea,—
50 Looked for the coming that might not be!
   What did the winds and the sea-birds say
   Of the cruel captain who sailed away?—
     Old Floyd Ireson, for his hard heart,
     Tarred and feathered and carried in a cart
55   By the women of Marblehead!
   Through the street, on either side,
   Up flew windows, doors swung wide;
   Sharp-tongued spinsters, old wives gray,
   Treble lent the fish-horn's bray.
60 Sea-worn grandsires, cripple-bound,
   Hulks of old sailors run aground,
   Shook head, and fist, and hat, and cane,
   And cracked with curses the hoarse refrain:
     "Here's Flud Oirson, fur his horrd horrt,
65   Torr'd an' futherr'd an' corr'd in a corrt
     By the women o' Morble'ead!"

   Sweetly along the Salem road
   Bloom of orchard and lilac showed.
   Little the wicked skipper knew
70 Of the fields so green and the sky so blue.
   Riding there in his sorry trim,
   Like an Indian idol glum and grim,
   Scarcely he seemed the sound to hear
   Of voices shouting, far and near:
75   "Here's Flud Oirson, fur his horrd horrt,
     Torr'd an' futherr'd an' corr'd in a corrt
     By the women o' Morble'ead!"

   "Hear me, neighbors!" at last he cried,—
   "What to me is this noisy ride?
80 What is the shame that clothes the skin
   To the nameless horror that lives within?
   Waking or sleeping, I see a wreck,
   And hear a cry from a reeling deck!
   Hate me and curse me,—I only dread
85 The hand of God and the face of the dead!"
     Said old Floyd Ireson, for his hard heart,
     Tarred and feathered and carried in a cart
     By the women of Marblehead!

Then the wife of the skipper lost at sea
90 Said, "God has touched him! why should we!"
Said an old wife mourning her only son,
"Cut the rogue's tether and let him run!"
So with soft relentings and rude excuse,
Half scorn, half pity, they cut him loose,
95 And gave him a cloak to hide him in,
And left him alone with his shame and sin.
  Poor Floyd Ireson, for his hard heart,
  Tarred and feathered and carried in a cart
    By the women of Marblehead!

COMMENTARY AND QUESTIONS

1. Like his friend and contemporary James Russell Lowell, Whittier employs local dialect. What does the use of dialect suggest about the attitude of poem's speaker toward the language of the people of Marblehead, Massachusetts? Do you think that dialect has a place in poetry? Where have you seen dialect used in other poems or prose? Do you think that the use of dialect is a step toward Americans writing in American English? Discuss.

2. Briefly outline the poem's narrative.

3. What other narrative poems have we read?

4. Describe the poem's form. Is the form successful in conveying emotion?

5. "Skipper Ireson's Ride" is a fictionalized account of a real event that occurred in 1808. To what extent do you think Whittier has softened the real violence of the event? Quote specific passages in your discussion.

REVIEW

1. What appears to be Whittier's primary contribution to the evolution of American poetry? Describe this contribution.

2. Is Whittier's poetry quaint, charming, but superficial, or is it well-crafted and penetrating? Discuss.

OLIVER WENDELL HOLMES
1809–1894

Born in Cambridge, Massachusetts, to Reverend Abiel Holmes, Oliver Wendell Holmes received his primary education in Cambridge. He then attended Phillips Academy, Andover, before entering the class of 1829 at Harvard College. The next year, hearing plans to destroy the Revolutionary War frigate *Constitution*, he quickly wrote "Old Ironsides," which became instantly popular and was published in newspapers nationally. A year later his publication of two essays entitled "The Autocrat of the Breakfast Table" helped establish the twenty-two-year-old Holmes as a skilled and witty essayist.

As well as being a prolific poet and essayist, Holmes was also a teacher of anatomy, first at Dartmouth College and then at Harvard. He began his medical career at twenty-seven after studying medicine in Paris and then receiving his degree from Harvard Medical School in 1836. The next year he married Amelia Lee Jackson, a Bostonian and daughter of a Massachusetts supreme court justice. Of the Holmeses' three children, the eldest, Oliver Wendell Holmes, Jr., was to become a distinguished U.S. Supreme Court justice. At Harvard Oliver Wendell, Sr., became a revered teacher and the author of at least one important medical essay. He was the Parkman Professor of Anatomy and Physiology at Harvard Medical school from 1847 to 1882 and the medical school's dean from 1847 to 1853.

Publishing his first volume of poems in 1836, Holmes enjoyed a long and fruitful literary career. His "Autocrat of the Breakfast Table" articles, later published in the *Atlantic Monthly*, helped to gain him wide popularity, as did his light poems and more serious works such as "The Chambered Nautilus," perhaps his finest poem.

53

The Chambered Nautilus[1]

This is the ship of pearl, which, poets feign,[2]
   Sails[3] the unshadowed main,—
   The venturous bark[4] that flings
On the sweet summer wind its purpled wings
5 In gulfs enchanted, where the Siren sings,
   And coral reefs lie bare,
Where the cold sea-maids rise to sun their streaming hair.

Its webs of living gauze no more unfurl;
   Wrecked is the ship of pearl!
10   And every chambered cell,
Where its dim dreaming life was wont to dwell,
As the frail tenant shaped his growing shell,
   Before thee lies revealed,—
Its irised[5] ceiling rent, its sunless crypt unsealed!

15 Year after year beheld the silent toil
   That spread his lustrous coil;[6]
   Still, as the spiral grew,
He left the past year's dwelling for the new,
Stole with soft step its shining archway through,
20   Built up its idle door,
Stretched in his last-found home, and knew the old no more.

Thanks for the heavenly message brought by thee,
   Child of the wandering sea,
   Cast from her lap, forlorn!
25 From thy dead lips a clearer note is born
Than ever Triton[7] blew from wreathèd horn!
   While on mine ear it rings,
Through the deep caves of thought I hear a voice that sings:—

Build thee more stately mansions, O my soul,
30   As the swift seasons roll!
   Leave thy low-vaulted[8] past!
Let each new temple, nobler than the last,
Shut thee from heaven with a dome more vast,
   Till thou at length art free,
35 Leaving thine outgrown shell by life's unresting sea!

---

1 **Chambered Nautilus:** mollusk found in the Indian and Pacific oceans and having a spiral shell with a series of air-tight chambers.
2 **feign:** to pretend.
3 **Sails:** the ancients believed the nautilus used a membrane for a sail.
4 **bark:** a large sailing vessel with three to five masts.
5 **irised:** beautifully colored.
6 **coil:** the spiraling shell.
7 **Triton:** a Greek god of the sea.
8 **low-vaulted:** an arched ceiling of roof.

COMMENTARY AND QUESTIONS

1. How does the chambered nautilus sail "the unshadowed main" (line 2)?

2. Who is the speaker in the last stanza?

3. What is the poem's dominant metaphor?

4. What is the poem's "heavenly message" (line 22) brought by the "child of the wandering sea" (line 23)?

5. Given his theories of Nature and the Over-Soul, what would Emerson have thought of this poem? As you answer this question, refer specifically to lines from Emerson and to the commentary on Emerson.

6. Explain the thematic connection between this poem and Bryant's "To a Waterfowl."

7. Holmes considered this his best poem. Describe the strengths and weaknesses of "The Chambered Nautilus."

Old Ironsides[1]

Ay, tear her tattered ensign[2] down!
   Long has it waved on high,
And many an eye has danced to see
   That banner in the sky;
5 Beneath it rung the battle shout,
   And burst the cannon's roar;—
The meteor of the ocean air
   Shall sweep the clouds no more.

Her deck, once red with heroes' blood,
10   Where knelt the vanquished foe,
When winds were hurrying o'er the flood,
   And waves were white below,
No more shall feel the victor's tread,
   Or know the conquered knee;—
15 The harpies of the shore shall pluck
   The eagle of the sea!

Oh, better that her shattered hulk
   Should sink beneath the wave;
Her thunders shook the mighty deep,
20   And there should be her grave;
Nail to the mast her holy flag,
   Set every threadbare sail,
And give her to the god of storms,
   The lightning and the gale!

---

[1] **Old Ironsides:** the U.S. frigate *Constitution.* The poem was written in a response to plans to destroy the famous warship of the Revolution.

[2] **ensign:** a flag displaying an insignia.

COMMENTARY AND QUESTIONS

1. What is the poem's central figure of speech?

2. Note the metrical pattern, alternating lines of iambic tetrameter (four iambs) and iambic trimeter (three iambs), the same pattern used in many old Protestant hymns. How does this pattern affect the poem?

3. What is the poem's appeal? Be as specific as possible.

REVIEW

1. Of what earlier American poetry, if any, does Holmes's work remind you? Be specific.

2. Which do you think is the best of these two poems by Holmes? Support your reasons with appropriate examples.

EDGAR ALLAN POE
1809–1849

Born in Boston, Massachusetts, the son of itinerent actors, Edgar Allan Poe was orphaned at age two and raised by John and Frances Allan, a wealthy couple in Richmond, Virginia. After going to school in England for five years, where business had brought the Allans, he was tutored in Richmond for admission to the University of Virginia. There Poe incurred gambling debts and withdrew from the university before the end of his first year. Shortly afterward, he argued with John Allan, left home, and joined the army. Poe suffered throughout his life from mental instability, an inherited tendency toward alcoholism, and the insecurity generated by John Allan's failure to understand and support his foster son. After a period in the army, Poe resigned and entered West Point, hoping to please John Allan; however, Poe, temperamentally unsuited to the military life, was expelled after failing both to apply himself to his studies and to obey the academy's rules.

Like Bryant and Freneau, Poe became a journalist, working in Richmond, Philadelphia, and New York. In 1836 he married his thirteen-year-old cousin Virginia and lived with her and her mother, Mrs. Clemm. Dismissed from more than one editorial position for problems relating to his drinking, Poe was never able to ensure financial security for his family. His early death appears to have been the result of alcoholism and the stresses of his life.

The death of Virginia in 1847, as well as a broken love affair of youth, inspired many of Poe's tales and poems including "The Raven" and "Annabel Lee," which depict the pain of lost love and a sense of extreme mental depression. Along with Nathaniel Hawthorne and Herman Melville, Poe is one of the nineteenth-century American writers who explored the dark, irrational side of the human condition. He is, in fact, the only American poet of his century who explored the nature of obsession and insanity, common themes in twentieth-century poetry and fiction.

A Dream Within a Dream

"A Dream Within a Dream," like most of Poe's poetry and fiction, depicts a gloomy, dreamlike state where concrete objects serve more as symbols of the spirit, which Poe called the soul, than as images of reality. A poem, said Poe, "excites by elevating the soul." Through employing insistent rhythms, heavy rhymes, and refrains (repetitions of whole lines) in poems like "Annabel Lee" and "The Raven," Poe hoped to lift his audience to the supernal realm, the realm of spiritual beauty. Unlike all of the other poets we have read so far, Poe did not aim to teach a moral lesson, but purely to depict his dark vision of beauty "beyond the grave." In placing beauty before moral truth, Poe foreshadowed modern literature.

Take this kiss upon the brow!
And, in parting from you now,
Thus much let me avow—
You are not wrong, who deem
5   That my days have been a dream;
Yet if hope has flown away
In a night, or in a day,
In a vision, or in none,
Is it therefore the less gone?
10   *All* that we see or seem
Is but a dream within a dream.

I stand amid the roar
Of a surf-tormented shore,
And I hold within my hand
15   Grains of the golden sand—
How few! yet how they creep
Through my fingers to the deep,
While I weep—while I weep!
O God! can I not grasp
20   Them with a tighter clasp?
O God! can I not save
One from the pitiless wave?
Is *all* that we see or seem
But a dream within a dream?

COMMENTARY AND QUESTIONS

1. What is the dream? What, then, is the "dream within the dream"?

2. What images does Poe use to depict the trials of life?

3. What do the "grains of golden sand" symbolize?

4. Explain how the rhyme scheme affects the poem's mood.

5. That life is actually a dream and reality is spiritual, not physical, is a common romantic perception. Emerson developed this idea in his theory of the Over-Soul. Contrast Emerson's poem "Brahma" to Poe's "A Dream Within a Dream."

Sonnet: To Science

Science! true daughter of Old Time thou art!
    Who alterest all things with thy peering eyes.
Why preyest thou thus upon the poet's heart,
    Vulture, whose wings are dull realities?
5 How should he love thee? or how deem thee wise,
    Who wouldst not leave him in his wandering
To seek for treasure in the jewelled skies,
    Albeit he soared with an undaunted wing?
Hast thou not dragged Diana[1] from her car[2]?
10   And driven the Hamadryad[3] from the wood
To seek a shelter in some happier star?
    Hast thou not torn the Naiad[4] from her flood,
The Elfin[5] from the green grass, and from me
    The summer dream beneath the tamarind[6] tree?

[1] **Diana:** Greek goddess of the moon.
[2] **car:** chariot.
[3] **Hamadryad:** a nymph who dwells in the forest, the spirit of a particular tree.
[4] **Naiad:** a nymph presiding over a brook, spring, or fountain.
[5] **Elfin:** pertaining to elves.
[6] **tamarind tree:** a tropical old-world tree bearing an edible fruit.

COMMENTARY AND QUESTIONS

1. How does Poe personify science?

2. Of what does Poe accuse science? Do you think the accusations are valid and important? In your opinion, has scientific discovery inhibited poetry? Discuss.

The Raven

Once upon a midnight dreary, while I pondered, weak and weary,
Over many a quaint and curious volume of forgotten lore,
While I nodded, nearly napping, suddenly there came a tapping,
As of some one gently rapping, rapping at my chamber door.
5 " 'Tis some visitor," I muttered, "tapping at my chamber door—
    Only this, and nothing more."

Ah, distinctly I remember it was in the bleak December,
And each separate dying ember wrought its ghost upon the floor.
Eagerly I wished the morrow;—vainly I had sought to borrow
10 From my books surcease of sorrows—sorrow for the lost Lenore—
For the rare and radiant maiden whom the angels name Lenore—
    Nameless here for evermore.

And the silken sad uncertain rustling of each purple curtain
Thrilled me—filled me with fantastic terrors never felt before;
15 So that now, to still the beating of my heart, I stood repeating
" 'Tis some visitor entreating entrance at my chamber door—
Some late visitor entreating entrance at my chamber door;—
  This it is, and nothing more."

Presently my soul grew stronger; hesitating then no longer,
20 "Sir," said I, "or Madam, truly your forgiveness I implore;
But the fact is I was napping, and so gently you came rapping,
And so faintly you came tapping, tapping at my chamber door,
That I scarce was sure I heard you"—here I opened wide the door;—
  Darkness there, and nothing more.

25 Deep into that darkness peering, long I stood there wondering, fearing,
Doubting, dreaming dreams no mortal ever dared to dream before;
But the silence was unbroken, and the darkness gave no token,
And the only word there spoken was the whispered word, "Lenore!"
This I whispered, and an echo murmured back the word, "Lenore!"
30   Merely this, and nothing more.

Back into the chamber turning, all my soul within me burning,
Soon again I heard a tapping somewhat louder than before.
"Surely," said I, "surely that is something at my window lattice;
Let me see, then, what thereat is, and this mystery explore—
35 Let my heart be still a moment and this mystery explore;—
  'Tis the wind and nothing more!"

Open here I flung the shutter, when, with many a flirt and flutter,
In there stepped a stately raven of the saintly days of yore.
Not the least obeisance made he; not an instant stopped or stayed he;
40 But, with mien of lord or lady, perched above my chamber door—
Perched upon a bust of Pallas[1] just above my chamber door—
  Perched, and sat, and nothing more.

Then this ebony bird beguiling my sad fancy into smiling,
By the grave and stern decorum of the countenance it wore,
45 "Though thy crest be shorn and shaven, thou," I said, "art sure no
    craven,
Ghastly grim and ancient raven wandering from the Nightly shore—
Tell me what thy lordly name is on the Night's Plutonian[2] shore!"
  Quoth[3] the raven, "Nevermore."

---

[1] **Pallas:** Pallas Athena, Greek goddess of wisdom.
[2] **Plutonian:** pertaining to Pluto, Roman god of the dead, ruler of the underworld.
[3] **Quoth:** uttered, said.

Much I marvelled this ungainly fowl to hear discourse so plainly,
50   Though its answer little meaning—little relevancy bore;
For we cannot help agreeing that no living human being
Ever yet was blessed with seeing bird above his chamber door—
Bird or beast upon the sculptured bust above his chamber door,
     With such name as "Nevermore."

55   But the raven, sitting lonely on the placid bust, spoke only
That one word, as if his soul in that one word he did outpour.
Nothing further then he uttered—not a feather then he fluttered—
Till I scarcely more than muttered "Other friends have flown before—
On the morrow *he* will leave me, as my hopes have flown before."
60   Then the bird said "Nevermore."

Startled at the stillness broken by reply so aptly spoken,
"Doubtless," said I, "what it utters is its only stock and store,
Caught from some unhappy master whom unmerciful Disaster
Followed fast and followed faster till his songs one burden bore—
65   Till the dirges of his Hope that melancholy burden bore
     Of 'Never—nevermore,' "

But the raven still beguiling all my sad soul into smiling,
Straight I wheeled a cushioned seat in front of bird and bust and door;
Then, upon the velvet sinking, I betook myself to linking
70   Fancy unto fancy, thinking what this ominous bird of yore—
What this grim, ungainly, ghastly, gaunt, and ominous bird of yore
     Meant in croaking "Nevermore."

This I sat engaged in guessing, but no syllable expressing
To the fowl whose fiery eyes now burned into my bosom's core;
75   This and more I sat divining, with my head at ease reclining
On the cushion's velvet lining that the lamp-light gloated o'er,
But whose velvet violet lining with the lamp-light gloating o'er,
     She shall press, ah, nevermore!

Then, methought, the air grew denser, perfumed from an unseen
     censer[4]
80   Swung by angels whose faint foot-falls tinkled on the tufted floor.
"Wretch," I cried, "thy God hath lent thee—by these angels he hath
     sent thee
Respite—respite and nepenthe[5] from thy memories of Lenore!
Quaff,[6] oh quaff this kind nepenthe, and forget this lost Lenore!"
     Quoth the raven, "Nevermore."

---

[4] **censer:** a container for incense.
[5] **nepenthe:** a legendary drug used to remedy grief.
[6] **quaff:** to drink heartily.

85   "Prophet" said I, "thing of evil!—prophet still, if bird or devil!—
Whether Tempter sent, or whether tempest tossed thee here ashore,
Desolate yet all undaunted, on this desert land enchanted—
On this home by Horror haunted—tell me truly, I implore—
Is there—is there balm in Gilead[7]?—tell me—tell me. I implore!"
90   Quoth the raven, "Nevermore."

"Prophet!" said I, "thing of evil—prophet still, if bird or devil!
By that Heaven that bends above us—by that God we both adore—
Tell this soul with sorrow laden if, within the distant Aidenn,[8]
It shall clasp a sainted maiden whom the angels name Lenore—
95   Clasp a rare and radiant maiden whom the angels name Lenore?"
     Quoth the raven, "Nevermore."

"Be that word our sign of parting, bird or fiend!" I shrieked, up-
     starting—
"Get thee back into the tempest and the Night's Plutonian shore!
Leave no black plume as a token of that lie thy soul hath spoken!
100   Leave my loneliness unbroken!—quit the bust above my door!
Take thy beak from out my heart, and take thy form from off my door!"
     Quoth the raven, "Nevermore."

And the raven, never flitting, still is sitting, still is sitting
On the pallid bust of Pallas, just above my chamber door;
105   And his eyes have all the seeming of a demon's that is dreaming,
And the lamp-light o'er him streaming throws his shadow on the floor;
And my soul from out that shadow that lies floating on the floor
     Shall be lifted—nevermore!

---

[7] **balm in Gilead:** a healing herb in an area referred to in the Bible (Jer. viii: 22).
[8] **Aidenn:** paradise.

COMMENTARY AND QUESTIONS

1. Briefly outline the poem's plot.
2. Why do you think that Poe has the raven perch on a bust of Pallas Athena?
3. Describe the speaker's state of mind.
4. How is Lenore important to the poem?
5. What is the poem's primary metrical pattern? What other sound devices does Poe employ heavily? How does the music of the poem affect the poem's meaning?
6. Why do you think "The Raven" has become a famous American poem?
7. Write a stanza in the style of "The Raven."

Annabel Lee

It was many and many a year ago,
   In a kingdom by the sea,
That a maiden there lived whom you may know
   By the name of ANNABEL LEE;
5 And this maiden she lived with no other thought
   Than to love and be loved by me.

I was a child and *she* was a child,
   In this kingdom by the sea:
But we loved with a love that was more than love—
10 I and my ANNABEL LEE;
With a love that the winged seraphs of heaven
   Coveted her and me.

And this was the reason that, long ago,
   In this kingdom by the sea,
15 A wind blew out of a cloud, chilling
   My beautiful ANNABEL LEE;
So that her highborn kinsmen came
   And bore her away from me,
To shut her up in a sepulchre
   In this kingdom by the sea.

The angels, not half so happy in heaven,
   Went envying her and me—
Yes!—that was the reason (as all men know,
   In this kingdom by the sea)
25 That the wind came out of the cloud by night,
   Chilling and killing my ANNABEL LEE.

But our love it was stronger by far than the love
   Of those who were older than we—
   Of many far wiser than we—
30 And neither the angels in heaven above,
   Nor the demons down under the sea,
Can ever dissever my soul from the soul
   Of the beautiful ANNABEL LEE:

For the moon never beams, without bringing me dreams
35 Of the beautiful ANNABEL LEE;
And the stars never rise, but I feel the bright eyes
   Of the beautiful ANNABEL LEE;
And so, the all night-tide, I lie down by the side
Of my darling,—my darling,—my life and my bride,
40 In her sepulchre there by the sea,
   In her tomb by the side of the sea.

COMMENTARY AND QUESTIONS

1. This poem, like many of Poe's short stories, is set in the dim, romanticized past. Why do you think certain romantic writers such as Edgar Allan Poe, Washington Irving, and Nathaniel Hawthorne set their tales in the "long ago and far away" rather than in the here and now? Discuss.

2. Describe the poem's plot.

3. After noting the poem's metrical pattern, rhyme scheme, and the final revelation in the last six lines, identify the source of "Annabel Lee" 's power.

4. Respond to the following statement: "The source of "Annabel Lee" 's power is its intoxicating combination of self-pity and self-righteousness." Support your response with specific examples from the poem.

REVIEW

1. Try to look at Poe's poems from the point of view of poets like Longfellow, Whittier, and Holmes. What do you think they thought of Poe's poetry? Explain your reasoning.

2. In comparison to the other poets we have studied, how do you rank Edgar Allan Poe?

3. Write a poem imitating Poe's style.

SIDNEY LANIER
1842–1881

The intense musical quality of his poems and their loving depictions of Southern landscape have made Sidney Lanier a significant figure in nineteenth-century American poetry. Born in Macon, Georgia, Lanier was the eldest of three children and the son of Robert Sampson Lanier, a lawyer. As the story goes, the seven-year-old Lanier, a precocious lover of music, fashioned a flute from a reed. At fifteen he entered Oglethorpe University, where he became interested in literature as well as music and read such English poets as Keats, Coleridge, Shelley, and Tennyson.

In 1861, a year after graduating from Oglethorpe at the head of his class, Lanier joined the Confederate army. He was later captured and spent four months in prison at Point Lookout, Maryland, where he continued to write poetry and entertained fellow prisoners by playing the flute which he carried with him throughout the war. He later described his experience as a prisoner of war in his novel *Tiger-Lilies*.

Returning home in 1865, Lanier suffered from tuberculosis, which had attacked him in prison and plagued him for the rest of his life. After marrying Mary Day in 1867, he followed an uneven career as a musician, lecturer, author of boys' books, novelist, and poet. Always burdened by both his poor health and insecure financial position, he endured a difficult life with few rewards. In the poems that follow, one can sense Lanier's melancholy, courage, and love for his native countryside.

The Mocking Bird

Superb and sole, upon a pluméd spray
That o'er the general leafage boldly grew,
He summ'd the woods in song[1]; or typic[2] drew
The watch of hungry hawks, the lone dismay

---

[1] **He summ'd the woods in song:** The mockingbird imitates all of the other birds in the woods, thus summing up the sounds of the woods.
[2] **typic:** typically.

5   Of languid doves when long their lovers stray,
And all birds' passion-plays that sprinkle dew
At morn in brake[3] or bosky[4] avenue.
Whate'er birds did or dreamed, this bird could say.
Then down he shot, bounced airily along
10 The sward, twitched in a grasshopper, made song
Midflight, perched, prinked,[5] and to his art again.
Sweet Science, this large riddle read me plain:
How may the death of that dull insect be
The life of yon[6] trim Shakspere on that tree?

[3] **brake:** an overgrown area, dense with brushwood.
[4] **bosky:** a wooded area.
[5] **prinked:** to primp, to neaten one's appearance.
[6] **yon:** yonder, over there.

COMMENTARY AND QUESTIONS

1. What do mockingbirds look like? How is their song unusual?

2. Paraphrase lines 6 and 7.

3. How do the line breaks in lines 9–14 affect our reading of the poem?

4. In what form is the poem written? How do the last two lines fulfill the requirements of this form?

5. What is the poem's theme?

6. Compare and contrast "The Mocking Bird" to an earlier American poem written about a bird, some other creature, or a natural object, such as a flower.

The Dying Words of Stonewall Jackson[1]

"Order A. P. Hill to prepare for battle."
"Tell Major Hawks to advance the Commissary train."
"Let us cross the river and rest in the shade."

The stars of Night contain the glittering Day
And rain his glory down with sweeter grace
Upon the dark World's grand, enchanted face—
     All loth[2] to turn away.

[1] **Stonewall Jackson:** Confederate General Thomas J. Jackson, General Robert E. Lee's "right arm."
[2] **loth:** also loath, unwilling or reluctant (not to be confused with *loath:* to dislike greatly).

5 And so the Day, about to yield his breath,
   Utters the stars unto the listening Night,
   To stand for burning fare-thee-wells of light
       Said on the verge of death.

   O hero-life that lit us like the sun!
10 O hero-words that glittered like the stars
   And stood and shone above the gloomy wars
       When the hero-life was done!

   The phantoms of a battle came to dwell
   I' the fitful vision of his dying eyes—
15 Yet even in battle-dreams, he sends supplies
       To those he loved so well.

   His army stands in battle-line arrayed:
   His couriers fly: all's done: now God decide!
   —And not till then saw he the Other Side
20   Or would accept the shade.

   Thou Land whose sun is gone, thy stars remain!
   Still shine the words that miniature his deeds.
   O thrice-beloved, where'er thy great heart bleeds,
       Solace has thou for pain!

COMMENTARY AND QUESTIONS

1. What do the stars in this elegy (a poem lamenting a death) stand for? In lines 19–21, what are "the Other Side," the "shade," and "Thou Land"?

2. Paraphrase the last sentence.

3. Written before Sidney Lanier reached the height of his poetic power, this poem is considered one of Lanier's minor works. How do you assess the poem's craft, its power to move the reader, and its historical value?

Song of the Chattahoochee[1]

   Out of the hills of Habersham,
   Down the valleys of Hall,[2]
I hurry amain[3] to reach the plain,
Run the rapid and leap the fall,
5 Split at the rock and together again,
   Accept my bed, or narrow or wide,

---

[1] **Chattahoochee:** a river in northern Georgia.
[2] **Habersham . . . Hall:** two counties in northern Georgia.
[3] **amain:** with strength and intensity.

And flee from folly on every side
With a lover's pain to attain the plain
    Far from the hills of Habersham,
10   Far from the valleys of Hall.

All Down the hills of Habersham,
    All through the valleys of Hall,
The rushes cried *Abide, abide,*
The willful waterweeds held me thrall,[4]
15 The laving[5] laurel turned my tide,
The ferns and the fondling grass said *Stay,*
The dewberry dipped for to work delay,
And the little reeds sighed *Abide, abide,*
    Here in the hills of Habersham,
20   *Here in the valleys of Hall.*

High o'er the hills of Habersham,
    Veiling the valleys of Hall,
The hickory told me manifold
Fair tales of shade, the poplar tall
25 Wrought me her shadowy self to hold,
The chestnut, the oak, the walnut, the pine,
Overleaning, with flickering meaning and sign,
Said, *Pass not, so cold, these manifold*
    Deep shades of the hills of Habersham,
30   *These glades in the valleys of Hall.*

And oft in the hills of Habersham,
    And oft in the valleys of Hall,
The white quartz shone, and the smooth brook-stone
Did bar me of passage with friendly brawl,
35 And many a luminous jewel lone
—Crystals clear or a-cloud with mist,
Ruby, garnet and amethyst—
Made lures with the lights of streaming stone
    In the clefts of the hills of Habersham,
40   In the beds of the valleys of Hall,

But oh, not the hills of Habersham,
    And oh, not the valleys of Hall
Avail: I am fain[6] for to water the plain.
Downward the voices of Duty call—
45 Downward, to toil and be mixed with the main,[7]
The dry fields burn, and the mills are to turn,

---

[4] **thrall:** held in bondage.
[5] **laving:** washing, bathing.
[6] **fain:** ready, willing, pleased, happy.
[7] **main:** sea.

And a myriad flowers mortally yearn,
And the lordly main from beyond the plain
    Calls o'er the hills of Habersham,
    Calls through the valleys of Hall.

COMMENTARY AND QUESTIONS

1. Who is the speaker?

2. Briefly summarize the poem's narative.

3. Describe the poem's tone.

4. Using specific examples, discuss the poem's musical qualities and their affect on meaning.

5. Compare "The Song of the Chattahoochee" to another particularly musical poem by one of the poets we have studied earlier.

REVIEW

1. What does Sidney Lanier have in common with Edgar Allan Poe, biographically and artistically? Can you draw any conclusions from these similarities.

2. Compare Lanier's nature poems to those by Bradstreet, Bryant, or Emerson. What does each poet's treatment of nature tell us about his or her life, the age in which they lived, and their views of life?

3. Write eight or more lines in the rhyme and rhythm of "Song of the Chattahoochee."

4. Compare "The Mocking Bird" to one of the other sonnets we have read. Explain which is better crafted and why.

Review of Part One

1. Survey the poems in this unit from Bradstreet to Lanier, and select three poets whom you feel are particularly significant to the development of American poetry. Providing examples from their work, discuss the poets' contributions.

2. Identify Emersonian ideas in the work of three other nineteenth-century poets.

3. Explain why a particular poem especially moved you.

4. Beginning with Freneau's romantic poems, discuss American romantic poetry in detail—its idea of nature, its love of fantasy, and its tendency to idealize and sentimentalize as well as to depict "the long ago and far" away rather than present reality. Working from your knowledge of American history, take into consideration not only what poets wrote about but also what they did not write about. Consider, for instance, why none of the poems in this unit deals with the dehumanizing effects of industrialization, technology, racism, and sexism.

5. Consider the lives of the poets we have read. What was the relationship of the poet to society in 1650? In 1750? In 1850?

6. Collect at least ten quotations that reflect the evolving attitudes of American poets toward nature. Then, using the quotations for support, explain this evolution.

Modern American Poetry

The Irish poet William Butler Yeats (1865–1939) spoke for most modern poets in America and Great Britain when he said, "We wanted to strip away everything that was artificial, to get at a style like speech, as simple as the simplist prose, like a cry of the heart" (quoted in *The New Poetry* [1917]). If you recall the heavy rhyme and meter of Poe's "The Raven" and Longfellow's "Hiawatha," you will have a sense of the poetic language that modern poets wanted to cast off in order to gain the freedom necessary to write in the rhythms of modern speech.

Walt Whitman, who published the first edition of his book *Leaves of Grass* in 1855, had actually written modern poetry ten years before Yeats was born. Whitman's long-lined, free verse poems, as liberated in their treatment of sex as they are in their form, have baffled, awed, outraged, and inspired readers. Yet today it is clear that Whitman, half a century ahead of his time, achieved the freedom from artificiality and the proselike simplicity that Yeats described. Significantly, Ralph Waldo Emerson, whose concept of the Over-Soul pervades Whitman's poetry, was the only influential American poet of Whitman's time to recognize that Whitman was writing a truly American poetry that could be instructive to future American poets.

While Whitman loudly and courageously sounded to the world what he called "my barbaric yawp," Emily Dickinson made her own understated challenge, telling to her readers what she called "the simple news that nature told." In 1890, the year her first collection was published, Dickinson's rhymed and metered poems appeared so simple and often so sentimental that it was more than half a century before most serious readers began to see that Dickinson's work was not always sentimental at all, but very often illuminating, complicated, and disturbing. Readers also began to notice that the off rhymes and broken meters in Dickinson's poetry were not only purposeful but essential in communicating complex meanings. Despite their many differences, both Whitman and Dickinson broke the European conventions that had distracted and inhibited earlier American poets. In the modern American poetry since Whitman and Dickinson, we see their two approaches repeated again and again.

In her 1917 introduction to an anthology called *The New American Poetry*, Harriet Monroe, founding editor of *Poetry Magazine,* which was devoted to publishing modern poets, explains that modern poetry sought an almost scientific objectivity: "In presenting the concrete object or the concrete environment, whether these be beautiful or ugly, [modern poetry] seeks to give more precisely the emotion arising from them. . . ." In other words, Monroe's modern poet, like the photographer, presents an object in a certain light and from a certain angle without extensive explanation or elaboration.

72

Edwin Arlington Robinson and Robert Frost succeeded in creating uniquely American voices in poems that worked within traditional structures. Their poems examined the human mind, reflecting the influence of psychology and modern man's sense of isolation in a world where traditional social and religious structures were weakening. Although Frost became the most popular American poet of this century, his adherence to formal patterns of rhyme and meter as well as his deceivingly simple themes made his work at first unfashionable and unappreciated in many academic and literary circles.

T. S. Eliot, who was born in St. Louis, Missouri, in 1888 and became a British subject in 1927, emerged in the 1920s as the dominant modern poet and remained so until his death in 1965. Since his work cannot readily be classified as American and since he is often considered a British poet, we do not include him in this text. Students interested in reading Eliot might begin with "Preludes," "The Love Song of J. Alfred Prufrock," and "The Hollow Men." Eliot, along with other poets called modernists—including Ezra Pound, Marianne Moore, H. D., Amy Lowell, William Carlos Williams, Wallace Stevens, and E. E. Cummings—experimented with new poetic forms and structures. As Harriet Monroe put it, "They [sought] a vehicle suited to their own epoch and their own creative mood, and resolutely reject[ed] all others."

Now, at the end of the twentieth century, it is clear that virtually all modern poets of the first half of the century—whether they thought of themselves as modernists or as formalist—shared two chracteristics. First, they approached their poems as objects to be described and illuminated but never explained. Whether the object be a jar on a mountain in Tennessee, a "goat-footed / balloonman," or a farmer rebuilding a stone wall, the modern poet shows us that object but rarely interprets it. The second characteristic of modern poets is that they often depict humankind as lonely and isolated. Yet despite modern poetry's emphasis upon craft, technique, experimentation, scientific objectivity, and human isolation, Emerson's romantic idea of the Over-Soul nonetheless endures in Whitman, Williams, Cummings, and others.

Finally, modern American poetry, like modern America, is diverse, not only stylistically but also culturally. Carl Sandburg's images of the Midwest, Robinson Jeffers's views of the California coast, John Crowe Ransom's scene of a southern women's college, and Langston Hughes's sounds and sights of Harlem show us that in the first part of the twentieth century America discovered itself—its native voices, its authentic places, and its dreams.

WALT WHITMAN
1819–1892

In 1836 when Ralph Waldo Emerson asked in his essay "Nature," "Why should we not have a poetry and philosophy of insight and not of tradition?" Walt Whitman was only seventeen years old. But in 1855 he answered Emerson's literary call to arms with the first publication of *Leaves of Grass*. In this thin collection of poems, Whitman deliberately turned from the conventional European poetic forms used by his American predecessors to an open, unrhymed, unmetered form reflective of the free American spirit. His free verse is also thematically free, making Whitman not only the first American poet to employ free verse but also the first to write generously of the city as well as the country, of industry as well as nature, of the body as well as the soul, of the woman as well as the man, of physical as well as spiritual love, and of African Americans, Orientals, and Native Americans as well as whites. Today Whitman stands as the most influential poet of his century and the first modern American poet.

His ancestors settled in Long Island around 1660 and farmed there for five generations. When the poet was four years old, his father took the family to Brooklyn, then a town of only ten thousand people. Walt, continuing to spend his summers in rural Huntington, Long Island, in the company of farmers and fisherman, experienced country life as well as town life, just across the river from the growing city of New York. Although his formal schooling ended when he was thirteen, Whitman was a brilliant student of life. He tells us,

> The least insect or animal, the senses, eyesight, love,
> The first step I say awed me and pleas'd me so much
> I have hardly gone and hardly wish'd to go any farther.

Whitman did go much farther than his first perceptions of nature, but his poetry never lost the raw, sensual, ecstatic quality we recall from our early contacts with the natural world.

From age thirteen until the Civil War, Whitman—like Freneau, Bryant, Whittier, and Poe—worked for newspapers, at first briefly in production and later as a writer and editor. Employed in Brooklyn, Long Island, Manhattan, and for three months in

New Orleans, Whitman held positions at ten papers. During these vital years, he not only wrote poems but also participated in local politics, developed an enduring love of opera and the theater, and read the Bible, Shakespeare, ancient Egyptian works, Greek tragedy, Dante, Carlyle, Emerson, and—like Emerson—ancient Hindu literature. It is clear that Whitman shares Emerson's belief in a "Unity" or "Oneness" that unites all creation, an idea influenced by Eastern thought as well as by the ancient Greek philosopher Plato.

When the Civil War began, Whitman moved to Washington, D.C. and lived there from 1862 to 1873. He found employment in government offices and, during the war, aided and cheered wounded soldiers by bringing them sweets and tobacco, writing letters for them, reading aloud, telling tales, dressing wounds, and sometimes helping with operations. During these years he wrote his Civil War poems, the finest being "When Lilac Last in the Dooryard Bloomed," an elegy for President Lincoln.

Whitman produced most of his great work, however, before the war. Despite its originality and power, the first edition of *Leaves of Grass* attracted little attention; yet Emerson read it and wrote this to Whitman: "I greet you at the beginning of a great career." Whitman published nine more editions of his book, adding and editing as he went. By the end of his life, having endured bitter criticism and misunderstanding, he had gained a large, enthusiastic readership in Europe and America.

After suffering a paralyzing stroke in 1872, Whitman moved to Camden, New Jersey, to live with his brother. Later he purchased a small house of his own. It was in these later years that he became known as "the good gray poet," was photographed and painted by the great American painter Thomas Eakins, visited by the English writer Oscar Wilde, and supported by donations from other writers and friends. He continued to revise *Leaves of Grass* until his death.

Poets to Come

Poets to come! orators, singers, musicians to come!
Not to-day is to justify me and answer what I am for,
But you, a new brood, native, athletic, continental, greater than before
    known,
Arouse! for you must justify me.

5   I myself but write one or two indicative words for the future,
I but advance a moment only to wheel and hurry back in the darkness.

I am a man who, sauntering along without fully stopping, turns a casual
    look upon you and then averts his face,
Leaving it to you to prove and define it,
Expecting the main things from you.

COMMENTARY AND QUESTIONS

1. How could future poets "justify" an earlier poet? As you read on, note what aspects of Whitman's style and content may have needed justification.

2. What do you think is the darkness Whitman alludes to in line 6?

3. In line 9, consider what might be the "main things."

from *Song of Myself*

In the short poem "Shut Not Your Doors" Whitman explains perhaps the most unusual quality of his poetry:

> The words of my book are nothing, but the drift of it everything
> A book separate, not link'd with the rest, nor felt by the intellect. . . .

The poet warns us that the traditional elements of English poetry—such as end rhyme, regular meter, measured stanzas, familiar line lengths of six to ten syllables, and familiar patterns of thought—are not part of his poetry.

In "Song of Myself" Whitman tells us, "every atom of my blood [is] form'd from this soul, this air." Later he says,

> I am the poet of the Body and the poet of the Soul . . . I am the poet of the woman
> . . . I am not the poet of goodness only, I do not decline to be a poet of wickeness also.

Reading these words, some dismiss Whitman as strange, incomprehensible, or egotistical; and indeed a poet who wrote lines as new and unusual as these had to have a strong ego in order to believe in himself. However, we, as readers of Emerson's poetry, recognize in Whitman's poetry the poetic portrayal of Emerson's Over-Soul. For instance, the first three-line stanza of "Song of Myself" establishes the speaker as the voice of the Over-Soul, "that Oneness" that flows through and unites every atom of the universe.

1

I celebrate myself, and sing myself,
And what I assume you shall assume,
For every atom belonging to me as good belongs to you.

I loafe and invite my soul,
5   I lean and loafe at my ease observing a spear of summer grass.

My tongue, every atom of my blood, form'd from this soil, this air,
Born here of parents born here from parents the same, and their
     parents the same,
I, now thirty-seven years old in perfect health begin,
Hoping to cease not till death.

10   Creeds and schools in abeyance,
Retiring back a while sufficed at what they are, but never forgotten,
I harbor for good or bad, I permit to speak at every hazard,
Nature without check with original energy.

2

Houses and rooms are full of perfumes, the shelves are crowded with
    perfumes,
15 I breathe the fragrance myself and know it and like it,
The distillation would intoxicate me also, but I shall not let it.

The atmosphere is not a perfume, it has no taste of the distillation, it is
    odorless,
It is for my mouth forever, I am in love with it,
I will go to the bank by the wood and become undisguised and naked,
20 I am mad for it to be in contact with me.

The smoke of my own breath,
Echoes, ripples, buzz'd whispers, love-root, silk-thread, crotch and vine,
My respiration and inspiration, the beating of my heart, the passing of
    blood and air through my lungs,
The sniff of green leaves and dry leaves, and of the shore and dark-
    color'd sea-rocks, and of hay in the barn,
25 The sound of the belch'd words of my voice loos'd to the eddies of the
    wind,
A few light kisses, a few embraces, a reaching around of arms,
The play of shine and shade on the trees as the supple boughs wag,
The delight alone or in the rush of the streets, or along the fields and
    hillsides,
The feeling of health, the full-noon trill, the song of me rising from bed
    and meeting the sun.

30 Have you reckon'd a thousand acres much? have you reckon'd the earth
    much?
Have you practis'd so long to learn to read?
Have you felt so proud to get at the meaning of poems?
Stop this day and night with me and you shall possess the origin of all
    poems,
You shall possess the good of the earth and sun, (there are millions of
    suns left,)
35 You shall no longer take things at second or third hand, nor look
    through the eyes of the dead, nor feed on the spectres in books,
You shall not look through my eyes either, nor take things from me,
You shall listen to all sides and filter them from your self.

6

A child said *What is the grass?* fetching it to me with full hands;
How could I answer the child? I do not know what it is any more
    than he.

40 I guess it must be the flag of my disposition, out of hopeful green stuff
    woven.

Or I guess it is the handkerchief of the Lord,
A scented gift and remembrancer designedly dropt,
Bearing the owner's name someway in the corners, that we may see and
    remark, and say *Whose?*

Or I guess the grass is itself a child, the produced babe of the
    vegetation.

45 Or I guess it is a uniform hieroglyphic,
And it means, Sprouting alike in broad zones and narrow zones,
Growing among black folks as among white,
Kanuck,[1] Tuckahoe,[2] Congressman, Cuff,[3] I give them the same, I
    receive them the same.

And now it seems to me the beautiful uncut hair of graves.
50 Tenderly will I use you curling grass,
It may be you transpire from the breasts of young men,
It may be if I had known them I would have loved them,
It may be you are from old people, or from offspring taken soon out of
    their mothers' laps,
And here you are the mothers' laps.

55 This grass is very dark to be from the white heads of old mothers,
Darker than the colorless beards of old men,
Dark to come from under the faint red roofs of mouths.

O I perceive after all so many uttering tongues,
And I perceive they do not come from the roofs of mouths for nothing.

60 I wish I could translate the hints about the dead young men and
    women,
And the hints about old men and mothers, and the offspring taken soon
    out of their laps.

What do you think has become of the young and old men?
And what do you think has become of the women and children?

They are alive and well somewhere,
65 The smallest sprout shows there is really no death,
And if ever there was it led forward life, and does not wait at the end to
    arrest it,
and ceas'd the moment life appear'd.

All goes onward and outward, nothing collapses,
And to die is different from what any one supposed, and luckier.

---

[1] **Kanuck:** a French Canadian.
[2] **Tuckahoe:** a tidewater Virginian who eats tuckahoe, an edible root.
[3] **Cuff:** a Negro.

34

70 Now I tell what I knew in Texas in my early youth,
(I tell not the fall of Alamo,
Not one escaped to tell the fall of Alamo,
The hundred and fifty are dumb yet at Alamo,)
'Tis the tale of the murder in cold blood of four hundred and twelve
    young men.

75 Retreating they had form'd in a hollow square with their baggage for
        breastworks,
Nine hundred lives out of the surrounding enemies, nine times their
        number, was the price they took in advance,
Their colonel was wounded and their ammunition gone,
They treated for an honorable capitulation, receiv'd writing and seal,
        gave up their arms and march'd back prisoners of war.

They were the glory of the race of rangers,
80 Matchless with horse, rifle, song, supper, courtship,
Large, turbulent, generous, handsome, proud, and affectionate,
Bearded, sunburnt, drest in the free costume of hunters,
Not a single one over thirty years of age.

The second First-day morning they were brought out in squads and
        massacred, it was beautiful early summer,
85 The work commenced about five o'clock and was over by eight.

None obey'd the command to kneel,
Some made a mad and helpless rush, some stood stark and straight,
A few fell at once, shot in the temple or heart, the living and dead lay
        together,
The maim'd and mangled dug in the dirt, the new-comers saw them
        there,
90 Some half-kill'd attempted to crawl away,
These were dispatch'd with bayonets or batter'd with the blunts of
        muskets,
A youth not seventeen years old seiz'd his assassin till two more came
        to release him.
The three were all torn and cover'd with the boy's blood.

At eleven o'clock began the burning of the bodies;
95 That is the tale of the murder of the four hundred and twelve
        young men.

48

I have said that the soul is not more than the body,
And I have said that the body is not more than the soul,
And nothing, not God, is greater to one than one's self is,
And whoever walks a furlong without sympathy walks to his own
    funeral drest in his shroud,

100 And I or you pocketless of a dime may purchase the pick of the earth,
And to glance with an eye or show a bean in its pod confounds the
    learning of all times,
And there is no trade or employment but the young man following it
    may become a hero,
And there is no object so soft but it makes a hub for the wheel'd
    universe,
And I say to any man or woman, Let your soul stand cool and
    composed before a million universes.

105 And I say to mankind, Be not curious about God,
For I who am curious about each am not curious about God,
(No array of terms can say how much I am at peace about God and
    about death.)

I hear and behold God in every object, yet understand God not in the
    least,
Nor do I understand who there can be more wonderful than myself.

110 Why should I wish to see God better than this day?
I see something of God each hour of the twenty-four, and each moment
    then,
In the faces of men and women I see God, and in my own face in the
    glass,
I find letters from God dropt in the street, and every one is sign'd by
    God's name,
And I leave them where they are, for I know that wheresoe'er I go,
115 Others will punctually come for ever and ever.

        51
The past and present wilt—I have fill'd them, emptied them,
And proceed to fill my next fold of the future.

Listener up there! what have you to confide to me?
Look in my face while I snuff the sidle⁴ of evening,
120 (Talk honestly, no one else hears you, and I stay only a minute longer.)

Do I contradict myself?
Very well then I contradict myself,
(I am large, I contain multitudes.)

I concentrate toward them that are nigh, I wait on the door-slab.

125 Who has done his day's work? who will soonest be through with his
    supper?
Who wishes to walk with me?

Will you speak before I am gone? will you prove already too late?

---

⁴ **snuff the sidle:** put out the last sideways rays of the evening sun; thus, bring in darkness.

52

The spotted hawk swoops by and accuses me, he complains of my gab
and my loitering.

I too am not a bit tamed, I too am untranslatable,
130   I sound my barbaric yawp over the roofs of the world.

The last scud of day holds back for me,
It flings my likeness after the rest and true as any on the shadow'd
wilds,
It coaxes me to the vapor and the dusk.

I depart as air, I shake my white locks at the runaway sun,
135   I effuse my flesh in eddies, and drift it in lacy jags.

I bequeath myself to the dirt to grow from the grass I love,
If you want me again look for me under your boot-soles.

You will hardly know who I am or what I mean,
But I shall be good health to you nevertheless,
140   And filter and fibre your blood.

Failing to fetch me at first keep encouraged,
Missing me one place search another,
I stop somewhere waiting for you.

COMMENTARY AND QUESTIONS

1. Cite several places in the poem where the speaker's voice seems to portray
Emerson's Over-Soul.

2. Comment on Whitman's statement that "words . . . are nothing, the drift is
everything."

3. Cite examples of where by contradicting himself Whitman expresses a truth.

4. What is the tone of the poem?

5. Consider what Whitman means in line 33 by "the origin of all poems."

6. According to part 6, what does *grass* mean in the poem?

7. Does part 34 fit into the poem? Discuss.

8. How do the first three lines of part 48 relate to traditional Jewish and Christian
teaching? Noting lines 110–115, consider Whitman's idea of God. Have you seen
these ideas in other poems, novels, stories, plays, or movies? Discuss.

9. What do the first two lines of part 51 tell us about Whitman's idea of time?
Compare this idea to Henry David Thoreau's famous statement in *Walden*:

> Time is but the stream I go a'fishing in; I drink at it, but while I drink, I see
> the sandy bottom and detect how shallow it is. Its thin current slides away
> but eternity remains.

10. Noting lines 129 and 130, discuss how Whitman is, "untranslatable," "bar-
baric," and not "tamed."

11. What does Whitman promise in the poem's last eight lines and how might he keep that promise?

12. Although Whitman's rhythms are rarely regular, they are powerful. Choose a passage you find particularly musical, mark each stressed syllable, and note the pattern made by these syllables. For instance, there may be a certain number of stressed syllables in a line, alternating numbers of stresses (for instance, three stresses in one line and four in the next), or some other pattern. Note also how repetitions of like sounds (alliteration, assonance, consonance, rhyme), repetitions of words and phrases, and pauses at line breaks and within lines create the poem's music. Now discuss the musical quality of the poem.

A Child's Amaze

Silent and amazed even when a little boy,
I remember I heard the preacher every Sunday put God in his
     statements,
As contending against some being or influence.

COMMENTARY AND QUESTIONS

1. Whitman uses the word *amaze* as a noun, meaning mental confusion. Why is the child mentally confused?

2. What does the poem suggest about the preacher and, by extension, about organized religion?

3. How does Whitman see the relationship between man and God?

A Farm Picture

Through the ample open door of the peaceful country barn,
A sunlit pasture field with cattle and horses feeding,
And haze and vista, and the far horizon fading away.

COMMENTARY AND QUESTIONS

1. Note that this poem has nine nouns and no main verb. What is the poem's primary effect and how does it achieve that effect?

2. Although "A Farm Picture" is slight, it is an unusual poem because Whitman wrote it before anyone had considered that a poem could simply be an image—a small, spare description of a scene. As you read on, you will learn about the imagist poets who wrote poems similar to but sparer than "A Farm Picture." Is this poem effective? Discuss.

When I Heard the Learn'd Astronomer

When I heard the learn'd astronomer,
When the proofs, the figures, were ranged in columns before me,
When I was shown the charts and diagrams, to add, divide, and
    measure them,
When I sitting heard the astronomer where he lectured with much
    applause in the lecture-room,
5   How soon unaccountable I became tired and sick,
Till rising and gliding out I wander'd off by myself,
In the mystical moist night-air, and from time to time,
Look'd up in perfect silence at the stars.

COMMENTARY AND QUESTIONS

1. What is the poem's theme and how does Whitman establish it?

2. Note that the poem is one sentence. How does this structure affect the poem's meaning?

3. In what sense is this poem romantic?

A Noiseless Patient Spider

A noiseless patient spider,
I mark'd where on a little promontory it stood isolated,
Mark'd how to explore the vacant vast surrounding,
It launch'd forth filament, filament, filament, out of itself,
Ever unreeling them, ever tirelessly speeding them.

5   And you O my soul where you stand,
Surrounded, detached, in measureless oceans of space,
Ceaselessly musing, venturing, throwing, seeking the spheres to connect
    them,
Till the bridge you will need be form'd, till the ductile anchor hold,
Till the gossamer thread you fling catch somewhere, O my soul.

COMMENTARY AND QUESTIONS

1. Identify the poem's central metaphor and explain how it extends the poem's theme.

2. Relate this poem to Emerson's theory of man's connection to the Over-Soul.

Beat! Beat! Drums!

Beat! beat! drums!—blow! bugles! blow!
Through the windows—through doors—burst like a ruthless force,
Into the solemn church, and scatter the congregation,
Into the school where the scholar is studying;

5 Leave not the bridegroom quiet—no happiness must he have now with
    his bride,
Nor the peaceful farmer any peace, ploughing his field or gathering his
    grain,
So fierce you whirr and pound you drums—so shrill you bugles blow.

Beat! beat! drums!—blow! bugles! blow!
Over the traffic of cities—over the rumble of wheels in the streets;
10 Are beds prepared for sleepers at night in the houses? no sleepers must
    sleep in those beds,
No bargainers' bargains by day—no brokers or speculators—would they
    continue?
Would the talkers be talking? would the singer attempt to sing?
Would the lawyer rise in the court to state his case before the judge?
Then rattle quicker, heavier drums—you bugles wilder blow.

15 Beat! beat! drums!—blow! bugles! blow!
Make no parley—stop for no expostulation,
Mind not the timid—mind not the weeper or prayer,
Mind not the old man beseeching the young man,
Let not the child's voice be heard, nor the mother's entreaties,
20 Make even the trestles to shake the dead where they lie awaiting the
    hearses,
So strong you thump O terrible drums—so loud you bugles blow.

COMMENTARY AND QUESTIONS

1. Note the word *whirr* in line 7. How do drums whirr?

2. What is the speaker's attitude toward war? How does Whitman convey that
attitude?

An Army Corps on the March

With its cloud of skirmishers in advance,
With now the sound of a single shot snapping like a whip, and now an
    irregular volley,
The swarming ranks press on and on, the dense brigades press on,
Glittering dimly, toiling under the sun—the dust-cover'd men,
5 In columns rise and fall to the undulations of the ground,
With artillery interspers'd—the wheels rumble, the horses sweat,
As an army corps advances.

COMMENTARY AND QUESTIONS

1. Here is another picture-poem, like "A Farm Picture." Whitman shows us a scene
without making comment on the scene's meaning. What appears to be the attitude
of the speaker toward the subject? Cite words or phrases that suggest this attitude or
theme.

2. Note that Whitman has punctuated the poem as a sentence. Is it a sentence? Discuss the effect of the poem's grammar and punctuation on meaning.

Cavalry Crossing a Ford

A line in long array where they wind betwixt green islands,
They take a serpentine course, their arms flash in the sun—hark to the
    musical clank,
Behold the silvery river, in it the splashing horses loitering stop to
    drink,
Behold the brown-faced men, each group, each person a picture, the
    negligent rest on the saddles,
5 Some emerge on the opposite bank, others are just entering the ford—
    while,
Scarlet and blue, and snowy white,
The guidon flags[1] flutter gayly in the wind.

[1] **guidon flags:** small flags carried by military troops.

COMMENTARY AND QUESTIONS

1. This short poem also relies primarily on images to convey meaning. Note that the speaker never judges the scene. What is the poem's tone?
2. How do the "gayly" waving flags affect the poem's meaning? What is the poem's purpose?

When Lilacs Last in the Dooryard Bloom'd

Although Whitman never mentions the president's name, it is clear that "When Lilacs Last in the Dooryard Bloom'd" is an elegy for Lincoln.
   Note that Whitman employs three central symbols: the lilacs, the star, and the hermit thrush. As you read the poem, determine what each symbol means.

1

When lilacs last in the dooryard bloom'd,
And the great star early droop'd in the western sky in the night,
I mourn'd, and yet shall mourn with ever-returning spring.

Ever-returning spring, trinity sure to me you bring,
5 Lilac blooming perennial and drooping star in the west,
And thought of him I love.

2

O powerful western fallen star!
O shades of night—O moody, tearful night!
O great star disappear'd—O the black murk that hides the star!
10 O cruel hands that hold me powerless—O helpless soul of me!
O harsh surrounding cloud that will not free my soul.

3

In the dooryard fronting an old farm-house near the white-wash'd
    palings,
Stands the lilac-bush tall-growing with heart-shaped leaves of rich
    green,
With many a pointed blossom rising delicate, with the perfume strong I
    love,
With every leaf a miracle—and from this bush in the dooryard,
With delicate-color'd blossoms and heart-shaped leaves of rich green,
A sprig with its flower I break.

4

In the swamp in secluded recesses,
A shy and hidden bird is warbling a song.
20 Solitary the thrush,[1]
The hermit withdrawn to himself, avoiding the settlements,
Sings by himself a song.

Song of the bleeding throat,
Death's outlet song of life, (for well dear brother I know,
25 If thou wast not granted to sing thou would'st surely die.)

5

Over the breast of the spring, the land, amid cities,
Amid lanes and through old woods, where lately the violets peep'd
    from the ground, spotting the gray debris,
Amid the grass in the fields each side of the lanes, passing the endless
    grass,
Passing the yellow-spear'd wheat, every grain from its shroud in the
    dark-brown fields uprisen,
30 Passing the apple-tree blows[2] of white and pink in the orchards,
Carrying a corpse to where it shall rest in the grave,
Night and day journeys a coffin.

---

[1] **thrush:** referred to in the next line as a "hermit," thus a hermit thrush, which has a beautiful,
    often celebrated song.
[2] **blows:** a mass of blossoms.

6

Coffin that passes through lanes and streets,
Through day and night with the great cloud darkening the land,
35 With the pomp of the inloop'd flags with the cities draped in black,
With the show of the States themselves as of crape-veil'd women
    standing,
With processions long and winding and the flambeaus[3] of the night,
With the countless torches lit, with the silent sea of faces and the
    unbared heads,
With the waiting depot, the arriving coffin, and the sombre faces,
40 With dirges through the night, with the thousand voices rising strong
    and solemn,
With all the mournful voices of the dirges pour'd around the coffin,
The dim-lit churches and the shuddering organs—where amid these
    you journey,
With the tolling tolling bells' perpetual clang,
Here, coffin that slowly passes,
45 I give you my sprig of lilac.

7

(Nor for you, for one alone,
Blossoms and branches green to coffins all I bring,
For fresh as the morning, thus would I chant a song for you O sane and
    sacred death.

All over bouquets of roses,
50 O death, I cover you over with roses and early lilies,
But mostly and now the lilac that blooms the first,
Copious I break, I break the sprigs from the bushes,
With loaded arms I come, pouring for you,
For you and the coffins all of you O death.)

8

55 O western orb sailing the heaven,
Now I know what you must have meant as a month since I walk'd,
As I walk'd in silence the transparent shadowy night,
As I saw you had something to tell as you bent to me night after night,[4]
As you droop'd from the sky low down as if to my side, (while the
    other stars all look'd on,)
60 As we wander'd together the solemn night, (for something I know not
    what kept me from sleep,)
As the night advanced, and I saw on the rim of the west how full you
    were of woe,

[3] **flambeaus:** lighted torches.
[4] **you . . . night:** Whitman claimed that President Lincoln used to nod as the two passed on
    the streets of Washington.

As I stood on the rising ground in the breeze in the cool transparent
    night,
As I watch'd where you pass'd and was lost in the netherward[5] black of
    the night,
As my soul in its trouble dissatisfied sank, as where you sad orb,
65 Concluded, dropt in the night, and was gone.

    9

Sing on there in the swamp,
O singer bashful and tender, I hear your notes, I hear your call,
I hear, I come presently, I understand you,
But a moment I linger, for the lustrous star has detain'd me,
70 The star my departing comrade holds and detains me.

    10

O how shall I warble myself for the dead one there I loved?
And how shall I deck my song for the large sweet soul that has gone?
And what shall my perfume be for the grave of him I love?

Sea-winds blown from east and west,
75 Blown from the Eastern sea and blown from the Western sea, till there
    on the prairies meeting,
These and with these and the breath of my chant,
I'll perfume the grave of him I love.

    11

O what shall I hang on the chamber walls?
And what shall the pictures be that I hang on the walls,
80 To adorn the burial-house of him I love?

Pictures of growing spring and farms and homes,
With the Fourth-month eve at sundown, and the gray smoke lucid and
    bright,
With floods of the yellow gold of the gorgeous, indolent, sinking sun,
    burning, expanding the air,
With the fresh sweet herbage[6] under foot, and the pale green leaves of
    the trees prolific,
85 In the distance the flowing glaze, the breast of the river, with a wind-
    dapple here and there,
With ranging hills on the banks, with many a line against the sky, and
    shadows,
And the city at hand with dwellings so dense, and stacks of chimneys,
And all the scenes of life and the workshops, and the workmen
    homeward returning.

---

[5] **netherward:** descending toward darkness.
[6] **herbage:** grass or similar vegetation.

12

Lo, body and soul—this land,
90   My own Manhattan with spires, and the sparkling and hurrying tides, and the ships,
The varied and ample land, the South and the North in the light, Ohio's shores and flashing Missouri,
And ever the far-spreading prairies cover'd with grass and corn.
Lo, the most excellent sun so calm and haughty,
The violet and purple morn with just-felt breezes,
95   The gentle soft-born measureless light,
The miracle spreading bathing all, the fulfill'd noon,
The coming eve delicious, the welcome night and the stars,
Over my cities shining all, enveloping man and land.

13

Sing on, sing on you gray-brown bird,
100   Sing from the swamps, the recesses, pour your chant from the bushes,
Limitless out of the dusk, out of the cedars and pines.

Sing on dearest brother, warble your reedy song,
Loud human song, with voice of uttermost woe.

O liquid and free and tender!
105   O wild and loose to my soul—O wondrous singer!
You only I hear—yet the star holds me, (but will soon depart,)
Yet the lilac with mastering odor holds me.

14

Now while I sat in the day and look'd forth,
In the close of the day with its light and the fields of spring, and the farmers preparing their crops,
110   In the large unconscious scenery of my land with its lakes and forests,
In the heavenly aerial beauty, (after the perturb'd winds and the storms,)
Under the arching heavens of the afternoon swift passing, and the voices of children and women,
The many-moving sea-tides, and I saw the ships how they sail'd,
And the summer approaching with richness, and the fields all busy with labor,
115   And the infinite separate houses, how they all went on, each with its meals and minutia of daily usages,
And the streets how their throbbings throbb'd, and the cities pent—lo, then and there,
Falling upon them all and among them all, enveloping me with the rest,
Appear'd the cloud, appear'd the long black trail,
And I knew death, its thought, and the sacred knowledge of death.
120   Then with the knowledge of death as walking one side of me,

And the thought of death close-walking the other side of me,
And I in the middle as with companions, and as holding the hands of
     companions,
I fled forth to the hiding receiving night that talks not,
Down to the shores of the water, the path by the swamp in the dimness,
125   To the solemn shadowy cedars and ghostly pines so still.

And the singer so shy to the rest receiv'd me,
The gray-brown bird I know receiv'd us comrades three,
And he sang the carol of death, and a verse for him I love.

From deep secluded recesses,
130   From the fragrant cedars and the ghostly pines so still,
Came the carol of the bird.

And the charm of the carol rapt[7] me,
As I held as if by their hands my comrades in the night,
And the voice of my spirit tallied the song of the bird.

135   *Come lovely and soothing death,*
Undulate round the world, serenely arriving, arriving,
In the day, in the night, to all, to each,
Sooner or later delicate death.

Prais'd be the fathomless universe,
140   *For life and joy, and for objects and knowledge curious,*
And for love, sweet love—but praise! praise! praise!
For the sure-enwinding arms of cool-enfolding death.

Dark mother always gliding near with soft feet,
Have none chanted for thee a chant of fullest welcome?
145   *Then I chant it for thee, I glorify thee above all,*
I bring thee a song that when thou must indeed come, come
     unfalteringly.

Approach strong deliveress,
When it is so, when thou hast taken them I joyously sing the dead,
Lost in the loving floating ocean of thee,
150   *Laved in the flood of thy bliss O death.*
From me to thee glad serenades,
Dances for thee I propose saluting thee, adornments and feastings for
     thee,
And the sights of the open landscape and the high-spread sky are
     fitting,
And life and the fields, and the huge and thoughtful night.

---

[7] **rapt:** deeply moved, enraptured.

155   *The night in silence under many a star,*
     The ocean shore and the husky whispering wave whose voice I know,
     And the soul turning to thee O vast and well-veil'd death,
     And body gratefully nestling close to thee.

     Over the tree-tops I float thee a song,
160   *Over the rising and sinking waves, over the myriad fields and the*
        prairies wide,
     Over the dense-pack'd cities all and the teeming wharves and ways,
     I float this carol with joy, with joy to thee O death.

       15

     To the tally of my soul,
     Loud and strong kept up the gray-brown bird,
165   With pure deliberate notes spreading filling the night.

     Loud in the pines and cedars dim,
     Clear in the freshness moist and the swamp-perfume,
     And I with my comrades there in the night.

     While my sight that was bound in my eyes unclosed,
170   As to long panoramas of visions.

     And I saw askant the armies,
     I saw as in noiseless dreams hundreds of battle-flags,
     Borne through the smoke of the battles and pierc'd with missiles I saw
        them,
     And carried hither and yon through the smoke, and torn and bloody,
175   And at last but a few shreds left on the staffs, (and all in silence,)
     And staffs all splinter'd and broken.

     I saw battle-corpses, myriads of them,
     And the white skeletons of young men, I saw them,
     I saw the debris and debris of all the slain soldiers of the war,
180   But I saw they were not as was thought,
     They themselves were fully at rest, they suffer'd not,
     The living remain'd and suffer'd, the mother suffer'd,
     And the wife and the child and the musing comrade suffer'd,
     And the armies that remain'd suffer'd.

       16

185   Passing the visions, passing the night,
     Passing, unloosing the hold of my comrades' hands,
     Passing the song of the hermit bird and the tallying song of my soul,
     Victorious song, death's outlet song, yet varying ever-altering song,
     As low and wailing, yet clear the notes, rising and falling, flooding the
        night,

190 Sadly sinking and fainting, as warning and warning, and yet again
         bursting with joy,
     Covering the earth and filling the spread of the heaven,
     As that powerful psalm in the night I heard from recesses,
     Passing, I leave thee lilac with heart-shaped leaves,
     I leave thee there in the door-yard, blooming, returning with spring.

195 I cease from my song for thee,
     From my gaze on thee in the west, fronting the west, communing with
         thee,
     O comrade lustrous with silver face in the night.

     Yet each to keep and all, retrievements out of the night,
     The song, the wondrous chant of the gray-brown bird,
200 And the tallying chant, the echo arous'd in my soul,
     With the lustrous and drooping star with the countenance full of woe,
     With the holders holding my hand nearing the call of the bird,
     Comrades mine and I in the midst, and their memory ever to keep, for
         the dead I loved so well,
     For the sweetest, wisest soul of all my days and lands—and this for his
         dear sake,
205 Lilac and star and bird twined with the chant of my soul,
     There in the fragrant pines and the cedars dusk and dim.

COMMENTARY AND QUESTIONS

1. What is the "trinity" referred to in line 4?

2. In line 46, the speaker places a sprig of lilac on the president's coffin. What does this action represent?

3. In part 8, how does the speaker compare the "western orb" to Lincoln?

4. In parts 9 and 10, what does the thrush seem to represent and how does the bird's song seem to affect the speaker?

5. In part 11 the speaker muses on what images would be appropriate to hang on the walls of Lincoln's burial chamber. What do the speaker's thoughts tell us about Whitman's idea of America and of President Lincoln. How does part 12 extend part 11?

6. Describe the tension expressed in the last line of part 13.

7. What is the "long black trail" in line 118?

8. In lines 120 and 125, why does the speaker bring to the thrush the knowledge and the thought of death?

9. Why does Whitman have the thrush sing? How does the theme of the thrush's song contribute to the poem's meaning?

10. How do lines 171–184 contribute to the poem's meaning?

11. Discuss line 205.

REVIEW

1. Using either "A Farm Picture" or a few musical lines from another poem, carefully consider how Whitman repeats similar sounds and arranges stressed syllables into patterns that contribute to the poem's meaning.

2. Free verse has been criticized for being too loose and too random to provide the structure necessary to intensify language. Free verse has also been accused of being flat and unmusical—simply prose written out in poetic lines. Does Whitman succeed in raising his free verse above the level of prose? Using specific examples, discuss how Whitman elevates his language without the aid of regular meter and rhyme.

3. We know that Whitman, who had his picture taken hundreds of times, well understood the power of photography. It has also been suggested that his understanding of the effect of steam locomotion may have influenced Whitman's rejection of the plodding iambic foot in favor of free verse, which projects the free and open tone of a nation, so to speak, on wheels. Using examples from his poems, discuss how photography, steam locomotion, and other inventions may have affected Whitman's poetry.

4. Using a number of examples, explain your personal response to Walt Whitman's poetry.

5. Write a few lines in the style of Walt Whitman.

EMILY DICKINSON
1830–1886

Emily Dickinson lived in Amherst, Massachusetts, a small town about ninety miles west of Boston. The daughter of Edward Dickinson—a prominent lawyer, a respected citizen, the treasurer of Amherst College, and for one term a member of the U.S. House of Representatives—Emily grew up in an enlightened atmosphere. She evidently was an active, engaging child who enjoyed her friendships and her school. Amherst Academy, which she attended from age nine to sixteen, not only taught children reading, writing, and arithmetic, but also offered courses in history, geology, Latin, and botany. "We have a very fine school," she once boasted to a friend. Not surprisingly to anyone who has read her poems about nature and "nature's creatures," botany appears to have been her favorite subject. We also have evidence of Dickinson's youthful intelligence, wit, and vitality in the following anonymous valentine, which she apparently wrote to a college friend of her brother Austin:

> Sir, I desire an interview; meet at sunrise, or sunset, or the new moon—the place is immaterial. In gold, or in purple . . . with sword, or with pen, or with plough—the weapons are less than the wielder. . . . (quoted in Richard Sewall, *The Life of Emily Dickinson*)

After attending Mount Holyoke Female Seminary (now Mt. Holyoke College) for a year, Dickinson returned to Amherst, where she was to remain, but for a few trips, for the rest of her life. Although there are many suggestions that Dickinson fell in love, we know little of these relationships. In a letter to Thomas Wentworth Higginson (received 26 April 1862), a prominent literary figure from whom Dickinson sought advice, she says this of her life:

> You ask of my Companions. Hills—Sir—and the Sundown—and a Dog . . . They are better than Beings—because they know—but do not tell—and the noise in the Pool, at Noon—excels my Piano. I have a Brother and a Sister—My Mother does not care for thought—and Father, too busy with his Briefs—to notice what we do.

In the same letter Dickinson tells Higginson that she has read John Keats, Robert and Elizabeth Browning, and the Bible. We know also that she had read and liked Thoreau and that Emerson, who had visited her home when he spoke at Amherst College, was a major influence. Ironically, she never read the other great nineteenth-century American poet, Walt Whitman, for she "was told he was disgraceful."

Despite the mystery surrounding Dickinson's personal life, we do possess the most important information about this poet: 1,775 poems. Only nine of these were published during her lifetime, partly because of her reluctance to publish and partly because her genius, though sensed by Higginson and others, was not yet understood and appreciated. In 1890, four years after her death, the poet's first collection of poems appeared and was immediately popular. Since then, readers have seen beyond the comfortable, pleasant aspects of Dickinson's poems to their bold, original, and modern illuminations of life's realities.

INTRODUCTORY COMMENT

Because Emily Dickinson did not entitle her poems, we have identified them here by their first lines. Note also that the punctuation and capitalization are inconsistent, perhaps because the poems were not written for publication. Some feel that Dickinson's dashes are musical devices, whereas others suggest that the dashes often represent pauses in the poet's thought.

" 'Faith' is a fine invention"

"Faith" is a fine invention
When Gentlemen can *see*—
But *Microscopes* are prudent
In an Emergency.

COMMENTARY AND QUESTIONS

1. In line 2, what does the poet mean by *see*?

2. What is the poem's theme and what does this theme suggest about the poet's view of life?

3. Do you detect humor in this poem? If so, where?

"A Bird came down the Walk—"

A Bird came down the Walk—
He did not know I saw—
He bit an Angleworm[1] in halves
And ate the fellow, raw,

_____

[1] **Angleworm:** earthworm.

And then he drank a Dew
From a convenient Grass—
And then hopped sidewise to the Wall
To let a Beetle pass—

He glanced with rapid eyes
10 That hurried all around—
They looked like frightened Beads, I thought—
He stirred his Velvet Head

Like one in danger, Cautious,
I offered him a Crumb
15 And he unrolled his feathers
And rowed him softer home—

Than Oars divide the Ocean,
Too silver for a seam—
Or Butterflies, off Banks of Noon
20 Leap, plashless as they swim.

COMMENTARY AND QUESTIONS

1. Note that the poem's meter is regular (te tum, te tum, te tum, / te tum, te tum, te tum) until the seventh line, when the rhythm breaks and grates on the ear. How, if at all, does this metrical irregularity complement the poem's meaning?

2. How does Dickinson create and extend the metaphor, air is water?

3. Contrast the tone of the last stanza to that of the first stanza. How does this contrast affect the poem's meaning?

4. What does the poem tell us about nature?

"Apparently with no surprise"

Apparently with no surprise
To any happy Flower
The Frost beheads it at its play—
In accidental power—
5 The blonde[1] Assassin passes on—
The Sun proceeds unmoved
To measure off another Day
For an Approving God.

[1] **blonde:** white.

COMMENTARY AND QUESTIONS

1. What is the "blonde Assassin"?

2. What appears to be the sun's attitude toward the beheaded flower?

3. Describe the poem's tone.

4. How is man, if at all, like the flower?

5. What does this poem suggest about the relationship of God and man?

"A Toad, can die of Light—"

A Toad, can die of Light—
Death is the Common Right
Of Toads and Men—
Of Earl and Midge[1]
5 The privilege—
Why swagger, then?
The Gnat's supremacy is large as Thine—

Life—is a different Thing—
So measure Wine—
10 Naked of Flask—Naked of Cask—
Bare Rhine[2]—
Which Ruby's mine?[3]

[1] **Midge:** a type of gnat.
[2] **Rhine:** a German wine; a German river.
[3] **Which Ruby's mine?:** Which red drop is mine?

COMMENTARY AND QUESTIONS

1. What does line 1 suggest about the nature of life, and how does the rest of the stanza develop this suggestion?

2. In the second stanza the speaker offers flowing wine as a symbol of life. Have you ever seen wine used as a symbol of life or of life's blood? Discuss.

3. Why does the speaker ask us to measure flowing wine? How is all life more like a flowing liquid than a collection of individual objects?

4. Why in the last line does the speaker ask us to identify a specific drop, a ruby, of wine? What is the tone of this line?

5. What does the poem say about life and death?

"I heard a Fly buzz—when I died—"

I heard a Fly buzz—when I died—
The Stillness in the Room
Was like the Stillness in the Air—
Between the Heaves of Storm—

5   The Eyes around—had wrung them dry—
    And Breaths were gathering firm
    For that last Onset—when the King
    Be witnessed—in the Room—

    I willed my Keepsakes—Signed away
10 What portion of me be
    Assignable—and then it was
    There interposed a Fly—

    With Blue—uncertain stumbling Buzz—
    Between the light—and me—
15 And then the Windows failed—and then
    I could not see to see—

COMMENTARY AND QUESTIONS

1. If you were to paint the scene in this poem, what objects would you include? What colors would you use?

2. At what time of year are we most likely to see large flies that make a "stumbling buzz"?

3. Paraphrase stanza 2.

4. Explain "the Window failed" in line 15.

5. Explain the two meanings of "see" in the last line.

6. This poem describes a person's death. How does the presence of the fly affect the poem's meaning?

" 'Hope' is the thing with feathers—"

"Hope" is the thing with feathers—
That perches in the soul—
And sings the tune without the words—
And never stops—at all—

5   And sweetest—in the Gale—is heard—
    And sore must be the storm—
    That could abash the little Bird
    That kept so many warm—

    I've heard it in the chillest land—
10 And on the strangest Sea—
    Yet, never, in Extremity,
    It asked a crumb—of Me.

COMMENTARY AND QUESTIONS

1. State the poem's central metaphor.

2. Discuss how the metaphor helps the reader to understand hope.

3. Contrast Dickinson's uses of metaphor in this poem to "A Toad, can die of Light." Which is more effective? Why?

"Some keep the Sabbath going to Church—"

Some keep the Sabbath going to Church—
I keep it, staying at Home—
With a Bobolink[1] for a Chorister—
And an Orchard, for a Dome[2]—

5   Some keep the Sabbath in Surplice[3]—
I just wear my Wings—
And instead of tolling the Bell, for Church,
Our little Sexton—sings.

God preaches, a noted Clergyman—
10   And the sermon is never long,
So instead of getting to Heaven, at last—
I'm going, all along.

[1] **Bobolink:** a striking black songbird with white and yellowish markings.
[2] **Dome:** a hemispherical roof, often part of a church's architecture.
[3] **Surplice:** a gown worn by a clergyman.

COMMENTARY AND QUESTIONS

1. How does the poem portray Dickinson's religious beliefs?

2. Compare this poem's idea of God to "Apparently with no surprise" and to similar poems by Emerson and Whitman.

3. Describe the poem's tone, and discuss how the tone affects the poem's meaning.

"I'm Nobody! Who are you?"

I'm Nobody! Who are you?
Are you—Nobody—Too?
Then there's a pair of us?
Don't tell! they'd advertise—you know!

5   How dreary—to be—Somebody!
How public—like a Frog—
To tell one's name—the livelong June—
To an admiring Bog!

COMMENTARY AND QUESTIONS

1. State the poem's theme, and explain how Dickinson uses imagery to objectify and clarify that theme.

2. What, if anything, is unusual about the poem's rhyme and meter?

3. Cite two or more unexpected words, and discuss what these words bring to the poem.

4. Although this poem has wide appeal, it has been criticized for having little artistic merit. What is your opinion of the poem?

"Wild Nights—Wild Nights!"

Wild Nights—Wild Nights!
Were I with thee
Wild Nights should be
Our luxury!

5   Futile—the Winds—
To a Heart in port—
Done with the Compass—
Done with the Chart!

Rowing in Eden—
10   Ah, the Sea!
Might I but moor—Tonight—
In Thee!

COMMENTARY AND QUESTIONS

1. On a literal level, what are the "Wild Nights"?

2. Paraphrase lines 9 and 10.

3. What is the poem's central metaphor, and how does Dickinson extend this metaphor?

"Success is counted sweetest"

Success is counted sweetest
By those who ne'er succeed.
To comprehend a nectar
Requires sorest need.

5   Not one of all the purple Host[1]
Who took the Flag today
Can tell the definition
So clear of Victory

---

[1] **purple Host:** a large number of people of high rank; the victorious army.

As he defeated—dying—
10 On whose forbidden ear
The distant strains of triumph
Burst agonized and clear!

COMMENTARY AND QUESTIONS

1. Paraphrase the first stanza.

2. What does the speaker mean by "took the flag today"?

3. In line 10, why is the ear "forbidden"?

4. Discuss the poem's theme and offer examples from your experience that either support or question this theme.

"Because I could not stop for Death—"

Because I could not stop for Death—
He kindly stopped for me—
The Carriage held but just Ourselves—
And Immortality.

5 We slowly drove—He knew no haste
And I had put away
My labor and my leisure too,
For His Civility—

We passed the School, where Children strove
10 At Recess—in the Ring—
We passed the Fields of Gazing Grain—
We passed the Setting Sun—

Or rather—He passed Us—
The Dews drew quivering and chill—
15 For only Gossamer[1], my Gown—
My Tippet[2]—only Tulle[3]—

We paused before a House that seemed
A Swelling of the Ground—
The Roof was scarcely visible—
20 The Cornice—in the Ground—

---

[1] **Gossamer:** a sheer, gauzy fabric.
[2] **Tippet:** a covering for the shoulders.
[3] **Tulle:** a fine net of silk.

Since then—'tis Centuries—and yet
Feels shorter than the Day
I first surmised the Horses' Heads
Were toward Eternity—

COMMENTARY AND QUESTIONS

1. This poem has been praised for the compelling way that it unites love and death. Describe how the relationship between the speaker and death suggests both love and death.

2. How does stanza 2 advance the poem's meaning?

3. Discuss the significance of line 13.

4. What is the house in stanza 5?

5. Explain the significance of the last stanza.

6. What does the poem tell us about the nature of death?

"My life closed twice before its close—"

My life closed twice before its close—
It yet remains to see
If Immortality unveil
A third event to me   .

5   So huge, so hopeless to conceive
As these that twice befell.
Parting is all we know of heaven,
And all we need of hell.

COMMENTARY AND QUESTIONS

1. Is the speaker in this poem alive or dead? In the context of line 1, discuss the significance of your conclusion.

2. In line 7, what does the speaker mean by "Parting"?

3. Explain the paradox in the last two lines.

"I'll tell you how the Sun rose—"

I'll tell you how the Sun rose—
A Ribbon at a time—
The Steeples swam in Amethyst—
The news, like Squirrels, ran—
5   The Hills untied their Bonnets—

The Bobolinks[1]—begun—
Then I said softly to myself—
"That must have been the Sun"!
But how he set—I know not—
10   There seemed a purple stile[2]
That little Yellow boys and girls
Were climbing all the while—
Till when they reached the other side,
A Dominie[3] in Gray—
15   Put gently up the evening Bars—
And led the flock away—

[1] **Bobolinks:** striking black songbirds with white and yellowish markings.
[2] **stile:** steps for crossing a fence or wall.
[3] **Dominie:** a clergyman.

COMMENTARY AND QUESTIONS

1. Describe the tone established in line 1.

2. Literally, how could the first three lines be true?

3. Where and how does the poem's tone change?

4. Literally, how could the children in lines 10–12 be "Yellow" and the stile be "purple"?

5. What do the last four lines suggest?

6. Compare this poem to "Because I could not stop for Death."

"Before I got my eye put out"

Before I got my eye put out
I liked as well to see—
As other Creatures, that have Eyes
And know no other way—

5   But were it told to me—Today—
That I might have the sky
For mine—I tell you that my Heart
Would split, for size of me—

The Meadows—mine—
10   The Mountains—mine—
All Forests—Stintless Stars—
As much of Noon as I could take
Between my finite eyes—

The Motions of the Dipping Birds
15 The Morning's Amber Road—
For mine—to look at when I liked—
The News would strike me dead—

So safer—guess—with just my soul
Upon the Window pane—
20 Where other Creatures put their eyes—
Incautious—of the Sun—

COMMENTARY AND QUESTIONS

1. What is the *eye* in line 1? What is the *soul* in line 18?

2. How are stars "stintless" and morning roads "amber"? What were the roads like around Amherst, Massachusetts, in the last century?

3. Consider the word *noon* as Dickinson uses it in line 12 of this poem and in line 19 of "A Bird came down the Walk." What does the word mean to Dickinson? Note that she often refers to light and to sun. Do you detect a theme in this light imagery?

4. State the poem's central idea and explain how the poet has used imagery to clarify this idea.

5. This poem conveys an awe of nature more powerful perhaps than any poem we have encountered thus far. How does Dickinson convey this awe?

"A Route of Evanescence"

A Route of Evanescence
With a revolving Wheel—
A Resonance of Emerald—
A Rush of Cochineal[1]—
5 And every Blossom on the Bush
Adjusts its tumbled Head—
The mail from Tunis,[2] probably,
An easy Morning's Ride—

[1] **Cochineal:** vivid red.
[2] **Tunis:** a city on the north coast of Africa.

COMMENTARY AND QUESTIONS

1. This poem describes a ruby-throated hummingbird, whose wing beat is so rapid that we see not wings but a blur, as the tiny metallic-green bird darts forward, sideways and backward, or hovers to sip nectar from flowers. Giving specific examples, discuss how Dickinson captures the flight of the hummingbird.

2. Discuss the last two lines. Why the allusion to Tunis? What is the implied metaphor and how is it appropriate?

3. Discuss the poem's tone. Is there a lightness or humor? If so, where?

4. Compare this poem to one of Whitman's short poems such as "A Farm Picture" or "An Army Corps on the March." What techniques do both poets employ? Which short poem do you prefer? Why?

"The Sky is low—the Clouds are mean."

The Sky is low—the Clouds are mean.
A Travelling Flake of Snow
Across a Barn or through a Rut
Debates if it will go—

5 A Narrow Wind complains all Day
How some one treated him
Nature, like Us is sometimes caught
Without her Diadem.[1]

___

[1] **Diadem:** a crown.

COMMENTARY AND QUESTIONS

1. Paraphrase lines 2–4.

2. How can wind be "narrow"?

3. Although this poem treats a somber subject, the coming of winter, the tone seems to resist seriousness. How, if at all, does the poem maintain a buoyancy?

4. How do you rank this poem against others by Dickinson? Explain your reasoning.

"These are the days when Birds come back—"

These are the days when Birds come back—
A very few—a Bird or two—
To take a backward look.

These are the days when skies resume
5 The old—old sophistries[1] of June—
A blue and gold mistake.

___

[1] **sophistries:** lies that appear to be logical.

Oh fraud that cannot cheat the Bee—
Almost thy plausibility
Induces my belief.

10 Till ranks of seeds their witness bear[2]—
And softly thro' the altered air
Hurries a timid leaf.

Oh Sacrament[3] of summer days,
Oh Last Communion[4] in the Haze—
15 Permit a child to join.

Thy sacred emblems to partake—
Thy consecrated bread to take
And thine immortal wine!

---

[2] **Till ranks of seeds their witness bear:** until the many seeds blown by the wind prove that
   the season is fall, not early summer.
[3] **Sacrament:** the Eucharist, Communion.
[4] **Communion:** The Christian belief that by eating blessed bread and drinking blessed wine,
   one consumes the body and blood of Christ and thus communes with God.

COMMENTARY AND QUESTIONS

1. How does Dickinson indicate the weather and season of the poem's setting?
Note important phrases.

2. How are the June skies "sophistries"?

3. What proves that the season is fall?

4. How is the day a "Sacrament of summer days" and a "Last Communion"?

5. Literally, how does the speaker "partake" of the day she calls a "Sacrament"?

6. What is the poem's central idea?

7. What images of Indian summer days does this poem capture?

8. Which poem more powerfully reflects Dickinson's feeling for nature, this one or
"Before I got my eye put out"? Discuss.

"There's a certain Slant of light,"

There's a certain Slant of light,
Winter Afternoons—
That oppresses, like the Heft
Of Cathedral Tunes—

5 Heavenly Hurt, it gives us—
We can find no scar,
But internal difference,
Where the Meanings, are—

None may teach it—Any—
10 'Tis the Seal Despair[1]—
An imperial affliction
Sent us of the Air—

When it comes, the Landscape listens—
Shadows—hold their breath—
15 When it goes, 'tis like the Distance
On the look of Death—

[1] **Seal Despair:** as if the low slanting light of winter afternoons were an official seal of despair.

COMMENTARY AND QUESTIONS

1. How can the late afternoon light of winter afternoons be oppressive?

2. What metaphors does Dickinson employ to help us understand how this light makes her feel?

3. This poem, "These are the Days the Birds come back," and "The Sky is low—the Clouds are mean" each describe particular weather in a particular season. Which poem is the most effective? Why?

4. Describe in prose or poetry a certain type of weather that you find particularly powerful.

"I started Early—Took my Dog—"

I started Early—Took my Dog—
And visited the Sea—
The Mermaids in the Basement
Came out to look at me—

5 And Frigates—in the Upper Floor
Extended Hempen Hands—
Presuming Me to be a Mouse—
Aground—upon the Sands—

But no Man moved Me—till the Tide
10 Went past my simple Shoe—
And past my Apron—and my Belt
And past my Bodice—too—

And made as He would eat me up—
As wholly as a Dew
15 Upon a Dandelion's Sleeve—
And then—I started—too—

And He—He followed—close behind—
I felt His Silver Heel
Upon my Ankle—Then my Shoes
20 Would overflow with Pearl—

Until We met the Solid Town—
No One He seemed to know—
And bowing—with a Mighty look—
At me—The Sea withdrew—

COMMENTARY AND QUESTIONS

1. Describe the literal action of the poem.

2. Where does the tone turn from light to serious? What other poems of Dickinson's use a light opening line to introduce a serious theme? What is the effect of this technique?

3. Contrast the fresh, innocent tone of lines 1 and 2 to the change that begins in the third stanza.

4. Compare the sea to death in "Because I could not stop for Death."

5. Discuss the poem's theme.

"Tell all the Truth but tell it slant—"

Tell all the Truth but tell it slant—
Success in Circuit[1] lies
Too bright for our infirm Delight
The Truth's superb surprise

5   As Lightning to the Children eased
With explanation kind
The Truth must dazzle gradually
Or every man be blind—

[1] **Circuit:** curving, circular.

COMMENTARY AND QUESTIONS

1. Paraphrase the first stanza.

2. Explain the comparison Dickinson makes in the last stanza.

3. Compare the theme and the imagery of this poem to "Before I got my eye put out."

4. Do you think this poem gives sound advice about how to tell people the truth?

5. Examine this poem as advice on how to write a poem. How, if at all, does Dickinson adhere to this advice?

REVIEW

1. The following characteristics not only distinguish the best of Dickinson's poetry from earlier American poetry but also introduce themes and methods that later became popular in the twentieth century:

> a realistic, unsentimental view of life and death
> surprising words (like *cochineal*)
> purposeful breaks or irregularities in rhyme and meter
> economy—saying a lot in a few words
> strong opening lines
> vivid, unusual detail
> unexpected points of view (such as having a dead person narrate)
> tones that shift in the middle of the poem
> eccentric punctuation and capitalization

Look over Dickinson's poems and find examples of each of these characteristics as well as other characteristics not listed.

2. Write a poem of at least eight lines in the style of Emily Dickinson. As your basic form, use the quatrains Dickinson borrowed from the hymns of her day, iambic tetrameter lines alternating with iambic trimeter lines:

> te tum te tum te tum te tum
> te tum te tum te tum
> te tum te tum te tum te tum
> te tum te tum te tum

Remember, Dickinson would use internal punctuation to vary the meter, and although she would probably rhyme every other line, she would have an off rhyme somewhere, like *gun* and *stone*. She might also deemphasize rhyme by having sentences continue uninterrupted from one line to the next.

3. Compare the poetry of Anne Bradstreet with that of Emily Dickinson. Think of the two hundred and fifty years separating their lives, their roles as women in their New England communities, their relationships to God and nature, and their poetic craft.

4. Compare Dickinson's attitudes toward God and nature to those of one of the following poets: Bryant, Emerson, Lanier, or Whitman.

EDWIN ARLINGTON ROBINSON
1869–1935

Like Bryant and Lanier, E. A. Robinson began writing poetry at an early age. He attended Harvard College from 1891 to 1893, when the financial difficulties resulting from his father's death forced him to return to his home in Gardiner, Maine. There he wrote two books of poems before moving to New York in 1897. Many of these early poems, some of the best and most memorable he would write, describe characters in Tilbury Town, a fictitious place modeled after Gardiner.

Robinson's years in New York were difficult because the poet could not make a comfortable living as a writer, and he refused to compromise his artistic ideals. Instead, he earned a living as best he could, while leaving time and energy to write. In 1911, however, he had the good fortune of spending the summer at the McDowell Colony, an artists' retreat in Peterboro, New Hampshire. There, free to write without distraction, he spent the rest of his summers.

When Robinson was fifty years old and had published eight books, his work finally became well-known and appreciated. Robinson earned honorary degrees from Yale and Bowdoin in 1922 and 1925, and three Pulitzer Prizes. Writing in traditional forms and employing simple language, Robinson eventually rivaled Robert Frost as the most popular poet of the time. Despite its apparent simplicity and lack of structural innovation, Robinson's poetry possesses three clearly modern traits: a fascination with nonrational human behavior; a relatively detached, reportorial presentation of events; and a natural, unembellished, native voice. This last trait, his strong voice that sounds like natural American speech yet functions within the rules of strict poetic forms, may well be his greatest achievement.

Dear Friends

Dear friends, reproach me not for what I do,
Nor counsel me, nor pity me; nor say
That I am wearing half my life away
For bubble-work that only fools pursue.

111

5   And if my bubbles be too small for you,
    Blow bigger then your own: the games we play
    To fill the frittered minutes of a day,
    Good glasses are to read the spirit through.

    And whoso reads may get him some shrewd skill;
10 And some unprofitable scorn resign,
    To praise the very thing that he deplores;
    So, friends (dear friends), remember, if you will,
    The shame I win for singing is all mine,
    The gold I miss for dreaming is all yours.

COMMENTARY AND QUESTIONS

1. Paying particular attention to "bubble-work" and "good glasses," paraphrase the first stanza.

2. What does the speaker mean by "singing" (line 13) and "good glasses" (line 8)?

3. Noting specifically the tone of the last three lines, describe the tone of the poem.

4. How does the poet perceive his relationship with his audience? Compare "Dear Friends" to Dickinson's "Success is counted sweetest."

An Old Story

    Strange that I did not know him then,
        That friend of mine!
    I did not even show him then
        One friendly sign;

5   But cursed him for the ways he had
        To make me see
    My envy of the praise he had
        For praising me.

    I would have rid the earth of him
        Once, in my pride! . . .
    I never knew the worth of him
        Until he died.

COMMENTARY AND QUESTIONS

1. Paraphrase the second stanza.

2. Note that the second stanza, which is part of a sentence that began in line 3, contains no punctuation until the final period. After rereading the stanza aloud without pausing at the ends of lines, comment on how the stanza's grammar and punctuation affect its voice. The term *voice* describes the way one "hears" a piece of writing as one reads.

3. State the theme of "An Old Story."

Cliff Klingenhagen

Cliff Klingenhagen had me in to dine
With him one day; and after soup and meat,
And all the other things there were to eat,
Cliff took two glasses and filled one with wine
5 And one with wormwood.[1] Then, without a sign
For me to choose at all, he took the draught
Of bitterness himself, and lightly quaffed
It off, and said the other one was mine.

And when I asked him what the deuce he meant
10 By doing that, he only looked at me
And grinned, and said it was a way of his.
And though I know the fellow, I have spent
Long time a-wondering when I shall be
As happy as Cliff Klingenhagen is.

[1] **wormwood:** a bitter drink.

COMMENTARY AND QUESTIONS

1. Nine lines of this poem end without *end-stops* (punctuation marks coming at the end of poetic lines). Discuss the effect of Robinson's allowing these sentences to spill from line to line without the interruption of commas, semicolons, and periods?

2. Why do you think that Cliff Klingenhagen drinks wormwood? What effect does this action have on the speaker?

3. State and discuss the poem's theme.

John Evereldown

"Where are you going to-night, to-night,—
    Where are you going, John Evereldown?
There's never the sign of a star in sight,
    Nor a lamp that's nearer than Tilbury Town.
5 Why do you stare as a dead man might?
Where are you pointing away from the light?
And where are you going to-night, to-night,—
    Where are you going, John Evereldown?"

"Right through the forest, where none can see,
10   There's where I'm going, to Tilbury Town.
The men are asleep,—or awake, may be,—
    But the women are calling John Evereldown.

Ever and ever they call for me,
And while they call can a man be free?
15 So right through the forest, where none can see,
    There's where I'm going, to Tilbury Town."

"But why are you going so late, so late,—
    Why are you going, John Evereldown?
Though the road be smooth and the path be straight,
20   There are two long leagues[1] to Tilbury Town.
Come in by the fire, old man, and wait!
Why do you chatter out there by the gate?
And why are you going so late, so late,—
    Why are you going, John Evereldown?"

25 "I follow the women wherever they call,—
    That's why I'm going to Tilbury Town.
God knows if I pray to be done with it all,
    But God is no friend to John Evereldown.
So the clouds may come and the rain may fall,
30 The shadows may creep and the dead men crawl,—
But I follow the women wherever they call,
    And that's why I'm going to Tilbury Town."

[1] **two long leagues:** One league is three miles, thus six miles.

COMMENTARY AND QUESTIONS

1. This songlike poem, with its narrative line (plot), repeated phrases, and folk quality, is a ballad. Summarize the narrative.

2. How do "old man" and "chatter" affect the poem's meaning?

3. What is the poem's central idea?

4. Does the ballad form seem appropriate for this poem? Discuss.

Reuben Bright

Because he was a butcher and thereby
Did earn an honest living (and did right),
I would not have you think that Reuben Bright
Was any more a brute than you or I:
5 For when they told him that his wife must die,
He stared at them, and shook with grief and fright,
And cried like a great baby half that night,
And made the women cry to see him cry.

And after she was dead, and he had paid
10 The singers and the sexton and the rest,
He packed a lot of things that she had made
Most mournfully away in an old chest
Of hers, and put some chopped-up cedar boughs
In with them, and *tore down* the slaughter-house.

COMMENTARY AND QUESTIONS

1. Note that this sonnet is composed of only two sentences and the second stanza, the sestet, employs only one end-stop, excluding the final period. Discuss the effect of the poem's punctuation and grammar.

2. Is "and did right" necessary to the poem's meaning, or does it simply create a rhyme for "bright"?

3. Explain why Reuben Bright "tore down the slaughterhouse."

Richard Cory

Whenever Richard Cory went down town,
We people on the pavement looked at him:
He was a gentleman from sole to crown,
Clean favored, and imperially slim.

5 And he was always quietly arrayed,
And he was always human when he talked;
But still he fluttered pulses when he said,
"Good-morning," and he glittered when he walked.

And he was rich,—yes, richer than a king,—
10 And admirably schooled in every grace:
In fine, we thought that he was everything
To make us wish that we were in his place.

So on we worked, and waited for the light,
And went without the meat, and cursed the bread;
15 And Richard Cory, one calm summer night,
Went home and put a bullet through his head.

COMMENTARY AND QUESTIONS

1. State the poem's central idea.

2. What do we know about the speaker's relationship to Richard Cory and the townspeople? How do these relationships affect the poem's meaning?

3. Cite the words and phrases that help us understand Richard Cory's reputation.

4. "Richard Cory" has been made into a song and into a play. How do you account for the poem's enduring popularity? Compare the Simon and Garfunkel song to the poem. Which do you prefer and why?

Walt Whitman

The master-songs are ended, and the man
That sang them is a name. And so is God
A name; and so is love, and life, and death,
And everything. But we, who are too blind
5 To read what we have written, or what faith
Has written for us, do not understand:
We only blink, and wonder.

Last night it was the song that was the man,
But now it is the man that is the song.
10 We do not hear him very much to-day:
His piercing and eternal cadence rings
Too pure for us—too powerfully pure,
Too lovingly triumphant, and too large;
But there are some that hear him, and they know
15 That he shall sing to-morrow for all men,
And that all time shall listen.

The master-songs are ended? Rather say
No songs are ended that are ever sung,
And that no names are dead names. When we write
20 Men's letters on proud marble or on sand,
We write them there forever.

COMMENTARY AND QUESTIONS

1. Describe the poem's form—rhyme pattern, meter, stanza pattern. How, if at all, does the form seem appropriate to the poem's subject?

2. Comment on lines 11–16. Do you agree with Robinson's view of Whitman?

3. Do you detect the influence of Whitman on Robinson? If so, where?

REVIEW

1. Which poem of Robinson's do you like the best? The least? Explain your reasons.

2. Three of these poems are sonnets. Study the rhyme schemes of each; identify the "turn" of thought; and explain whether each sonnet is Italian, English, or a hybrid. Are these poems well-constructed, allowing ideas to assert themselves naturally, without interference from the technical demands of the sonnet form? Discuss, using specific examples.

3. To what extent does Robinson create a natural American voice, despite the constraints of form and the traditional assumption that poets should use lofty, embellished language? Can you think of any fiction writers of the time who also were experimenting with the patterns and vocabulary of natural native speech?

4. Discuss the psychological themes in these poems. How do they help establish Robinson as a modern poet?

5. What other common characteristics do these poems share?

ROBERT FROST
1874–1963

Although many people associate Robert Frost with New England, he was born in San Francisco and lived there until his father died in 1885. Frost came to New England at age eleven and learned a different way of life and a different dialect of English, which may well have sharpened his skill of listening carefully to the way people talk. On the subject of listening, he later said, "Words exist in the mouth, not in books," meaning that the poet must capture the tones and patterns of real speech. He said once in a letter that one way to hear what he called "the abstract sound of sense" is to listen to "voices behind the door that cuts off the words." We see, therefore, in much of Frost's poetry—particularly, his long narratives like "The Fear" and "Home Burial"—not a nineteenth-century idea of poetic language, but rather the sound of authentic American speech.

Frost graduated from Lawrence High School in Lawrence, Massachusetts in 1892 and the next year spent less than a semester at Dartmouth College, claiming that true education did not take place in academic settings. In 1895 he married Eleanor White, his high school sweetheart and, along with Frost, co-recipient of the high school's valedictorian honors. Two years later he attended Harvard University for eighteen months as a special student, withdrawing just before his wife gave birth to their second child.

In Derry, New Hampshire from 1900 to 1906, Frost worked a farm, which he eventually inherited from his paternal grandfather. During these years he accumulated much of the specific rural knowledge that we see in his poems about farm people and nature. Then from 1906 to 1911 Frost taught at Pinkerton Academy in Derry. He wrote many of his most famous poems during these difficult years of farming and teaching. During this time, the family had little money and the American publishers had shown only slight interest in Frost's poetry. So in 1912 when he was 38 years old, Frost sold his farm and took his wife and four children to England. There he published his first two books, *A Boy's Will* (1913) and *North of Boston* (1914), met some of the important writers and poets of his time, and developed the characteristic voice for which his poetry is famous. Although English poets like Edward Thomas admired Frost's use of traditional forms, the eccentric and influential American Ezra Pound encouraged Frost to employ free verse instead of rhymed and metered patterns. Frost's refusal to abandon traditional form set him apart from other American poets such as T. S. Eliot, Wallace Stevens, and William Carlos Williams, making Frost appear old-fashioned. Poets and editors were blind to Frost's new American music that captured what he called "the abstract vitality of our speech." These early years of the century seemed to be the time to cast off the formalisms of the past and to find new ways to interpret contemporary life. Of course Frost's extremely American voice and the music it made were important modern innovations, and his dark themes did explore twentieth-century problems such as human isolation and alienation. Nevertheless, it was not until the last decade of his long life that Robert Frost saw his work appreciated by prominent American critics.

After Frost had gotten his start in England, he returned to America in 1915 at the outbreak of World War I and began working as a poet-in-residence, first for a year at the University of Michigan and later at Amherst, Harvard, and other colleges and universities. Despite the rural setting and colloquial voice of his poetry, Robert Frost was in fact the first American poet of many to earn a living as a poet in universities and colleges. This work gave Frost time to write and a sufficient income to live comfortably.

Frost became more popular in his lifetime than any American poet since Longfellow, whose life intersected Frost's by eight years. Collected editions of his poems were published, starting in 1930, three times before his death; he won four Pulitzer Prizes; in 1958 the Library of Congress appointed him poetry consultant; and in 1961 he participated in the inauguration of President John F. Kennedy. On the other hand, four of his six children died during Frost's lifetime, and the poet suffered many other personal tragedies. Since his death in 1963, his image as the kindly old New Hampshire farmer-poet has been replaced by one of a contentious, single-minded, crafty, poetic genius, always willing to do battle for the cause of his art.

The Pasture

I'm going out to clean the pasture spring;
I'll only stop to rake the leaves away
(And wait to watch the water clear, I may):
I shan't be gone long.—You come too.

5   I'm going out to fetch the little calf
That's standing by the mother. It's so young
It totters when she licks it with her tongue.
I shan't be gone long.—You come too.

COMMENTARY AND QUESTIONS

1. Why do you think Frost used this poem at the beginning of collections of his poems?

2. Describe the poem's tone.

3. What does "The Pasture" suggest about the poems that will follow?

Mending Wall

Something there is that doesn't love a wall,
That sends the frozen-ground-swell under it
And spills the upper boulders in the sun,
And makes gaps even two can pass abreast.
5   The work of hunters is another thing:
I have come after them and made repair
Where they have left not one stone on a stone,
But they would have the rabbit out of hiding,
To please the yelping dogs. The gaps I mean,
10 No one has seen them made or heard them made,
But at spring mending-time we find them there.
I let my neighbor know beyond the hill;
And on a day we meet to walk the line
And set the wall between us once again.
15 We keep the wall between us as we go.
To each the boulders that have fallen to each.
And some are loaves and some so nearly balls
We have to use a spell to make them balance:
"Stay where you are until our backs are turned!"
20 We wear our fingers rough with handling them.
Oh, just another kind of outdoor game,
One on a side. It comes to little more:
There where it is we do not need the wall:
He is all pine and I am apple orchard.
25 My apple trees will never get across
And eat the cones under his pines, I tell him.
He only says, "Good fences make good neighbors."
Spring is the mischief in me, and I wonder
If I could put a notion in his head:
30 "Why do they make good neighbors? Isn't it
Where there are cows? But here there are no cows.
Before I built a wall I'd ask to know
What I was walling in or walling out,
And to whom I was like to give offense.
35 Something there is that doesn't love a wall,
That wants it down." I could say "Elves" to him,
But it's not elves exactly, and I'd rather
He said it for himself. I see him there,
Bringing a stone grasped firmly by the top
40 In each hand, like an old-stone savage armed.
He moves in darkness as it seems to me,
Not of woods only and the shade of trees.
He will not go behind his father's saying,
And he likes having thought of it so well
45 He says again, "Good fences make good neighbors."

COMMENTARY AND QUESTIONS

1. What is the speaker's attitude toward mending his wall each year? Cite some words or phrases that help establish that attitude.

2. Do "good fences make good neighbors"? Discuss this question, using examples from your life or from certain events in history.

3. Frost wrote this poem and most of his other long poems in *blank verse*, which is unrhymed iambic pentameter, a traditional English form suited for long narrative poems. (Do not confuse *blank verse* with *free verse*, which prescribes no particular rhyme or meter.) Blank verse allows the reader to follow the narrative without the distraction of end rhymes, whereas the iambic pentameter provides the poet with a structure to help measure rhythm and line length. Do you think blank verse is effective in this poem? Discuss.

Home Burial

This narrative poem describes a conflict between a man and a woman whose first child has died. As you read the poem, note the locations of the characters and the hints that the conflict we are hearing has a history and probably a future.

He saw her from the bottom of the stairs
Before she saw him. She was starting down,
Looking back over her shoulder at some fear.
She took a doubtful step and then undid it
5   To raise herself and look again. He spoke
Advancing toward her: "What is it you see
From up there always?—for I want to know."
She turned and sank upon her skirts at that,
And her face changed from terrified to dull.
10 He said to gain time: "What is it you see?"
Mounting until she cowered under him.
"I will find out now—you must tell me, dear."
She, in her place, refused him any help,
With the least stiffening of her neck and silence.
15 She let him look, sure that he wouldn't see,
Blind creature; and awhile he didn't see.
But at last he murmured, "Oh," and again, "Oh."

"What is it—what?" she said.

                              "Just that I see."

"You don't," she challenged. "Tell me what it is."

20 "The wonder is I didn't see at once.
I never noticed it from here before.
I must be wonted[1] to it—that's the reason.

[1] **wonted:** accustomed.

The little graveyard where my people are!
So small the window frames the whole of it.
25 Not so much larger than a bedroom, is it?
There are three stones of slate and one of marble,
Broad-shouldered little slabs there in the sunlight
On the sidehill. We haven't to mind *those*.
But I understand: it is not the stones,
But the child's mound——"

                              "Don't, don't, don't,

30   don't," she cried.

She withdrew, shrinking from beneath his arm
That rested on the banister, and slid downstairs;
And turned on him with such a daunting look,
He said twice over before he knew himself:
35 "Can a man speak of his own child he's lost?"

"Not you!—Oh, where's my hat? Oh, I don't need it!
I must get out of here. I must get air.—
I don't know rightly whether any man can."

"Amy! Don't go to someone else this time.
40 Listen to me. I won't come down the stairs."
He sat and fixed his chin between his fists.
"There's something I should like to ask you, dear."

"You don't know how to ask it."

                              "Help me, then."

Her fingers moved the latch for all reply.

45 "My words are nearly always an offense.
I don't know how to speak of anything
So as to please you. But I might be taught,
I should suppose. I can't say I see how.
A man must partly give up being a man
50 With womenfolk. We could have some arrangement
By which I'd bind myself to keep hands off
Anything special you're a-mind to name.
Though I don't like such things 'twixt[2] those that love.
Two that don't love can't live together without them.
55 But two that do can't live together with them."
She moved the latch a little. "Don't—don't go.
Don't carry it to someone else this time.
Tell me about it if it's something human.
Let me into your grief. I'm not so much

[2] **twixt:** between

60 Unlike other folks as your standing there
    Apart would make me out. Give me my chance.
    I do think, though, you overdo it a little.
    What was it brought you up to think it the thing
    To take your mother-loss of a first child
65 So inconsolably—in the face of love.
    You'd think his memory might be satisfied——"

    "There you go sneering now!"

                          "I'm not, I'm not!

    You make me angry. I'll come down to you.
    God, what a woman! And it's come to this,
70 A man can't speak of his own child that's dead."

    "You can't because you don't know how to speak.
    If you had any feelings, you that dug
    With your own hand—how could you?—his little grave;
    I saw you from that very window there,
75 Making the gravel leap and leap in air,
    Leap up, like that, like that, and land so lightly
    And roll back down the mound beside the hole.
    I thought, Who is that man? I didn't know you.
    And I crept down the stairs and up the stairs
80 To look again, and still your spade kept lifting.
    Then you came in. I heard your rumbling voice
    Out in the kitchen, and I don't know why,
    But I went near to see with my own eyes.
    You could sit there with the stains on your shoes
85 Of the fresh earth from your own baby's grave
    And talk about your everyday concerns.
    You had stood the spade up against the wall
    Outside there in the entry, for I saw it."
    "I shall laugh the worst laugh I ever laughed.
90 I'm cursed. God, if I don't believe I'm cursed."

    "I can repeat the very words you were saying:
    'Three foggy mornings and one rainy day
    Will rot the best birch fence a man can build.'
    Think of it, talk like that at such a time!
95 What had how long it takes a birch to rot
    To do with what was in the darkened parlor?
    You *couldn't* care! The nearest friends can go
    With anyone to death, comes so far short
    They might as well not try to go at all.
100 No, from the time when one is sick to death,
    One is alone, and he dies more alone.

Friends make pretense of following to the grave,
But before one is in it, their minds are turned
And making the best of their way back to life
105 And living people, and things they understand.
But the world's evil. I won't have grief so
If I can change it. Oh, I won't, I won't!"

"There, you have said it all and you feel better.
You won't go now. You're crying. Close the door.
110 The heart's gone out of it: why keep it up?
Amy! There's someone coming down the road!"

"You—oh, you think the talk is all. I must go—
Somewhere out of this house. How can I make you——"

"If—you—do!" She was opening the door wider.
115 "Where do you mean to go? First tell me that.
I'll follow and bring you back by force. I *will!*—"

COMMENTARY AND QUESTIONS

1. Describe the locations and the movements of the characters during the first twelve lines.

2. What has the woman been looking at, and why does it take the man awhile to understand?

3. How would the meaning change if "grave" were substituted for "mound" in line 30?

4. What does "this time" in line 39 imply?

5. Why does the man say he is cursed?

6. In line 91–96 what is the man's point, and why is the woman angered? How, if at all, are these views stereotypic? With which view do you sympathize?

7. What if the poem had ended at line 110? Discuss the importance of lines 111–116. Do you like this conclusion? How does it compare to conclusions in other of Frost's poems?

8. Examine the point of view Frost chose for this poem. How does the narrator affect the poem? Why do you think Frost used a large amount of dialogue? Is this dialogue effective?

9. In what form is "Home Burial" written? Comment on Frost's use of this form.

10. How may the theme and subject matter of this poem be more modern than Frost's first readers realized?

The Fear

A lantern-light from deeper in the barn
Shone on a man and woman in the door
And threw their lurching shadows on a house
Nearby, all dark in every glossy window.

5   A horse's hoof pawed once the hollow floor,
And the back of the gig[1] they stood beside
Moved in a little. The man grasped a wheel.
The woman spoke out sharply, "Whoa, stand still!—
I saw it just as plain as a white plate,"
10 She said, "as the light on the dashboard ran
Along the bushes at the roadside—a man's face.
You *must* have seen it too."

                              "I didn't see it.

Are you sure——"

                    "Yes, I'm sure!"

                                   "—it was a face?"

"Joel, I'll have to look. I can't go in,
15 I can't, and leave a thing like that unsettled.
Doors locked and curtains drawn will make no difference.
I always have felt strange when we came home
To the dark house after so long an absence,
And the key rattled loudly into place
20 Seemed to warn someone to be getting out
At one door as we entered at another.
What if I'm right, and someone all the time—
Don't hold my arm!"

                    "I say it's someone passing."

"You speak as if this were a traveled road.
25 You forget where we are. What is beyond
That he'd be going to or coming from
At such an hour of night, and on foot too?
What was he standing still for in the bushes?"

"It's not so very late—it's only dark.
30 There's more in it than you're inclined to say.
Did he look like——?"

                        "He looked like anyone.
I'll never rest tonight unless I know.
Give me the lantern."

                      "You don't want the lantern."

She pushed past him and got it for herself.

___

[1] **gig:** a two-wheeled carriage drawn by a horse.

35   "You're not to come," she said. "This is my business.
     If the time's come to face it, I'm the one
     To put it the right way. He'd never dare—
     Listen! He kicked a stone. Hear that, hear that!
     He's coming towards us. Joel, go in—please.
40   Hark!—I don't hear him now. But please go in."
     "In the first place you can't make me believe it's——"

     "It is—or someone else he's sent to watch.
     And now's the time to have it out with him
     While we know definitely where he is.
45   Let him get off and he'll be everywhere
     Around us, looking out of trees and bushes
     Till I shan't dare to set a foot outdoors.

     And I can't stand it. Joel, let me go!"

     "But it's nonsense to think he'd care enough."

50   "You mean you couldn't understand his caring.
     Oh, but you see he hadn't had enough—
     Joel, I won't—I won't—I promise you.
     We mustn't say hard things. You mustn't either."

     "I'll be the one, if anybody goes!
55   But you give him the advantage with this light.
     What couldn't he do to us standing here!
     And if to see was what he wanted, why,
     He has seen all there was to see and gone."

     He appeared to forget to keep his hold,
60   But advanced with her as she crossed the grass.

     "What do you want?" she cried to all the dark.
     She stretched up tall to overlook the light
     That hung in both hands, hot against her skirt.

     "There's no one; so you're wrong," he said.

                                "There is.—
65   What do you want?" she cried, and then herself
     Was startled when an answer really came.

     "Nothing." It came from well along the road.

     She reached a hand to Joel for support:
     The smell of scorching woolen made her faint.
70   "What are you doing around this house at night?"

     "Nothing." A pause: there seemed no more to say.

And then the voice again: "You seem afraid.
I saw by the way you whipped up the horse.
I'll just come forward in the lantern-light
And let you see."

75   "Yes, do.—Joel, go back!"

She stood her ground against the noisy steps
That came on, but her body rocked a little.

"You see," the voice said.

                         "Oh." She looked and looked.

"You don't see—I've a child here by the hand.
80 A robber wouldn't have his family with him."

"What's a child doing at this time of night——?"

"Out walking. Every child should have the memory
Of at least one long-after-bedtime walk.
What, son?"

                    "Then I should think you'd try to find
85 Somewhere to walk——"

                              "The highway, as it happens—
We're stopping for the fortnight² down at Dean's."

"But if that's all—Joel—you realize—
You won't think anything. You understand?
You understand that we have to be careful.
90 This is a very, very lonely place.—
Joel!" She spoke as if she couldn't turn.
The swinging lantern lengthened to the ground,
It touched, it struck, it clattered and went out.

² **fortnight:** two weeks.

COMMENTARY AND QUESTIONS

1. This poem is set at night. A man named Joel and a woman, we assume his wife, confront another man that the woman, but not Joel, has seen "plain as a white plate" in the bushes beside the road. Describe the conflict between the husband and the wife, and tell how that conflict helps us understand the relationship between the three people.

2. After noting the various contexts in which the lantern appears, discuss whether or not it serves as a symbol.

3. How does the presence of the man's young son and the line, "We're stopping for a fortnight down at Dean's" (line 86) affect the situation—especially our understanding of the relationship between the husband and wife?

4. Discuss the poem's conclusion. What questions are left unanswered? Should Frost have answered them? Why or why not?

5. Does the dialogue in this poem seem real and believable? Discuss.

Mowing

There was never a sound beside the wood but one,
And that was my long scythe[1] whispering to the ground.
What was it it whispered? I knew not well myself;
Perhaps it was something about the heat of the sun,
5   Something, perhaps, about the lack of sound—
And that was why it whispered and did not speak.
It was no dream of the gift of idle hours,
Or easy gold at the hand of fay[2] or elf:
Anything more than the truth would have seemed too weak
10   To the earnest love that laid the swale[3] in rows,
Not without feeble-pointed spikes of flowers
(Pale orchises[4]), and scared a bright green snake.
The fact is the sweetest dream that labor knows.
My long scythe whispered and left the hay to make.[5]

[1] **scythe:** an implement used for mowing (cutting) hay or other grasslike plants; it is nearly a yard long, curved, single-edged blade tapering from three inches down to one and a half, and afixed to a five-foot-long bent handle. The mower sweeps the sharp blade in semicircular motions that slice (rather than chop) the hay, making a quiet, whispering sound.
[2] **fay:** a fairy or elf.
[3] **swale:** a low, moist tract of land.
[4] **pale orchises:** a wild, white orchid that grows in wet places.
[5] **make:** to dry in the sun.

COMMENTARY AND QUESTIONS

1. In the first six lines, what sounds does Frost use to suggest the swishing sound of the scythe? What are the poetic terms for these repeated sounds?

2. What "scared a bright green snake" in line 12? Note that "Not without . . . (pale orchises)" is set off by commas.

3. Paraphrase lines 6–12, being sure to consider the meanings of "it" in line 7, the cut stems of the flowers mowed down by the scythe (line 11), and the snake (line 12) disturbed by the mower.

4. Discuss line 13. What is the "fact"? Is it the mown swale or any tangible thing as contrasted to an intangible dream or illusion? Or is it the poem itself, which is an intangible inspiration made into a tangible object of art?

Good Hours

I had for my winter evening walk—
No one at all with whom to talk,
But I had the cottages in a row
Up to their shining eyes in snow.

5 And I thought I had the folk within:
I had the sound of a violin;
I had a glimpse through curtain laces
Of youthful forms and youthful faces.

I had such company outward bound.
10 I went till there were no cottages found.
I turned and repented, but coming back
I saw no window but that was black.

Over the snow my creaking feet
Disturbed the slumbering village street
15 Like profanation, by your leave,[1]
At ten o'clock of a winter eve.

[1] **by your leave:** with your permission.

COMMENTARY AND QUESTIONS

1. Like some of Emily Dickinson's poems, "Good Hours" begins on a positive theme and half way through changes directions to consider something disturbing. How does this technique work in this poem?

2. Discuss Frost's use of "repent" in line 11.

3. Unlike "The Fear" this poem employs a heavy aa, bb, cc, etc. rhyme scheme, with each rhyme chiming perfectly. The lines also contain four stressed syllables and a somewhat irregular mix of unstressed syllables. Note also that eleven of the sixteen lines are end-stopped. After marking the four stressed syllables in each line, comment on how the poem's music affects the poem's meaning.

4. What is the poem's central idea?

The Road Not Taken

Two roads diverged in a yellow wood,
And sorry I could not travel both
And be one traveler, long I stood
And looked down one as far as I could
5 To where it bent in the undergrowth;

Then took the other, as just as fair,
And having perhaps the better claim,
Because it was grassy and wanted wear;
Though as for that, the passing there
10 Had worn them really about the same,

And both that morning equally lay
In leaves no step had trodden black.
Oh, I kept the first for another day!
Yet knowing how way leads on to way,
15 I doubted if I should ever come back.

I shall be telling this with a sigh
Somewhere ages and ages hence:
Two roads diverged in a wood, and I—
I took the one less traveled by,
20 And that has made all the difference.

COMMENTARY AND QUESTIONS

1. Like many of Frost's more popular poems, "The Road not Taken" appears to mean less than it does. What is poem's apparent meaning?

2. Discuss the importance of the following words and phrases: "as just as fair" (line 6), "perhaps" (line 7), "really about the same" (line 10), "equally" (line 11).

3. Readers usually assume the last line is a happy ending. Do you agree? Discuss.

4. State the poem's central idea.

The Oven Bird[1]

There is a singer everyone has heard,
Loud, a mid-summer and a mid-wood bird,
Who makes the solid tree trunks sound again.
He says that leaves are old and that for flowers
5 Mid-summer is to spring as one to ten.
He says the early petal-fall is past,
When pear and cherry bloom went down in showers
On sunny days a moment overcast;
And comes that other fall we name the fall.
10 He says the highway dust over all.
The bird would cease and be as other birds
But that he knows in singing not to sing.
The question that he frames in all but words
Is what to make of a diminished thing.

---

[1] **Oven Bird:** a migratory songbird that nests on the ground and usually remains in thick wooded cover. Its loud call sounds like, "TEACHer, TEACHer, TEACHer, TEACHer," growing louder with each repetition.

COMMENTARY AND QUESTIONS

1. How does Frost express the loudness of the oven bird's call?
2. What is the "early petal-fall" referred to in line 6?
3. In line 9, what are the two meanings of "fall"?
4. Explain the paradox (a contradiction that in some way is true) in line 12.
5. What is the "diminished thing"?
6. What is the poem's theme?

Birches

When I see birches bend to left and right
Across the lines of straighter darker trees,
I like to think some boy's been swinging them.
But swinging doesn't bend them down to stay
5   As ice storms do. Often you must have seen them
Loaded with ice a sunny winter morning
After a rain. They click upon themselves
As the breeze rises, and turn many-colored
As the stir cracks and crazes¹ their enamel.
10 Soon the sun's warmth makes them shed crystal shells
Shattering and avalanching on the snow crust—
Such heaps of broken glass to sweep away
You'd think the inner dome of heaven had fallen.
They are dragged to the withered bracken² by the load,
15 And they seem not to break; though once they are bowed
So low for long, they never right themselves:
You may see their trunks arching in the woods
Years afterwards, trailing their leaves on the ground
Like girls on hands and knees that throw their hair
20 Before them over their heads to dry in the sun.
But I was going to say when Truth broke in
With all her matter of fact about the ice storm,
I should prefer to have some boy bend them
As he went out and in to fetch the cows—
25 Some boy too far from town to learn baseball,
Whose only play was what he found himself,
Summer or winter, and could play alone.
One by one he subdued his father's trees
By riding them down over and over again

¹ **crazes:** to produce a network of fine cracks.
² **bracken:** a kind of fern; any large, coarse fern.

30   Until he took the stiffness out of them,
      And not one but hung limp, not one was left
      For him to conquer. He learned all there was
      To learn about not launching out too soon
      And so not carrying the tree away
35   Clear to the ground. He always kept his poise
      To the top branches, climbing carefully
      With the same pains you use to fill a cup
      Up to the brim, and even above the brim.
      Then he flung outward, feet first, with a swish,
40   Kicking his way down through the air to the ground.
      So was I once myself a swinger of birches.
      And so I dream of going back to be.
      It's when I'm weary of considerations,
      And life is too much like a pathless wood
45   Where your face burns and tickles with the cobwebs
      Broken across it, and one eye is weeping
      From a twig's having lashed across it open.
      I'd like to get away from earth awhile
      And then come back to it and begin over.
50   May no fate willfully misunderstand me
      And half grant what I wish and snatch me away
      Not to return. Earth's the right place for love:
      I don't know where it's likely to go better.
      I'd like to go by climbing a birch tree,
55   And climb black branches up a snow-white trunk
      Toward heaven, till the tree could bear no more,
      But dipped its top and set me down again.
      That would be good both going and coming back.
      One could do worse than be a swinger of birches.

COMMENTARY AND QUESTIONS

1. How important is the boy's father to this poem? What if, for instance, the birches that the boy subdued belonged to no one in particular? How, if at all, would the meaning of the poem change?

2. Cite some places where Frost portrays birch-swinging as something likelife.

3. Paying particular attention to the meaning of the phrase "climbing a birch tree," paraphrase lines 48–59.

4. Note that lines 4–22, about 30 percent of the poem, digress from swinging birches. Is this digression necessary to the poem's final effect? Explain your answer.

5. State the poem's central idea.

"Out, Out[1]—"

The buzz saw[2] snarled and rattled in the yard
And made dust and dropped stove-length sticks of wood,
Sweet-scented stuff when the breeze drew across it.
And from there those that lifted eyes could count
5   Five mountain ranges one behind the other
Under the sunset far into Vermont.
And the saw snarled and rattled, snarled and rattled,
As it ran light, or had to bear a load.
And nothing happened: day was all but done.
10   Call it a day, I wish they might have said
To please the boy by giving him the half hour
That a boy counts so much when saved from work.
His sister stood beside them in her apron
To tell them "Supper." At the word, the saw,
15   As if to prove saws knew what supper meant,
Leaped out at the boy's hand, or seemed to leap—
He must have given the hand. However it was,
Neither refused the meeting. But the hand!
The boy's first outcry was a rueful laugh,
20   As he swung toward them holding up the hand,
Half in appeal, but half as if to keep
The life from spilling. Then the boy saw all—
Since he was old enough to know, big boy
Doing a man's work, though a child at heart—
25   He saw all spoiled. "Don't let them cut my hand off—
The doctor, when he comes. Don't let him, sister!"
So. But the hand was gone already.
The doctor put him in the dark of ether.
He lay and puffed his lips out with his breath.
30   And then—the watcher at his pulse took fright.
No one believed. They listened at his heart.
Little—less—nothing!—and that ended it.
No more to build on there. And they, since they
Were not the one dead, turned to their affairs.

[1] **Out, Out—:** These words are borrowed from Shakespeare's *Macbeth*. Macbeth, having just heard of Lady Macbeth's death and anticipating his own, refers to life as a candle: "Out, out brief candle!"

[2] **buzz saw:** a circular saw blade two or more feet in diameter, usually unprotected and, often on farms, driven by a tractor engine. This method of cutting wood preceded the chainsaw.

COMMENTARY AND QUESTIONS

1. How do the s sounds in lines 1–3 and 7 complement the meaning of these lines?

2. How does the sentence beginning in line 13 contribute to the effect of the boy's sudden and fatal injury?

3. Note the way the narrator describes the setting, explains the event (a true story Frost had heard from the boy's father), then describes the boy's death and the reactions of the people present. How does the narrator's way of telling this story affect the poem's theme? State the poem's theme.

4. Compare "Out, Out—" to other poems about death by Robinson, Dickinson, Whitman, or other poets you have read.

The Sound of Trees

I wonder about the trees.
Why do we wish to bear
Forever the noise of these
More than another noise
5   So close to our dwelling place?
We suffer[1] them by the day
Till we lose all measure of pace,
And fixity in our joys,
And acquire a listening air.
10   They are that that talks of going
But never gets away;
And that talks no less for knowing,
As it grows wiser and older,
That now it means to stay.
15   My feet tug at the floor
And my head sways to my shoulder
Sometimes when I watch trees sway,
From the window or the door.
I shall set forth for somewhere,
20   I shall make the reckless choice
Some day when they are in voice
And tossing so as to scare
The white clouds over them on.
I shall have less to say,
25   But I shall be gone.

[1] **suffer:** tolerate, endure.

COMMENTARY AND QUESTIONS

1. Paraphrase the first two sentences, lines 1–9.

2. According to the speaker, what kind of people are the trees like?

3. Where and how does the poem's focus shift from trees?

4. What is the tone of the last three lines and what does it tell us about the speaker? This poem conveys a sense of discontent as much by the music its words make as by its theme. Note how the rhythm tends toward but usually resists the comfortable, regular meter present, for instance, in the iambic trimeter lines (tee tum tee tum tee tum) 6, 11, and 14. Note also how roughly and quickly the last line reads. After marking the stressed syllables in each line, use specific examples to discuss how rhythm affects the poem's meaning.

5. What is the poem's theme?

Design

I found a dimpled spider, fat and white,
On a white heal-all[1], holding up a moth
Like a white piece of rigid satin cloth—
Assorted characters of death and blight
5   Mixed ready to begin the morning right,
Like the ingredients of a witches' broth—
A snow-drop spider, a flower like a froth,
And dead wings carried like a paper kite.

What had that flower to do with being white,
10   The wayside blue and innocent heal-all?
What brought the kindred spider to that height,
Then steered the white moth thither in the night?
What but design of darkness to appall?—
If design govern in a thing so small.

[1] **heal-all:** a plant with tightly clustered violet-blue flowers, reputed to have healing powers.

COMMENTARY AND QUESTIONS

1. After reading the footnote on the heal-all and rereading lines 9 and 10, explain the irony in the name of the flower within the context of this poem. What other ironies appear in the poem?

2. What image or images are particularly powerful? Discuss.

3. Discuss the poem's theme and then compare it to a Dickinson poem that also depicts death in nature.

Stopping by Woods on a Snowy Evening

Whose woods these are I think I know.
His house is in the village, though;
He will not see me stopping here
To watch his woods fill up with snow.

5 My little horse must think it queer
   To stop without a farmhouse near
   Between the woods and frozen lake
   The darkest evening of the year.

   He gives his harness bells a shake
10 To ask if there is some mistake.
   The only other sound's the sweep
   Of easy wind and downy flake.

   The woods are lovely, dark and deep,
   But I have promises to keep,
15 And miles to go before I sleep,
   And miles to go before I sleep.

COMMENTARY AND QUESTIONS

1. What will probably happen if the speaker remains stopped by the "lovely, dark and deep" woods on "the darkest evening of the year"? How does this probability affect the poem's meaning?

2. Frost said that when he could not think of a way to end this poem, he used the old technique of repeating the last line. Is the ending effective? How does the repetition affect the poem's meaning?

3. Note and comment on the relationship between sentences, lines, and stanzas.

4. This poem uses a compelling rhyme scheme (aaba, bbcb, ccdc, dddd), perfect rhymes, perfect iambic tetrameter meter (tee tum tee tum tee tum tee tum), and four quatrains. How does this regularity affect the poem's meaning?

5. This may well be the most often quoted American poem of this century. What accounts for its enduring popularity? What is your opinion of the poem?

REVIEW

1. Identify a common attitude or theme in Robert Frost's poetry.

2. Using specific poems as examples, compare Frost's view of nature to that of another poet we have studied.

3. In what sense is Frost a modern poet? How is he traditional?

4. Is Frost essentially a New England poet or a poet who happens to write about New England? Is this distinction useful? Why or why not?

5. Describe Frost's poetry.

6. What is your opinion of Frost's poetry? Offer specific examples to illustrate your points.

7. Examine Frost's sonnets. Do they fit into the conventional English or Italian structures? Does Frost unite content and form gracefully? Who do you think is the better sonneteer—Frost or Robinson? Explain your reasoning.

8. Write a poem of eight or more lines in the style of Robert Frost.

CARL SANDBURG
1868–1967

Carl Sandburg's long-lined, free verse poems, often employing catalogs descriptive of the American people and landscape, are clearly reminiscent of Walt Whitman. As we look closely at his portrayals of characters and places, however, we see that this raw, stark twentieth-century realism often sets Sandburg's work well apart from the more romanticized realism of Whitman's poetry.

Born in Galesburg, Illinois, the child of Swedish immigrants, Carl Sandburg left school at thirteen and worked at various jobs, such as harvesting, dishwashing, and house painting. In 1897, a year before enlisting in the Spanish-American War, he rode with hoboes in railroad boxcars as far west as Kansas, stopping along the way to work at odd jobs. After serving eight months in Puerto Rico as an infantryman, he returned to Galesburg and attended Lombard College for four years, where he captained the basketball team, wrote for student publications, and excelled in his classes. In 1902, however, he left college without a degree and set off again to travel the country by boxcar. These travels strengthened Sandburg's already strong identity with working people. Eventually living in Wisconsin and later moving to Chicago, Sandburg married and worked as a reporter, an editor, and a political organizer.

In 1914 his career as a poet was launched when nine of his "Chicago Poems" appeared in *Poetry,* the then-new literary magazine that was publishing the prominent young poets of the time. Although we are concerned with Sandburg's life as a poet, he was also a journalist, historian, and biographer, his biography of Abraham Lincoln winning the Pulitzer Prize. In his career as a poet Sandburg won another Pulitzer Prize and the Poetry Society of America's Gold Medal. He received honorary degrees from many colleges and universities, including Northwestern, Syracuse, Dartmouth, Rollins, and his own Lombard; in 1928 he was the Phi Betta Kappa poet at Harvard. Active until the end of his life, he was in 1960 a consultant in Hollywood for *The Greatest Story Ever Told,* a film about the life of Christ, and in 1962 became a member of the National Committee for the Support of Public Schools.

Although Sandburg's popularity has diminished in the last twenty-five years, it is still clear that his poetry captures both the exuberance and the confusion of the American people at the beginning of this century.

137

Chicago

Hog Butcher for the World,
Tool Maker, Stacker of Wheat,
Player with Railroads and the Nation's Freight Handler;
Stormy, husky, brawling,
5   City of the Big Shoulders:

They tell me you are wicked and I believe them, for I have seen your
     painted women under the gas lamps luring the farm boys.
And they tell me you are crooked and I answer: Yes, it is true I have
     seen the gunman kill and go free to kill again.
And they tell me you are brutal and my reply is: On the faces of women
     and children I have seen the marks of wanton hunger.
And having answered so I turn once more to those who sneer at this
     my city, and give them back the sneer and say to them:
10   Come and show me another city with lifted head singing so proud to be
     alive and coarse and strong and cunning.
Flinging magnetic curses amid the toil of piling job on job, here is a tall
     bold slugger set vivid against the little soft cities;
Fierce as a dog with tongue lapping for action, cunning as a savage
     pitted against the wilderness,
     Bareheaded,
     Shoveling,
     Wrecking,
     Planning,
     Building, breaking, rebuilding,
Under the smoke, dust all over his mouth, laughing with white teeth,
Under the terrible burden of destiny laughing as a young man laughs,
15   Laughing even as an ignorant fighter laughs who has never lost a battle,
Bragging and laughing that under his wrist is the pulse, and under his
     ribs the heart of the people.
                       Laughing!
Laughing the stormy, husky, brawling laughter of Youth, half-naked,
     sweating, proud to be Hog Butcher, Tool Maker, Stacker of Wheat,
     Player with Railroads and Freight Handler to the Nation.

COMMENTARY AND QUESTIONS

1. "Chicago" is the kind of poem that cries out to be spoken, even shouted. After noting its long lines, free verse, parallel structures, and repeated words and phrases, explain how the poem gains its vitality.

2. Compare "Chicago" to a similar poem by Whitman. Tell which you prefer and why.

Happiness

I asked professors who teach the meaning of life to tell me what is
    happiness.
And I went to famous executives who boss the work of thousands
    of men.
They all shook their heads and gave me a smile as though I was trying
    to fool with them.
And then one Sunday afternoon I wandered out along the Desplaines
    river[1]
5 And I saw a crowd of Hungarians under the trees with their women and
    children and a keg of beer and an accordion.

[1] **Desplaines river:** a river in Illinois.

COMMENTARY AND QUESTIONS

1. Why do the executives and engineers shake "their heads and smile" at the
speaker's question?

2. Sandburg ends the poem with an image of happy people. Is this an effective
ending? Why or why not?

3. Discuss the poem's theme in terms of your own experience.

4. Compare this poem to Whitman's "When I Heard the Learn'd Astronomer."

Mag

I wish to God I never saw you, Mag.
I wish you never quit your job and came along with me.
I wish we never bought a license and a white dress
For you to get married in the day we ran off to a minister
5 And told him we would love each other and take care of each other
Always and always long as the sun and the rain lasts anywhere.
Yes, I'm wishing now you lived somewhere away from here
And I was a bum on the bumpers a thousand miles away dead broke.
    I wish the kids had never come
10   And rent and coal and clothes to pay for
     And a grocery man calling for cash,
      Every day cash for beans and prunes.
    I wish to God I never saw you, Mag.
    I wish to God the kids had never come.

COMMENTARY AND QUESTIONS

1. Describe the poem's voice and examine how Sandburg creates this voice.

2. State the poem's theme and consider to what extent, if at all, American poets before Sandburg had dealt with it.

Limited[1]

I am riding on a limited express, one of the crack[2] trains of the nation.
Hurtling across the prairie into blue haze and dark air go fifteen all-steel
    coaches holding a thousand people.
(All the coaches shall be scrap and rust and all the men and women
    laughing in the diners and sleepers shall pass to ashes.)
I ask a man in the smoker where he is going and he answers: "Omaha."

[1] **limited:** a train having a limited number of cars and a limited number of stops in order to
    provide fast service.
[2] **crack:** excellent.

COMMENTARY AND QUESTIONS

1. Explain the irony of the last line.

2. What does the poem suggest about people's view of life and death?

Fog

Although Sandburg claimed he was not an imagist, a movement led at first by Ezra Pound and later by Amy Lowell, "Fog" bears the mark of the imagist theory. According to the imagists, a poem should describe a specific thing, make every word essential, and let the image (the thing described) speak for itself; the poem should not explain to the reader what the image means.

The fog comes
on little cat feet.

It sits looking
over harbor and city
5   on silent haunches
and then moves on.

COMMENTARY AND QUESTIONS

1. What is the poem's central metaphor?

2. Discuss this statement: "Fog" is all image and no theme.

3. Compare "Fog" to one of Whitman's short "picture poems."

Killers

I am singing to you
Soft as a man with a dead child speaks;
Hard as a man in handcuffs,
Held where he cannot move:

5   Under the sun
Are sixteen million men,
Chosen for shining teeth,
Sharp eyes, hard legs,
And a running of young warm blood in their wrists.

10   And a red juice runs on the green grass;
And a red juice soaks the dark soil.
And the sixteen million are killing . . . and killing and killing.

I never forget them day or night:
They beat on my head for memory of them;
15   They pound on my heart and I cry back to them,
To their homes and women, dreams and games.

I wake in the night and smell the trenches,
And hear the low stir of sleepers in lines—
Sixteen million sleepers and pickets in the dark:
20   Some of them long sleepers for always,
Some of them tumbling to sleep tomorrow for always,
Fixed in the drag of the world's hearbreak,
Eating and drinking, toiling . . . on a long job of killing.
    Sixteen million men.

COMMENTARY AND QUESTIONS

1. To what does "sixteen million men" refer?

2. How does the first-person narration affect the poem's meaning?

3. Discuss two or three words that you feel are particularly interesting and effective.

4. Examine the title and its relationship to the theme.

REVIEW

1. How do these poems, originally published in 1914 and 1916, reflect American concerns and attitudes in the early years of this century?

2. Whose poetry do you find more moving—Whitman's or Sandburg's? Discuss.

3. Write a poem of five or more lines in the style of Sandburg.

WALLACE STEVENS
1879–1955

Do you agree with Wallace Stevens's statement: "The things that we build or grow or do are so little when compared to the things that we suggest or believe or desire"? In this practical country of ours, where society places great importance on doing and accomplishing—earning good marks, winning at sports, possessing impressive things—Stevens's statement sounds almost radical because it seems to reject the American work ethic. Yet in reality, Stevens was a classic American high achiever.

Born in Reading, Pennsylvania, he grew up the son of a lawyer and attended Harvard for three years as a special student. In 1901 he entered New York Law School and was admitted to the bar in 1904. Twelve years later he joined the legal department of Hartford Accident and Indemnity Company and moved with his wife to Hartford, Connecticut. He became vice president in 1934 and remained with the company until his death in 1955. Composing poems on his way to work and on weekends, Stevens always kept separate his careers as poet and businessman. In 1950 he won the Bollingen Prize for poetry and in 1955 the Pulitzer Prize for poetry.

Much has been made of Stevens's conventional life-style because it contrasts dramatically with his unconventional poetry, which so often places the odd or the strange next to the comfortable and the expected. Not since Poe, who influenced the French symbolist poets who in turn influenced Stevens, have we seen such unusual language, strange imagery, and frequent use of symbolism. Unlike Whitman, Dickinson, and Frost, who write from an Emersonian view of the universe, Stevens does not believe that a Universal Oneness flows through all things, uniting all creation. Poets in Emerson's tradition tend to employ simple language to describe the physical world of particular objects, each reflecting the Universal Being. On the contrary, Stevens believed that because the universe was disorderly and chaotic, the primary resource of the poet is not nature but the imagination: "The things that we . . . suggest or believe or desire." Through imagination, Stevens hoped, the poet could create an order that would help shape our chaotic universe.

And yet in the poems that follow you will detect a love of American places and things—the sounds of their names, the feelings they engender—and an almost embarrassed tendency to romanticize. Perhaps this conflict between the poet's mind rejecting the old beliefs of the last century and the poet's heart loving the sights, smells, sounds, textures, and names of the real world, provided Stevens with the energy to shape his imagination into elegant modern poems that still continue to influence the course of American poetry.

Ploughing on Sunday

The white cock's tail
Tosses in the wind.
The turkey-cock's tail
Glitters in the sun.

5　Water in the fields.
The wind pours down.
The feathers flare
And bluster in the wind.

Remus,[1] blow your horn!
10　I'm ploughing on Sunday,
Ploughing North America,
Blow your horn!

Tum-ti-tum,
Ti-tum-tum-tum!
15　The turkey-cock's tail
Spreads to the sun.

The white cock's tail
Streams to the moon.
Water in the fields.
20　The wind pours down.

[1] **Remus:** founded Rome with his twin brother Romulus. When the brothers quarreled over the plans for the city, Romulus was slain.

COMMENTARY AND QUESTIONS

1. How, if at all, does the title suggest this poem may question traditonal Christian values?

2. Explain how meter, the repetition of like sounds, and other elements contribute to the poem's voice and its tone.

3. Choose two or three words and discuss how Stevens uses them in unusual ways that bring life to the poem.

4. Why do you think the speaker has alluded to Remus? What do they have in common?

5. What kind of a day is Stevens's Sunday as contrasted to Edward Taylor's and Ralph Waldo Emerson's.

6. Compare "Ploughing on Sunday" to Dickinson's "Some keep the Sabbath going to Church."

The Emperor of Ice-Cream

Call the roller of big cigars,
The muscular one, and bid him whip
In kitchen cups concupiscent[1] curds.
Let the wenches dawdle in such dress
5   As they are used to wear, and let the boys
Bring flowers in last month's newspapers.
Let be be finale of seem.[2]
The only emperor is the emperor of ice-cream.

Take from the dresser of deal,
10   Lacking the three glass knobs, that sheet
On which she embroidered fantails[3] once
And spread it so as to cover her face.
If her horny feet protrude, they come
To show how cold she is, and dumb.
15   Let the lamp affix its beam.
The only emperor is the emperor of ice-cream.

---

[1] **concupiscent:** a strong desire; sexual desire.
[2] **"Let . . . seem":** Stevens paraphrased this line as, "Let being become the conclusion or denouement of appearing to be."
[3] **fantails:** pigeons.

COMMENTARY AND QUESTIONS

1. This was Stevens's favorite poem because, he said, it "deliberately wears a commonplace costume and yet seems to me to contain something of the essential gaudiness of poetry." Describe the poem's "commonplace costume" and its "gaudiness."

2. Given Stevens's rejection of the Emersonian world view and his reliance on the imagination as his primary resource, why do you think Stevens thought that poetry should be gaudy—showy, tasteless?

3. How do lines 7 and 8 complete the meaning of the first six lines?

4. What is the scene described in lines 9–14?

5. What does the emperor of ice cream seem to represent and over what does he appear to rule?

Anecdote of the Jar

I placed a jar in Tennessee,
And round it was, upon a hill.
It made the slovenly wilderness
Surround that hill.

5   The wilderness rose up to it,
And sprawled around, no longer wild.
The jar was round upon the ground
And tall and of a port in air.

It took dominion everywhere.
10   The jar was gray and bare.
It did not give of bird or bush,
Like nothing else in Tennessee.

COMMENTARY AND QUESTIONS

1. What does the poem suggest about Stevens's view of nature?

2. If we see the jar as a symbol of art, what does the poem tell us about the relationship between art and nature?

3. Although the "gray and bare" jar dominated the "slovenly wilderness," which is nature, the jar "did not give of bird or bush." What point is Stevens making about art's powers and its limitations?

4. How does this poem help us understand that Stevens is a modernist and clearly not an Emersonian?

5. Note the poem's metrical structure. Is it at all regular? If so, how? How does the poem's structure (meter, line length, stanza length) contribute to the poem's meaning?

Vacancy in the Park

March . . . Someone has walked across the snow,
Someone looking for he knows not what.

It is like a boat that has pulled away
From a shore at night and disappeared.

5   It is like a guitar left on a table
By a woman, who has forgotten it.

It is like the feeling of a man
Come back to see a certain house.

The four winds blow through the rustic arbor,
10   Under its mattresses of vines.

COMMENTARY AND QUESTIONS

1. What does *it* refer to in lines 3, 5, 6, and 7?

2. How is *it* like *a boat, a guitar,* and *the feeling* as described in lines 3–8?

3. Discuss *mattresses*—its connotations and its contribution to the poem's conclusion.

4. Of what does the poem remind you?

REVIEW

1. Stevens's poems are often referred to as "elegant," meaning that in some way they are clear, clean, perfect—despite their "gaudiness." Perhaps the key to understanding their elegance is to see that Stevens measures his lines and stanzas, carefully weighing every syllable. Compare the structure of one of Stevens's poems to a section of Whitman's "Song of Myself."

2. Using two or three poems by each poet as examples, compare Stevens's use of symbolism to Poe's.

3. Using three or more poems as examples, discuss the "gaudiness" of Stevens's poems.

4. Paying particular attention to the qualities reviewed earlier (elegance, symbolism, and "gaudiness"), write a poem in the style of Wallace Stevens.

5. According to Lawrance Thompson and R. H. Winnich's biography *Robert Frost, The Later Years,* Stevens encountered Frost at a hotel in Florida and jokingly said, "you write about—subjects" to which Frost replied, "you write about—bric-a-brac." What did each poet mean? To what extent is each remark true? How does the interchange help us understand the conflict between Frost and modernists like Stevens, Williams, and Pound?

EZRA
POUND
1885–1972

The most colorful and revolutionary poet of his time, Ezra Pound influenced William Carlos Williams, T. S. Eliot, H. D., Amy Lowell, and other young poets. The following ideas of Pound's have powerfully affected American poetry: (1) every word in a poem must be important to the poem's effect, (2) rather than fitting a prescribed metrical pattern, a poem's music should follow the natural rhythms of the spoken language, and (3) whereas abstractions (words like *freedom, love,* and *tyranny*) confuse ideas and weaken emotions, concrete images of things clarify and strengthen ideas and emotions.

Pound was born in Hailey, Idaho, and spent two years as a special student at the University of Pennsylvania, where he met William Carlos Williams, who would remain a lifelong friend, and Hilda Doolittle, the poet H. D. He then transferred to Hamilton College and later returned to Penn, where he received his master's degree in 1906. After teaching briefly at Wabash College, Pound went abroad and settled for a time in England, where he came to know and influence the important writers of his time. T. S. Eliot, who was long considered the greatest modernist poet, said that Pound was the better craftsman. During this period in London when he was translating Italian, French, Chinese, and Japanese, writing relatively short lyrical poems, and spending time with other writers, Pound was most influential. With his long red hair, a pointed beard, a mustache, and a cape, he was also most flamboyant in his early period.

In 1920 Pound went to Paris, where he helped T. S. Eliot edit his great poem "The Waste Land." Leaving Paris in 1924, he settled in Rapallo, Italy, where he began work on his famous long poem, *The Cantos.* Pound received in 1928 the *Dial* award "for distinguished service to American letters." During the following years he shifted his focus from literary to political, becoming increasingly critical of the American government. In World War II he broadcast fascist propaganda to the United States by short-wave radio and in 1945 was arrested for treason. Declared legally insane, he spent twelve years in Saint Elizabeth Hospital in Washington, D.C. In 1958, through the help of other poets, he was released. He then returned to Italy, where he lived until his death in 1972.

A Pact

I make a pact with you, Walt Whitman—
I have detested you long enough.
I come to you as a grown child
Who has had a pig-headed father;
5   I am old enough now to make friends.
It was you that broke the new wood,
Now is a time for carving.
We have one sap and one root—
Let there be commerce between us.

COMMENTARY AND QUESTIONS

1. According to "A Pact," what does Pound think he owes to Walt Whitman?

2. How, as a poet, was Whitman "pig-headed"?

3. How does Pound think he will improve on what Whitman began?

4. Paraphrase the last line.

The Plunge

I would bathe myself in strangeness:
These comforts heaped upon me, smother me!
I burn, I scald so for the new,
New friends, new faces,
5   Places!
Oh to be out of this,
This that is all I wanted
       —save the new.

And you,
10   Love, you the much, the more desired!
Do I not loathe all walls, streets, stones,
All mire, mist, all fog,
All ways of traffic?
You, I would have flow over me like water,
15   Oh, but far out of this!
Grass, and low fields, and hills,
And sun,
Oh, sun enough!
Out, and alone, among some
20   Alien people!

COMMENTARY AND QUESTIONS

1. What do the first eight lines suggest about the kind of poetry Pound wanted to see?

2. Whom does the second stanza seem to address?

3. Why do you think Pound wants to be "alone, among some /Alien people"?

4. What is the poem's central idea?

Separation on the River Kiang

"Separation on the River Kiang" is written in the Chinese tradition of poems of leave-taking. Pound, who did not read Chinese, based his versions of Chinese on the notes of a friend who had studied Japanese interpretations of the original poems. Thus Pound's versions of the two Chinese poems collected here reflect much more of Pound's creative genius than would literal translations.

> Ko-jin goes west for Kō-kaku-ro,
> The smoke-flowers are blurred over the river.
> His lone sail blots the far sky.
> And now I see only the river,
> 5   The long Kiang, reaching heaven.
> _Rihaku (Li T'ai Po)_

COMMENTARY AND QUESTIONS

1. Describe the poem's tone.

2. Discuss the images and the rhythms that contribute most to the tone. You may want to mark the stressed syllables, noting patterns of stresses.

3. Explain how the last line completes the poem's meaning.

In a Station of the Metro

Pound was inspired to write this poem after emerging from the metro train in Paris and seeing "suddenly a beautiful face, and then another and another and then a beautiful child's face and then another beautiful woman."

> The apparition of these faces in the crowd;
> Petals on a wet, black bough.

COMMENTARY AND QUESTIONS

1. What is the effect of the poem's first four words? Are they necessary? Why or why not? Note particularly _apparition._

2. What kind of petals are likely to be on a "wet, black bough"? What time of year? How do these inferences affect your reading of the poem?

3. What idea or feeling does this poem convey?

4. Where do you see the influence of oriental poetry?

The River-Merchant's Wife: A Letter

> While my hair was still cut straight across my forehead
> I played about the front gate, pulling flowers.
> You came by on bamboo stilts, playing horse,
> You walked about my seat, playing with blue plums.
> 5 And we went on living in the village of Chōkan:
> Two small people, without dislike or suspicion.
>
> At fourteen I married My Lord you.
> I never laughed, being bashful.
> Lowering my head, I looked at the wall.
> 10 Called to, a thousand times, I never looked back.
>
> At fifteen I stopped scowling,
> I desired my dust to be mingled with yours
> Forever and forever and forever.
> Why should I climb the look out?
>
> 15 At sixteen you departed,
> You went into far Ku-tō-en, by the river of swirling eddies,
> And you have been gone five months.
> The monkeys make sorrowful noise overhead.
>
> You dragged your feet when you went out.
> 20 By the gate now, the moss is grown, the different mosses,
> Too deep to clear them away!
> The leaves fall early this autumn, in wind.
> The paired butterflies are already yellow with August
> Over the grass in the West garden;
> 30 They hurt me. I grow older.
> If you are coming down through the narrows of the river Kiang,
> Please let me know beforehand,
> And I will come out to meet you
> As far as Chō-fū-Sa.

By Rihaku (Li T'ai Po)

COMMENTARY AND QUESTIONS

1. Describe the speaker and her tone of voice.
2. What details help us understand the speaker's mood?
3. Do you like this poem? How does it move the reader?

REVIEW

1. Emerson called for American poetry to revolt against European tradi-
tion, and Whitman answered the call with his loosely structured, highly
descriptive free verse. Cite some specific ways that Pound continued
Whitman's tradition of revolt.

2. Cite at least three similarities between Whitman and Pound and three more between Emerson and Pound.

3. Identify and discuss a few lines of Pound's that you consider to be particularly musical. In your discussion, contrast Pound's rhythms with lines from Stevens and Williams.

4. Pound was particularly interested that Chinese characters, the symbols used to represent words, are simplified pictures of things, not of sounds. He pointed out that the Chinese language communicates abstractions through images of concrete things. For instance, the color red is symbolized by putting together abbreviated pictures of *rose, iron rust, cherry,* and *flamingo*—four concrete objects. Why do you think that Pound was drawn to Chinese poetry? How do you think it may have affected his own poetry?

5. In what aspects of Williams's poetry do we detect Pound's influence?

6. Which poem of Pound's do you like the best? Why?

WILLIAM CARLOS WILLIAMS
1883–1963

William Carlos Williams once said this to an audience:

> All art is sensual. Listen . . . Don't try to work [a modern poem] out. Listen to it. Let it come to you. . . . Let the thing spray in your face. Get the feeling of it. . . . It may be that you will . . . have a sensation that you may later find will clarify itself. . . . So that I say, don't attempt to understand the modern poem. Listen to it! And it should be HEARD. In other words: if it ain't a pleasure, it ain't a poem!"

These statements give us two important insights into Williams's work: It relies a great deal on imagery and music to communicate meaning, and it conveys an almost romantic affection for the real world. Williams's friend Wallace Stevens wrote in an introduction to Williams's *Selected Poems,* "He is a romantic poet. This will horrify him. Yet the proof is everywhere." Williams probably did not agree with Stevens. But, romantic or not, Williams viewed his free verse, imagistic poems as objects to be encountered and experienced, not as abstract romantic feelings. Like Whitman before him, Williams also focused on the facts of everyday life, rather than on romantic dreams. And yet, like Whitman again, Williams's love of America—its people and places—seems to romanticize his otherwise modern, apparently objective descriptions of life.

Born in Rutherford, New Jersey, William Carlos Williams went to elementary school there and then, for two years, attended schools in Geneva and Paris. During high school Williams attended Horace Mann School in New York City, where an English teacher the students called Uncle Billy Abbott helped Williams, as he wrote in his *Autobiography,* to "feel the excitement of great books." After Horace Mann, Williams was admitted directly to the University of Pennsylvania Medical School, where he began to pursue his two lifelong occupations: medicine and poetry. At Penn, Williams enjoyed his studies but also wrote and read on his own. There he met Ezra Pound, who became a lifelong friend and the greatest single influence in Williams's poetry.

152

After graduating from medical school in 1906, Williams published privately in 1909 his first collection of poems; studied pediatrics at the University of Leipzig in Germany in 1909 and 1910; married Florence Herman of Rutherford in 1912; and, with Pound's assistance a year later, published *Tempers,* his first significant book. He then settled in his hometown of Rutherford, becoming a respected pediatrician and an important modern poet. Williams won, among other distinctions, the Guarantors Prize from *Poetry* magazine in 1931 and the Pulitzer Prize in 1963. His latest *Selected Poems* represents work from sixteen volumes of poetry, ranging from 1913 to 1958. Today his work has a strong and growing influence on contemporary poetry.

Apology

Why do I write today?

The beauty of
the terrible faces
of our nonentities
5   stirs me to it:

colored women
day workers—
old and experienced—
returning home at dusk
10   in cast off clothing
faces like
old Florentine oak.[1]

Also

the set pieces[2]
15   of your faces stir me—
leading citizens—
but not
in the same way.

[1] **Florentine oak:** lined, darkened, 600-year-old hardwood.
[2] **set pieces:** carefully planned, implying a lack of spontaneity.

COMMENTARY AND QUESTIONS

1. How does the poem's first line set the relationship between the speaker and the reader?

2. Why are the faces of "our nonentities" "terrible" and the faces of "leading citizens" "set pieces"?

3. Discuss the effect of "Also," line 13.

4. How is the poem, as the title tells us, an apology?

Smell!

Oh strong ridged and deeply hollowed
nose of mine! what will you not be smelling?
What tactless asses we are, you and I, boney nose,
always indiscriminate, always unashamed,
5   and now it is the souring flowers of the bedraggled
poplars: a festering pulp on the wet earth
beneath them. With what deep thirst
we quicken our desires
to that rank odor of a passing springtime!
10   Can you not be decent? Can you not reserve your ardors
for something less unlovely? What girl will care
for us, do you think, if we continue in these ways?
Must you taste everything? Must you know everything?
Must you have a part in everything?

COMMENTARY AND QUESTIONS

1. How many sentences are in this poem, and how many of these sentences are interrogative? How do these grammatical structures affect the poem?

2. Using words like *festering, rank, ardors,* and *bedraggled,* Williams elevates the level of diction in this poem. Would simpler words work better? Why or why not?

3. Describe the poem's tone.

4. Write this poem out in long, Whitmanesque lines, and then comment on its similarity to certain passages from *Song of Myself.*

The Red Wheelbarrow

so much depends
upon

a red wheel
barrow

5   glazed with rain
water

beside the white
chickens.

COMMENTARY AND QUESTIONS

1. Note that this poem is a sixteen-word sentence. Describe and comment on the arrangement of the words, taking into account the total number of syllables and the stressed syllables in each line.

2. Compare the structure of this poem to the structure of "A Portrait of the Times."

3. Describe the source of this poem's power.

4. Compare this poem to Whitman's "A Farm Picture." How might Whitman have influenced Williams?

This Is Just to Say

I have eaten
the plums
that were in
the icebox

5   and which
you were probably
saving
for breakfast

Forgive me
10 they were delicious
so sweet
and so cold

COMMENTARY AND QUESTIONS

1. What do you think accounts for the enduring popularity of this poem and of "The Red Wheelbarrow"?

2. Discuss how the arrangement of the words and the punctuation contributes to the poem's meaning.

3. What does the poem imply about the speaker and his life?

Nantucket

Flowers through the window
lavender and yellow

changed by white curtains—
Smell of cleanliness—

5   Sunshine of late afternoon—
On the glass tray

a glass pitcher, the tumbler
turned down, by which

a key is lying—And the
10 immaculate white bed

COMMENTARY AND QUESTIONS

1. This poem is a series of modified nouns with no predicate and no main verb to set the things in motion. What is the effect of the poem's grammar?

2. Do you like "Nantucket"? Discuss.

Danse Russe

If I when my wife is sleeping
and the baby and Kathleen
are sleeping
and the sun is a flame-white disc
5 in silken mists
above shining trees,—
if I in my north room
dance naked, grotesquely
before my mirror
10 waving my shirt round my head
and singing softly to myself:
"I am lonely, lonely.
I was born to be lonely,
I am best so!"
15 If I admire my arms, my face
my shoulders, flanks, buttocks
against the yellow drawn shades,—

Who shall say I am not
the happy genius of my household?

COMMENTARY AND QUESTIONS

1. How can a man living with a wife and two daughters be lonely? Why is he "best" (line 14) when he is lonely?

2. Discuss how certain images contribute to the poem's tone and its meaning.

3. "Danse Russe" has been praised as an honest poem. In what sense is it honest?

4. Discuss the last two lines in relation to the rest of the poem.

The Dance

In Brueghel's[1] great picture, The Kermess,[2]
the dancers go round, they go round and
around, the squeal and the blare and the

---

[1] **Brueghel's:** Pieter Brueghel (1525–1569), a Flemish artist whose paintings portrayed peasant life. The spellings in lines 1 and 12 are both considered to be correct.

[2] **The Kermess:** the carnival, fair, or dance.

tweedle of bagpipes, a bugle and fiddles
5   tipping their bellies (round as the thick-
sided glasses whose wash they impound)
their hips and their bellies off balance
to turn them, Kicking and rolling about
the Fair Grounds, swinging their butts, those
10   shanks must be sound to bear up under such
rollicking measures, prance as they dance
in Breughel's great picture, The Kermess.

COMMENTARY AND QUESTIONS

1. Judging from what you know of Williams, why do you think he was attracted to Brueghel's colorful, detailed painting of sixteenth-century peasants dancing and playing music at a town fair?

2. Reread the poem aloud, stressing its music. Is the rhythm appropriate to the poem's content? What if lines 2–4 read like this?

the dancers go round and around
to the tweedle of bagpipes, the squeal
of the fiddle, and blare of the flashing bugle.

How is this rhythm and syntax (word order) unlike Williams's style?

3. List the concrete nouns and action verbs. Then discuss their effect on the poem.

REVIEW

1. Some of Williams's short poems are reminiscent of oriental poetry. As you have seen, Ezra Pound, the person who most influenced Williams's idea of how a poem should be written, was interested in Chinese and Japanese poetry. Judging from the oriental influence in Pounds' "In a Station of the Metro" and "Taking Leave of a Friend," do you detect in poems like "The Red Wheelbarrow" and "Nantucket" a kinship to Oriental poetry?

2. Which poem do you like least? Best? Discuss.

3. Compare Williams's line to Stevens's. Which, if either, seems more regular. Can you make any generalizations about the way each poet breaks his lines? How easily could they be distinguished from a line of Whitman's?

4. Why do you think that Williams emphasized imagery and natural rhythms?

5. Compared to Whitman, Frost, and Robinson, how well do you think that Williams captured the natural rhythms of American speech? Use specific examples to discuss.

6. Write a short imagistic poem in the style of Williams.

H. D.
(HILDA
DOOLITTLE)
1886–1961

Hilda Doolittle was born in Bethlehem, Pennsylvania, where her father taught astronomy and mathematics at Lehigh University. Later, when her father accepted a position at the University of Pennsylvania, the family moved to Upper Darby, outside of Philadelphia. After attending private schools in the area, H. D. enrolled at Bryn Mawr College, where she met Marianne Moore. During that time she also met William Carlos Williams and Ezra Pound, who were studying at Penn. In his *Autobiography* Williams describes H. D. as "tall, blonde and with a long jaw but gay blue eyes. . . . There was much about her which is found in wild animals at times, a breathless impatience. . . . her beauty . . . was unquestioned." Briefly engaged to Pound when she was nineteen, H. D., like Williams, Moore, and other poets of the day, was strongly influenced by Pound's ideas about imagism (the theory that a poem should describe a specific thing, making every word essential and letting the image speak for itself); and it was Pound who later gave to her her pseudonym—H. D., Imagiste—and who helped her publish in *Poetry* magazine.

Poetry's editor Harriet Monroe echoed Williams's observation about H. D.'s freedom of spirit: "The amazing thing about H. D.'s poetry is the wildness of it . . . she is, quite unconsciously, a lithe, hard, bright-winged spirit of nature to whom humanity is but an incident" (*Poetry*, August 1925). As you read the poems included here, think of H. D.'s relationship to nature in comparison to that of other poets we have read.

In 1911 H. D. went to England, where she continued her friendship with Pound and in 1913 married the English poet Richard Aldington. After their marriage collapsed six years later, H. D. traveled to Europe, lived in Switzerland until returning to London in 1939, and in 1945 resettled in Switzerland, where she remained for most of her life. In 1961 H. D. became the first woman to win the Award of Merit Medal from the American Academy of Arts and letters. She wrote eight books of poems, including the long poem *Helen in Egypt,* three works of nonfiction, and four novels. Much of H. D.'s prose focused on her associations with real people such as Richard Aldington, Ezra Pound, Sigmund Freud, and D. H. Lawrence. Although H. D. is still known best as an imagist, her longer poems and prose have broadened her reputation.

Pear Tree

Silver dust[1]
lifted from the earth,
higher than my arms reach,
you have mounted,
5   O silver,
higher than my arms reach
you front us with great mass;

no flower ever opened
so staunch a white leaf,
10   no flower ever parted silver
from such rare silver;

O white pear,
your flower-tufts
thick on the branch
15   bring summer and ripe fruits
in their purple hearts.

[1] **silver dust:** The leaves of pear trees have a pale or silver hue, almost a dusty quality; and the undersides of the leaves are paler still.

COMMENTARY AND QUESTIONS

1. One might say "grow out of the ground" or perhaps "rise from the earth" to describe a tree's growth. What is the effect of the speaker's describing the pear tree's growth as "Silver dust / lifted from the earth"?

2. Describe the effect of the silver and white in this poem. Why are these colors unexpected?

3. What does purple suggest?

4. Discuss the tone and meaning of the poem.

Moonrise

Will you glimmer on the sea?
will you fling your spear-head
on the shore?
what note shall we pitch?
5   we have a song,
on the bank we share our arrows;
the loosed string tells our note:

O flight,
bring her swiftly to our song.
10   She is great,
we measure her by the pine trees.

COMMENTARY AND QUESTIONS

1. How, if at all, does the moon "fling [its] spear-head / on the shore?"

2. The Greek goddess of the moon, Artemis (Diana in Roman mythology), was also a goddess of chastity and the hunt. With this in mind, describe the speaker's relationship with the moon.

3. What is the "flight" referred to in line 8? What is the "song" in line 9?

4. Explain the last line.

5. Compare the inclusion of "pine trees" in line 11 with "purple" in the last line of "Pear Tree."

Oread[1]

Whirl up, sea—
whirl your pointed pines,
splash your great pines
on our rocks,
5   hurl your green over us,
cover us with your pools of fir.

[1] **Oread:** a nymph who lives in the mountains.

COMMENTARY AND QUESTIONS

1. Discuss the grammar of this poem.

2. How is the phrase "pools of fir" a kind of conclusion to the poem? Compare this last line to the last line of the previous poems.

3. This is one of H. D.'s most famous and respected imagist poems. Do you think it merits this acclaim? Why or why not?

REVIEW

1. Note and discuss the techniques H. D. commonly uses in these imagist poems.

2. Compare one of H. D.'s imagist poems to one by either Williams, Pound, or Lowell.

3. Compare H. D.'s relationship to nature with Emily Dickinson's. How and from what point (within or apart from) does each poet regard nature?

4. Write a poem in the style of H. D.

AMY LOWELL
1874–1925

Born into a prominent Boston family, Amy Lowell was the cousin of the nineteenth-century American poet James Russell Lowell, and of the modern poet Robert Lowell (1917–1978). Her eldest brother, Abbott Lawrence Lowell, became a distinguished president of Harvard University. She received her education in private schools, and in 1902, as she tells us, "discovered that poetry . . . was [her] natural mode of expression." From that time forth she devoted herself to both perfecting the art of poetry and advancing the understanding of modern poetic principles.

Amy Lowell's first poem was published eight years later in the *Atlantic Monthly* and her first book, *Dome of Many-colored Glass*, appeared in 1912, when she was thirty-eight. The next year she met Ezra Pound in England and became associated with the imagists, a group that she would eventually lead. Publishing regularly from then on, she wrote 650 poems, which filled eleven volumes; an ambitious biography of John Keats; and many critical essays. Her book *Fir-flower Tablets*, like Pound's book *Cathay*, presents versions of Chinese poems that, as Lowell put it, turned "literal translations of poems as near to the spirit of the originals as it was in my power to do." Note that in Amy Lowell—as in Emerson and Pound, who were the most influential poets of their respective times—we see a fascination with Oriental poetry and thought. In her introduction to *Fir-flower Tablets* she tells the reader, "It is curious that there has lately sprung up in America and England a type of poetry which is so closely allied to the Chinese in method and intention as to be very striking." She is speaking here of Imagist poems such as Williams's "The Red Wheelbarrow" and Pound's "In a Station of the Metro."

Perhaps more important than her interest in Oriental poetry is her recognition of Emily Dickinson's genius a good thirty years before Dickinson's general reputation had been elevated above that of a popular but sentimental nineteenth-century poet. "To my mind, Lowell wrote, "Emily Dickinson is one of the greatest woman poets. . . . She wrote a half a century ahead of her time."

During the last ten of her fifty-one years, Amy Lowell became an internationally known lecturer and reader. Her eccentricities—such as cigar smoking, writing nights, and sleeping days—her imposing physical presence, and her brilliant performances

162

made Lowell a persuasive advocate of modern poetry. At the time of her unexpected death, she had in progress three books of poems, which were published posthumously.

The Taxi

When I go away from you
The world beats dead
Like a slackened drum.
I call out for you against the jutted stars
5 And shout into the ridges of the wind.
Streets coming fast,
One after the other,
Wedge you away from me,
And the lamps of the city prick my eyes
10 So that I can no longer see your face.
Why should I leave you,
To wound myself upon the sharp edges of the night?

COMMENTARY AND QUESTIONS

1. What is a slackened drum? What does the simile in lines 1–3 imply?
2. How are stars "jutted"?
3. How do streets "wedge" the person being addressed away from the speaker?
4. Discuss what the speaker means by "the sharp edges / of the night."
5. What is the poem's central idea?

The Cyclists

Spread on the roadway,
With open-blown jackets,
Like black, soaring pinions,[1]
They swoop down the hillside,
    The Cyclists.

5 Seeming dark-plumaged
Birds, after carrion,
Careening and circling,
Over the dying
    Of England.

[1] **pinions:** birds' wings.

She lies with her bosom
10 Beneath them, no longer
The Dominant Mother,
The Virile—but rotting
   Before time.

The smell of her, tainted,
Has bitten their nostrils.
15 Exultant they hover,
And shadow the sun with
   Foreboding.

COMMENTARY AND QUESTIONS

1. How are the open jackets of the bicyclists like the wings of birds? How can England be both "The Dominant Mother" and "The Virile"? Does this apparent contradiction work in the poem?

2. This poem was published in 1914, the year that World War I began. How might this historical event affect one's understanding of the poem?

3. Count the number of syllables in each line. If you discover a pattern, discuss how this pattern affects the poem.

4. Discuss the poem's theme.

Anticipation

I have been temperate always,
But I am like to be very drunk
With your coming.
There have been times
5 I feared to walk down the street
Lest I should reel with the wine of you,
And jerk against my neighbours
As they go by.
I am parched now, and my tongue is horrible in my mouth,
10 But my brain is noisy
With the clash and gurgle of filling wine-cups.

COMMENTARY AND QUESTIONS

1. Compare this poem to Emily Dickinson's "Wild Nights—Wild Nights." How are their themes similar? Which conveys stronger emotion? How?

2. Are there any other aspects of this poem that remind you of Dickinson? Please be specific.

REVIEW

1. How is Lowell's poetry similar to that of Pound and Williams? How is her poetry unique?

2. Discuss both your favorite and least favorite poem included here.

3. Amy Lowell traced imagism (the reliance on clear, concentrated visual images and relatively simple language to convey feeling and thought) back to Dickinson, as well as to earlier English writers. Do you detect roots of imagism in Dickinson's poems? Please be specific.

MARIANNE MOORE
1887–1972

Perhaps more than any other modern poet, Marianne Moore threw off conventional ideas of poetry and treated her subject with an almost scientific objectivity. Following Pound's idea that an image is "an intellectual and emotional complex in an instant of time" (from "A Retrospect," in *Pavanes and Divisions* [1918]), she focused, particularly in her early poems, on objects, describing them with astonishing clarity. The ideas in her poems, like her abruptly broken poetic lines and unexpected rhymes, always surprise, forcing us to see reality in new, sometimes uncomfortable ways.

Born in Saint Louis, Missouri, Marianne Moore moved in 1896 with her family to Carlisle, Pennsylvania. After graduating from Bryn Mawr College in 1909, she attended a commercial college for a year, traveled to Europe, and taught from 1911 to 1915 at a U.S. Indian School in Carlisle. In 1915 her poems first appeared in *The Egotist* and *Poetry* magazines—the five poems in *Poetry* gaining her attention as a modern poet. In 1918 she moved to New York City, where she remained for fifty-four years. Moving from Manhattan to Brooklyn in 1929, she became a free-lance writer, as well as an avid and famed Brooklyn Dodgers fan.

In her distinguished career Moore won many awards, including a Shelley Memorial Award, a Guggenheim Fellowship, a joint grant from the American Academy of Arts and Letters and the National Institute of Arts and Letters, a Bollingen Prize, and a Pulitzer Prize. She also received many honorary degrees, including a doctorate in literature from Harvard University.

from *Baseball and Writing*

Suggested by post-game broadcasts

Fanaticism? No. Writing is exciting
and baseball is like writing.
   You can never tell with either
     how it will go
5   or what you will do;
   generating excitement—
   a fever in the victim—
   pitcher, catcher, fielder, batter.
     Victim in what category?
10 *Owl*man watching from the press box?
     To whom does it apply?
     Who is excited? Might it be I?

COMMENTARY AND QUESTIONS

1. How, according to the speaker, is writing like baseball?

2. In what sense, if at all, are "pitcher, catcher, fielder, batter" victims?

3. Who is the "*Owl*man in the pressbox" and how is he another category of victim? How is the *Owl*man like the writer? How is the writer a victim?

4. How is the sports fan like the reader?

5. Discuss the poem's line breaks, rhythms, and rhymes. What general effect do they achieve? What is the tone of the poem?

A Jelly-Fish

Visible, invisible,
   a fluctuating charm
an amber-tinctured amethyst
   inhabits it, your arm
5 approaches and it opens
   and it closes; you had meant
to catch it and it quivers;
   you abandon your intent.

COMMENTARY AND QUESTIONS

1. To what word does "it" in line 5 refer?

2. In this poem Moore adheres closely to the imagist's belief in describing the object of the poem in detail and letting the description tell its own story. Beyond the description of the jellyfish, tell what action occurs in this poem?

3. Does the poem's action together with its description suggest that the poem is about more than "you" reaching an arm toward a jellyfish, the jellyfish quivering, and then the "you abandon[ing] your intent"? Discuss.

4. Discuss the effect of the poem's line breaks, rhymes, and punctuation.

Poetry

I, too, dislike it.
    Reading it, however, with a perfect contempt for it, one discovers in
    it, after all, a place for the genuine.

COMMENTARY AND QUESTIONS

1. Comment on how the arrangement of the sentences and lines affects the poem's meaning.

2. Considering the poems you have read by Marianne Moore and also imagistic poems by other poets, discuss Moore's idea that poetry is "a place for the genuine"? Use specific examples.

REVIEW

1. Judging from these few poems and others you may have read, discuss what is unusual about Marianne Moore's poetry—the line breaks, rhymes, rhythms, subjects, approaches to her subjects, themes, and other aspects of her art?

2. Make a useful comparison between one of Moore's poems and another poem we have discussed.

3. Tell which of Moore's poems is the most interesting to you and why.

ROBINSON JEFFERS
1887–1962

Robinson Jeffers was born in Pittsburgh, Pennsylvania, the son of a theology professor who introduced his young son to Greek, Latin, and Hebrew. When his parents traveled to Europe and the Near East, Jeffers attended schools in Switzerland and Germany. After returning to Pittsburgh, he entered at age fifteen the University of Western Pennsylvania. When his family moved to Pasadena, California, he attended Occidental College, where he was well liked, active in student publications, and respected for his excellent academic performance. After graduating from Occidental in 1905, he studied medicine for three years but eventually abandoned that pursuit to write poetry.

Having already hiked and climbed in Europe, Jeffers was immediately drawn to the mountains and the coast of California. In 1913 he married Una Kuster, who supported Jeffers's writing throughout his life. The next year they moved to Carmel, where he lived and wrote until his death.

The wild country of California became the subject of many of Jeffers's best poems; like Dickinson, Frost, and others, Jeffers was moved by nature's beauty and its brutality. His work also reflects a strong distrust of humanity and its institutions. Like Emerson, Dickinson, and Stevens, who were also brought up in strong Christian traditions, Jeffers rebelled against his father's Presbyterian faith, turning for inspiration from human institutions to nature.

Summer Holiday

When the sun shouts and people abound
One thinks there were the ages of stone and the age of bronze
And the iron age; iron the unstable metal;
Steel made of iron, unstable as his mother; the towered-up cities
5   Will be stains of rust on mounds of plaster.

169

Roots will not pierce the heaps for a time, kind rains will cure them,
Then nothing will remain of the iron age
And all these people but a thigh-bone or so, a poem
Stuck in the world's thought, splinters of glass
10 In the rubbish dumps, a concrete dam far off in the mountain . . .

COMMENTARY AND QUESTIONS

1. What appears to be the poem's setting?

2. How does the title inform (help us understand) the poem?

3. State the poem's theme.

4. Discuss the effect of Jeffers's somewhat illogical insertion of an abstract idea, "a poem / Stuck in the world's thought," in a list of concrete images—"thigh-bone," "splinters of glass," "a concrete dam."

5. Do the last four lines conclude the poem well or do they simply make an abrupt end to a list?

Hurt Hawks

I

The broken pillar[1] of the wing jags[2] from the clotted shoulder,
The wing trails like a banner in defeat,
No more to use the sky forever but live with famine
And pain a few days: cat nor coyote
5 Will shorten the week of waiting for death, there is game without
  talons.
He stands under the oak-bush and waits
The lame feet of salvation; at night he remembers freedom
And flies in a dream, the dawns ruin it.
He is strong and pain is worse to the strong, incapacity is worse.
10 The curs of the day come and torment him
At distance, no one but death the redeemer will humble that head,
The intrepid readiness, the terrible eyes.
The wild God of the world is sometimes merciful to those
That ask mercy, not often to the arrogant.
15 You do not know him, you communal people, or you have forgotten
  him;
Intemperate and savage, the hawk remembers him;
Beautiful and wild, the hawks, and men that are dying, remember him.

---

[1] **pillar:** a slender vertical support or column, suggesting here a wing bone that has supported the hawk's flight.
[2] **jags:** projects sharply.

II

I'd sooner, except the penalties, kill a man than a hawk; but the great
   redtail[3]
Had nothing left but unable misery
20 From the bone too shattered for mending, the wing that trailed under
   his talons when he moved.
We had fed him six weeks, I gave him freedom,
He wandered over the foreland[4] hill and returned in the evening, asking
   for death,
Not like a beggar, still eyed with the old
Implacable arrogance. I gave him the lead gift in the twilight. What fell
   was relaxed,
25 Owl-downy, soft feminine feathers; but what
Soared: the fierce rush: the night-herons by the flooded river cried fear
   at its rising
Before it was quite unsheathed[5] from reality.

[3] **redtail:** a common hawk, length eighteen inches, wingspan forty-eight inches.
[4] **foreland:** a projecting land mass, in this case overlooking the sea.
[5] **unsheathed:** to remove a sword or knife from its case (sheath).

COMMENTARY AND QUESTIONS

1. How is the hawk injured?

2. Why will neither "cat nor coyote" "shorten the week of waiting for death"?

3. Focusing on "the wild God of the world," paraphrase and discuss lines 13–18.

4. What is the "lead gift" in line 24?

5. What is the speaker's attitude toward the hawk and toward humanity?

6. Discuss the importance of the poem's last three lines.

7. Why does the title refer to the plural "hawks" when the poem is about one hawk?

8. Consider the speaker's dilemma and compare it, if you wish, to your own or others' experiences with wild animals.

Carmel Point

The extraordinary patience of things!
This beautiful place defaced with a crop of suburban houses—
How beautiful when we first beheld it,
Unbroken field of poppy[1] and lupin[2] walled with clean cliffs;
5 No intrusion but two or three horses pasturing,

[1] **poppy:** a red, orange, or white wildflower.
[2] **lupin:** (also spelled lupine) blue-violet, pink, or white wildflowers growing in spikelike clusters.

Or a few milch[3] cows rubbing their flanks on the outcrop rockheads—
Now the spoiler has come: does it care?
Not faintly. It has all time. It knows the people are a tide
That swells and in time will ebb, and all
10 Their works dissolve. Meanwhile the image of the pristine beauty
Lives in the very grain of the granite,
Safe as the endless ocean that climbs our cliff.—As for us:
We must uncenter our minds from ourselves;
We must unhumanize our views a little, and become confident
15 As the rock and ocean that we were made from.

[3] **milch:** milk.

COMMENTARY AND QUESTIONS

1. In line 13 what does the speaker mean by "uncenter our minds from ourselves"? How, if at all, does the poem's theme relate to Emerson's thought?

2. Discuss the effect of the short sentences in lines 7 and 8.

3. Relate lines 13–15 to line 1.

4. What is the poem's theme?

5. Respond to the following and speculate on what modern poet might have written it:

"This poem would be far more engaging and powerful if it relied on its fine images and omitted nearly all of its narrative, which could be adequately implied in a title. For instance,

A CROP OF SUBURBAN HOUSES AT CARMEL POINT
  we first beheld it
  unbroken
  field of poppy and lupin
  walled with clean cliffs
  two or three horses
  a few cows rubbing their flanks
  on the outcrop
              rockheads
  grain of granite
              rock and ocean

As you can see, my purified and intensified version of 'Carmel Point' loses none of the poem's essential meaning."

Vulture

I had walked since dawn and lay down to rest on a bare hillside
Above the ocean. I saw through half-shut eyelids a vulture wheeling
    high up in heaven,
And presently it passed again, but lower and nearer, its orbit narrowing,
    I understood then

That I was under inspection. I lay death-still and heard the flight-
    feathers
5   Whistle above me and make their circle and come nearer.
I could see the naked red head between the great wings
Bear downward staring. I said, "My dear bird, we are wasting time here.
These old bones will still work; they are not for you." But how
    beautiful he looked, gliding down
On those great sails; how beautiful he looked, veering away in the sea-
    light over the precipice. I tell you solemnly
10   That I was sorry to have disappointed him. To be eaten by that beak
    and become part of him, to share those wings and those eyes—
What a sublime end of one's body, what an enskyment[1]; What a life
    after death.

[1] **enskyment:** the placing of something in the sky.

COMMENTARY AND QUESTIONS

1. State and discuss the poem's theme.
2. How would being eaten by a vulture be "a sublime end of one's body" (line 11)?
3. What do you find most effective about this poem? Discuss.

REVIEW

1. What themes or subjects occur in Jeffers's poetry? Which ones appeared in other modern poems and which have not been explored by other modern poets?
2. Note the length of Jeffers's lines, his line breaks, and the rhythms of his poems. Then discuss his free verse as compared to that of either Whitman, Williams, or Moore.
3. Discuss Jeffers's attitude toward humanity and nature.
4. Discuss your opinion of these poems.

JOHN CROWE RANSOM
1888–1974

John Crowe Ransom is the first formalist we have encountered since E. A. Robinson and Robert Frost. That is, he writes in traditional poetic patterns rather than in the free verse espoused by most of the moderns. In his essay "Poets Without Laurels," which appears in his book *The World's Body*, he wrote,

> Poets used to be bards and patriots, priests and prophets, keepers of the public conscience, and, naturally, men of public importance. . . . [Modern poets] have failed more and more flagrantly and more and more deliberately, to identify themselves with the public interests.

Ransom then goes on to criticize modern poetry for presenting a subject without offering "moral or theoretical conclusions."

The facts of Ransom's life suggest reasons for his traditional approach to poetry. The son of a Methodist minister, Ransom was born in Pulaski, Tennessee, and grew up in small Southern towns where stories of the Southern past were still told and retold. He entered Vanderbilt University at age fifteen, where he studied Latin, Greek, and philosophy. Upon graduation Ransom received a Rhodes Scholarship to Oxford, where he began reading the modern poetry of the day and writing his own poems. After serving as a lieutenant in World War I, Ransom returned to his alma mater to teach English. He remained there for twenty-five years before taking a position at Kenyon College, where he founded the *Kenyon Review*, which was to become one of the most respected literary reviews in the country.

Ransom wrote most of his best poetry before 1927, when he, Allen Tate, Robert Penn Warren, and others formed the Agrarians, a group that maintained rural agrarian values and resisted the social effects of industrialization. The group published *The Fugitive*, a journal that displayed the poetry and essays of their members. Later in his career Ransom became prominent as a spokesperson for the New Criticism. This theory, which dominated literary criticism for thirty years, maintained that one must judge a work of literature by the text alone and not through the historical context in which it was written or through the biography of its author. Aside from his critical essays, Ransom wrote three books of poems. He won the Bollingen Prize in 1964.

Janet Waking

Beautifully Janet slept
Till it was deeply morning. She woke then
And thought about her dainty-feathered hen,
To see how it had kept.

5   One kiss she gave her mother.
Only a small one gave she to her daddy
Who would have kissed each curl of his shining baby;
No kiss at all for her brother.

"Old Chucky, old Chucky!" she cried,
10 Running across the world upon the grass
To Chucky's house, and listening. But alas,
Her Chucky had died.

It was a transmogrifying[1] bee
Came droning down on Chucky's old bald head
15 And sat and put the poison. It scarcely bled,
But how exceedingly

And purply did the knot
Swell with the venom and communicate
Its rigor! Now the poor comb[2] stood up straight
20 But Chucky did not.

So there was Janet
Kneeling on the wet grass, crying her brown hen
(Translated far beyond the daughters of men)
To rise and walk upon it.

25 And weeping fast as she had breath
Janet implored us, "Wake her from her sleep!"
And would not be instructed in how deep
Was the forgetful kingdom of death.

---

[1] **transmogrifying:** changing into a different shape or form.
[2] **comb:** a fleshy, red ridge that grows on the crown of a chicken and other fowl.

COMMENTARY AND QUESTIONS

1. Describe the speaker's attitude toward his subject and discuss how this attitude affects the tone of the poem.

2. Identify two or three unexpected or surprising words and discuss how they affect the poem.

3. Discuss two or three passages where the imagery is particularly vivid.

4. Note the poem's rhyme scheme, the number of syllables in each line, the form of the stanzas, and the lines and stanzas that are not end-stopped (that do not end with punctuation). Then discuss the impact of these elements of form on the poem.

5. What do we know about Janet and her family? Which details seem most significant?

6. What does this poem suggest about the nature of life and death?

Blue Girls

Twirling your blue skirts, travelling the sward
Under the towers of your seminary,[1]
Go listen to your teachers old and contrary
Without believing a word.

5   Tie the white fillets[2] then about your hair
And think no more of what will come to pass
Than bluebirds that go walking on the grass
And chattering on the air.

Practise your beauty, blue girls, before it fail;
10   And I will cry with my loud lips and publish
Beauty which all our power shall never establish,
It is so frail.

For I could tell you a story which is true;
I know a woman with a terrible tongue,
15   Blear[3] eyes fallen from blue,
All her perfections tarnished—yet it is not long
Since she was lovelier than any of you.

[1] **seminary:** a private school for girls.
[2] **fillets:** a narrow strip of ribbon worn as a headband.
[3] **blear:** blurred or dimmed.

COMMENTARY AND QUESTIONS

1. Briefly paraphrase the poem, paying special attention to "publish" (line 10) and "establish" (line 11).

2. What is the speaker's attitude toward the "blue girls"?

3. What is the poem's theme?

4. How does the variation of line and rhyme in the last stanza affect the poem?

5. Do you like this poem? Discuss.

REVIEW

1. How, if at all, do these carefully rhymed and metered poems qualify as modern?

2. What beyond their formal structure do Ransom's poems have in common?

E. E. CUMMINGS
1894–1962

E. E. Cummings commonly joins two or more words into one, interrupts phrases with parenthetical remarks that seem to have no explicit relationship with the words they interrupt, and breaks conventional rules of punctuation, capitalization, and syntax (word order). These striking characteristics of his poetry still, after more than half a century, assert Cummings's strong belief that one must find one's unique way to communicate feelings and ideas. Readers who are distracted by these immediately evident characteristics may not realize that in some ways Cummings is a romantic poet—a modern romantic but nevertheless romantic. For instance, in his introduction to the *Collected Poems,* Cummings writes, "Knowledge is a polite word for dead but not buried imagination," emphasizing his typically romantic mistrust of traditional wisdom and his trust in the human imagination. On the subjects of love and the unimportance of the material world, Cummings wrote in a journal:

> I am someone who proudly and humbly affirms that love is the mystery of mysteries and that nothing measurable matters.

Like Emerson, Edward Estlin Cummings was the son of a prominent Unitarian minister. Growing up in Cambridge, Massachusetts, and attending Harvard, where his father taught, Cummings felt the pressures of tradition. After graduating from Harvard in 1915 and receiving his master's degree the following year, he joined the Ambulance Corps in France and through a mistake by French intelligence, was imprisoned for three months. His novel *The Enormous Room* is based on his experience in prison.

Cummings was drafted in the last year of World War I, and after being discharged he lived for two years in Paris, where he painted and wrote. His first important publication as a poet was in *The Dial* in 1920. In 1923 Cummings returned to the United States to live in New York City's Greenwich Village, where he was to remain. During his active career, he won two Guggenheim fellowships, and a Bollingen Prize in poetry, and in 1952–1953 he was the Charles Eliot Norton Professor of Poetry at Harvard.

178

"Buffalo Bill's"

Buffalo Bill's
defunct
      who used to
      ride a watersmooth-silver
5   stallion
and break onetwothreefourfive pigeonsjustlikethat
                              Jesus

he was a handsome man
                  and what i want to know is
10 how do you like your blueeyed boy
Mister Death

COMMENTARY AND QUESTIONS

1. What does the historical Buffalo Bill suggest about America? What forces, if any, have made Buffalo Bill "defunct?" Why does the speaker refer to Buffalo Bill as a "blueeyed boy?"

2. "Jesus" (line 7) makes immediate sense as an exclamation of admiration. Could "Jesus" also refer to the "he" that begins the next line? Why do you think Cummings places "Jesus" alone in the middle line of the poem and at its far right side? If you hold the poem sideways so that its left margin is at the bottom and its uneven right side is up, you will see that "Jesus" becomes the highest word in the poem's "skyline." How does the inclusion of "Jesus" affect the poem's meaning?

3. Discuss the effect of the spacing of words in line 6.

"in Just-"

in Just-
spring   when the world is mud-
luscious the little
lame balloonman

5 whistles   far   and wee

and eddieandbill come
running from marbles and
piracies and it's
spring

10 when the world is puddle-wonderful

the queer
old balloonman whistles
far   and   wee
and bettyandisbel come dancing

15 from hop-scotch and jump-rope and
    it's
    spring
    and
            the

20   goat-footed

    balloonMan   whistles
    far
    and
    wee

COMMENTARY AND QUESTIONS

1. What Greek mythological creature is goat-footed and how does the allusion to this creature affect the poem's meaning? What other words suggest that the balloonman is not innocent?

2. Citing specific words and phrases, explain how the poem evokes the sensual aspects (sights, sounds, smells, tastes, touches) of spring.

3. Using specific examples, discuss how the placement and spacing of words affects the poem's meaning.

4. What is the poem's theme?

5. Do you like this poem? Discuss.

" 'next to of course god america i"

"next to of course god america i
love you land of the pilgrims' and so forth oh
say can you see by the dawn's early my
country 'tis of centuries come and go
5   and are no more what of it we should worry
in every language even deafanddumb
thy sons acclaim your glorious name by gorry
by jingo by gee by gosh by gum
why talk of beauty what could be more beautiful
10 than these heroic happy dead
who rushed like lions to the roaring slaughter
they did not stop to think they died instead
then shall the voice of liberty be mute?"

He spoke. And drank rapidly a glass of water

COMMENTARY AND QUESTIONS

1. Describe the poem's speaker and that person's effect on the poem.

2. After citing examples, discuss the effect of Cummings's mixing clichéd phrases with unexpected words and ideas.

3. Compare this poem to one of Whitman's poems that questions war.

4. How does the punctuation of the first thirteen lines affect the poem's meaning?

5. What answer does the speaker expect to the question in line 13? What answer does the author expect from the reader?

"when serpents bargain for the right to squirm"

when serpents bargain for the right to squirm
and the sun strikes to gain a living wage—
when thorns regard their roses with alarm
and rainbows are insured against old age

5   when every thrush may sing no new moon in
if all screech-owls have not okayed his voice
—and any wave signs on the dotted line
or else an ocean is compelled to close

when the oak begs permission of the birch
10 to make an acorn—valleys accuse their
mountains of having altitude—and march
denounces april as a saboteur

then we'll believe in that incredible
unanimal mankind(and not until)

COMMENTARY AND QUESTIONS

1. In what form is the poem written and how strictly does it abide by that form? Do you like the off rhymes or would you prefer perfect rhymes? Discuss.

2. How is April a "saboteur" of March?

3. How, if at all, does this poem affect your opinion of Cummings as a craftsman?

4. What is the poem saying about modern American life? What is the poem's theme?

REVIEW

1. Cummings called "next to of course god america i" a sonnet. To what extent does it qualify as a sonnet? What does Cummings's definition of a sonnet suggest about his attitude toward formal poetry?

2. Discuss to what extent certain of these poems are romantic. How are they also modern?

3. Compare Cummings's use of titles, punctuation, and capitalization to Dickinson's use of these tools.

4. Write a poem in the style of E. E. Cummings.

LANGSTON HUGHES
1902–1967

The most respected and widely read poet of the Harlem Renaissance, Langston Hughes wrote in the rhythms and language of African American culture, rather than in the tradition of English poetry.

Born in Joplin, Missouri, Hughes was raised by his mother and grandmother, and spent parts of his childhood in Missouri, Kansas, Illinois, and Ohio. An excellent student, he wrote poetry for school publications and read poets such as Walt Whitman, Carl Sandburg, Edwin Arlington Robinson, and Amy Lowell. Later he was encouraged by Vachel Lindsay, a poet who, like Hughes, wrote musical poetry about the common man.

Hughes attended Columbia University for a year, then traveled to Africa and France. After returning to the United States, he began placing his poems in magazines and in 1926 published *The Weary Blues,* the first of ten books of poems. In 1932 to 1933, he traveled to the Soviet Union and later to central Asia. Although best known as a poet, Hughes wrote novels, short stories, and plays. His interest in promoting African American drama led him to take part in the establishment of African American theaters in New York, Chicago, and Los Angeles.

As well as using African American English as a legitimate vehicle for poetry, Hughes also employed the rhythms and moods of blues and other types of African American music popular in the 1920s. Although ancient poetry was sung, and the last five hundred years of European poetry had often joined words with song (in ballads, for instance), the two art forms had largely grown apart. Hughes's use of the cadences of African American music to imitate the sounds of African American life reunited poetry with the ancient past and helped create a new tradition that many African American poets have followed. In an age when the work of modern poets like Wallace Stevens, T. S. Eliot, and Ezra Pound was criticized as ambiguous, sometimes musically baffling, and unnecessarily complex, Hughes's poetry was, for many, a welcome antidote.

American Heartbreak

I am the American heartbreak—
Rock on which Freedom
Stumps its toe—
The great mistake
5   That Jamestown
Made long ago.

COMMENTARY AND QUESTIONS

1. Explain how the reference to Jamestown relates to the poem.

2. Who is "I"? What other American poets have used the first person in a similar way? Compare and discuss.

3. Note the poem's grammar, and comment on how it affects the poem.

4. Discuss the importance of lines 2 and 3 to the poem's effect.

Harlem

What happens to a dream deferred?

Does it dry up
like a raisin in the sun?
Or fester like a sore—
5   And then run?
Does it stink like rotten meat?
Or crust and sugar over—
like a syrupy sweet?

Maybe it just sags
10   like a heavy load.

Or does it explode?

COMMENTARY AND QUESTIONS

1. To what dream does the poem refer and how has it been "deferred"?

2. How do the images in the second and third stanzas contribute to the poem's effect?

3. Discuss the effect of the last line.

Nightmare Boogie[1]

I had a dream
and I could see
a million faces
black as me!
5 A nightmare dream:
Quicker than light
All them faces
Turned dead white!
Boogie-woogie,
10 Rolling bass,
Whirling treble
of cat-gut lace.

[1] **Boogie:** boogie woogie; a style of jazz piano characterized by a repeated rhythmic and melodic pattern in the bass.

COMMENTARY AND QUESTIONS

1. How does this poem seem to imitate the boogie woogie?
2. Paraphrase lines 3–8.
3. How do the last three lines affect the poem's meaning?

Daybreak in Alabama

When I get to be a composer
I'm gonna write me some music about
Daybreak in Alabama
And I'm gonna put the purtiest songs in it
5 Rising out of the ground like a swamp mist
And falling out of heaven like soft dew.
I'm gonna put some tall tall trees in it
And the scent of pine needles
And the smell of red clay after rain
10 And long red necks
And poppy colored faces
And big brown arms
And the field daisy eyes
Of black and white black white black people
15 And I'm gonna put white hands
And black hands and brown and yellow hands
And red clay earth hands in it
Touching everybody with kind fingers
And touching each other natural as dew

20 In that dawn of music when I
    Get to be a composer
    And write about daybreak
    In Alabama.

COMMENTARY AND QUESTIONS

1. What are the poem's strongest images and how do they affect its meaning?

2. Discuss the effect of the poem's repetition and its two-sentence structure. In particular, how does the long second sentence affect the way one reads the poem aloud?

3. Discuss the poem's theme.

REVIEW

1. What does Hughes's poetry have in common with that of Whitman and Sandburg?

2. What poetic techniques does Hughes most commonly use?

3. Do you detect anywhere the influence of imagism in Hughes's poetry?

4. Find examples of poetic song lyrics and compare them to "Nightmare Boogie."

5. What do you like most about Hughes's poetry? Least? Discuss.

COUNTEE CULLEN
1903–1946

Countee Cullen was the only major poet of the Harlem Renaissance to be born in New York City. The son of a Methodist minister, he was an excellent student, possessing, as James Weldon Johnson put it, "a lively and penetrating curiosity about life." According to Johnson, this curiosity became "the mainspring of nearly all his poetry." After receiving recognition for his poems in high school, he graduated from New York University in 1925 and then entered Harvard, where he earned his master's degree.

At age twenty-two, Cullen published *Color,* the first and some think the best of his seven volumes of poetry. He also wrote a novel, a translation of Euripides' *Medea,* two children's books, and criticism. Cullen received a Guggenheim Fellowship and spent 1928 in France. There he married Yolande Du Bois, the daughter of W. E. B. Du Bois, educator and founder of the National Association for the Advancement of Colored People (NAACP). This marriage lasted only a year, however, and after returning to New York, Cullen became a teacher in the New York City school system.

Critics praise Cullen's fine ear for the music of poetry and his mastery of traditional forms. These formal poems, influenced especially by the English romantic poets John Keats (1795–1821) and Percy Bysshe Shelley (1792–1822), stand in sharp contrast to Langston Hughes's more original forms based on the natural rhythms of African American speech and music. Both poets, despite their different views on form, write powerfully about the African American experience.

Incident
(For Eric Walrond)

> Once riding in old Baltimore,
>   Heart-filled, head-filled with glee,
> I saw a Baltimorean
>   Keep looking straight at me.

5 Now I was eight and very small,
       And he was no whit bigger,
   And so I smiled, but he poked out
       His tongue, and called me, "Nigger."

   I saw the whole of Baltimore
10   From May until December;
   Of all the things that happened there
       That's all that I remember.

COMMENTARY AND QUESTIONS

1. Mark the stressed syllables in this poem and comment on how the poem's music contributes to its meaning.

2. Now read the poem out loud, omitting these words: old (line 1), keep (line 4), Now (line 5), And (line 7). How does the absence of these words effect the poem's meaning? What is the primary function of these words?

3. What is the poem's theme? How, if at all, is the title a clue to Cullen's method of conveying his point?

Yet Do I Marvel

   I doubt not God is good, well-meaning, kind,
   And did He stoop to quibble could tell why
   The little buried mole continues blind,
   Why flesh that mirrors Him must some day die,
5 Make plain the reason tortured Tantalus[1]
   Is baited by the fickle fruit, declare
   If merely brute caprice dooms Sisyphus[2]
   To struggle up a never-ending stair.
   Inscrutable His ways are, and immune
10 To catechism by a mind too strewn
   With petty cares to slightly understand
   What awful brain compels His awful hand.
   Yet do I marvel at this curious thing:
   To make a poet black, and bid him sing!

[1] **Tantalus:** a king in Greek mythology who was condemned in Hades to stand in water, under a tree loaded with fruit. The water and the fruit receded when he tried to drink or eat, thus *tantalizing* Tantalus.
[2] **Sisyphus:** a king condemned in Hades to perpetually roll a large rock up a hill. Once reaching the top of the hill, the rock always rolled back down.

COMMENTARY AND QUESTIONS

1. Paraphrase lines 2 and 3.

2. In a sentence or two, summarize the meaning of the poem's first twelve lines.

3. How do the last two lines affect the poem's meaning?

4. Is this poem successful as a sonnet? Compare it to a sonnet by another poet we have read.

REVIEW

1. Describe Countee Cullen's style.

2. Contrast Cullen's style with that of Langston Hughes.

Review of Part Two

1. Identify and discuss the influence of Emerson's thought in at least three of the poets in Part II.

2. Illustrate through examples the influence of Walt Whitman on at least three other poets.

3. Using appropriate examples, discuss two different, if not contradictory, strains of modern American poetry. Trace each of these strains, or types, to its source.

4. Using examples from at least three poets, discuss the origins and development of imagism.

5. Select a short poem from Part I of this book, and rewrite it in the imagist style.

6. Identify a recurring theme in modern American poetry, and discuss what this theme tells us about the first half of the twentieth century.

7. Select a free verse poem and show how, despite the absence of a formal pattern of rhyme and meter, the poem has its own particular form.

8. Discuss the pros and cons of free verse poetry. Do you prefer it to formal poetry? Why or why not?

9. Discuss in some detail the work of your favorite poet from this period. Write at least eight lines in the style of this poet.

Recent American Poetry

Listen for the echo of Ralph Waldo Emerson in these four lines from Robert Lowell's poem "Epilogue":

> Those blessed structures, plot and rhyme—
> why are they no help to me now
> I want to make
> something imagined, not recalled?

In this poem, written a century after Emerson called for an American poetry "of insight and not of tradition," another influential American poet recognizes that traditional tools such as plot and rhyme are not always as useful to poets working in contemporary dimensions. New jobs, in other words, require new tools. In fact, regular patterns of end rhymes and long plots are less common in modern American poetry than in poetry of the last century. In this century, however, American poets have paid special attention to voice, visual imagery, and place.

Written at the end of Lowell's career, "Epilogue" comes after Lowell had followed Robert Frost, William Carlos Williams, and others in creating a conversational voice. Lowell's voice, more than any of his American predecessors, recounted apparently true, undisguised details from the poet's personal life. Sylvia Plath, Anne Sexton, and others also wrote this personal kind of verse that came to be called Confessional Poetry. More important, however, the inclusion of details from private life has become characteristic of modern American poetry, as has the informal voice that allows the speaker to relate personal events naturally and convincingly. Women writers like Adrienne Rich, Molly Peacock, and Sharon Olds are not only a part of this tradition but through it have developed a voice that is at once private and public, conveying the concerns of modern American women. Similarly Gwendolyn Brooks, Robert Hayden, Michael Harper, and Rita Dove develop and extend the African American voice in American poetry. Perhaps more than Langston Hughes and Countee Cullen, these poets create voices that succeed in speaking for African Americans as well as for humankind. This development of the colloquial voice is also evident in the freshness of Beat poets Allen Ginsberg and Lawrence Ferlinghetti, who in their long, Whitmanesque lines tap the vital language of the urban street.

Farther on in "Epilogue," Robert Lowell refers to his poems as snapshots, and in the last lines he writes,

part three

> We are poor passing facts,
> warned by that to give
> each figure in the photograph
> his living name.

In other words, Lowell says that since we are only facts that will pass away and be forgotten, the modern poem, like the snapshot, must preserve the details of real life. This idea not only underlies many modern poets' desire to record the facts of personal experience but also points out a second characteristic of recent American poetry—reliance upon the visual image as a primary poetic device. Since Walt Whitman, who was photographed more than any other poet of his time and who filled his poems with catalogs of images, American poetry has revealed much of its meaning through optic detail. Although you may recall the sharp picture in an Imagist poem like William Carlos Williams's "The Red Wheelbarrow," remember also the more surreal images in Wallace Stevens's "The Emperor of Ice Cream." For while Stevens used his gaudy abstractions to portray the world of imagination, poets like Robert Bly, James Wright, John Haines, Gary Snyder, and others juxtapose realistic description with abstract images in an effort to put us in touch with the transcendent or spiritual part of our nature, reminiscent of what Emerson called "the Unity" of all being. Thus modern poets employ imagery both to record and thus dignify the physical world as well as to suggest a spiritual realm beyond the physical.

Arising naturally from voices that carry images of private lives comes an interest in physical place. Although many contemporary poets purposely avoid the potential limitations of specific geographical location, others name not only real people but real places. Titles like the following illustrate this contemporary interest in place: Robert Hayden's "Night, Death, Mississippi," James Wright's "Outside Fargo, North Dakota," and "In Ohio," Lawrence Ferlinghetti's "The Pennycandystore Beyond the El," Allen Ginsberg's "A Supermarket in California," and Gary Snyder's "August on Sourdough, a Visit from Dick Brewer." These real places remind us that—unlike in the last century, when few American poets lived outside of the Northeast—the geography of contemporary American poetry is as diverse as its themes and forms. Reading poems set in various parts of the country, we sense that we are reading more than a collection of poems, but rather a form of news—recent news complete with sounds and sights of real people in the real places of the American heart.

THEODORE ROETHKE
1908–1963

In the romantic tradition of Ralph Waldo Emerson and Walt Whitman, Theodore Roethke recognizes a spirit that flows through all things and writes poems that call forth nature's power to demonstrate what Emerson called the Oneness. "I can sense," he wrote when he was in college, "the moods of nature almost instinctively . . . alone under an open sky . . . I'm tremendously exalted" (from *On the Poet and His Craft: Selected Prose of Theodore Roethke,* ed. Ralph J. Mills, Jr.). Considered by some to be a confessional poet, Roethke revealed and analyzed his psychological torments. His self-absorption, however, also reminds one of Whitman, who believed that because all things are part of one spirit, the contemplation of one's self is the contemplation of all selves. Also in the romantic tradition, Roethke wrote compelling love poems that balanced the sentimental with the real.

Theodore Roethke was born in Saginaw, Michigan, where his family ran a greenhouse business, originally begun by the poet's grandfather. The greenhouse, which was for Roethke a center of life, became an important symbol in his poetry. Although as a child he resisted school, he read widely before entering the University of Michigan, where he received a bachelor's degree in 1929 and a master's degree in 1936. He later attended Harvard, where he received encouragement to publish his poetry.

A devoted and passionate teacher, Roethke taught at Lafayette College, the University of Pennsylvania, and Bennington College before settling to teach for sixteen years at the University of Washington in Seattle. He was honored with two Pulitzer Prizes for poetry, a Bollingen Prize, and two National Book Awards. The author of six volumes of poems, Theodore Roethke has become a major influence on American poetry.

193

Open House

My secrets cry aloud.
I have no need for tongue.
My heart keeps open house,
My doors are widely swung.
5   An epic of the eyes
My love, with no disguise.

My truths are all foreknown,
This anguish self-revealed.
I'm naked to the bone,
10 With nakedness my shield.
Myself is what I wear:
I keep the spirit spare.

The anger will endure,
The deed will speak the truth
15 In language strict and pure.
I stop the lying mouth:
Rage warps my clearest cry
To witless agony.

COMMENTARY AND QUESTIONS

1. Like Robert Frost's "The Pasture," "Open House" is the first poem in a poet's collected works. What does Roethke tell us to expect in his poetry? Compare and contrast "Open House" to "The Pasture."

2. Describe the structure of "Open House" and comment on how this structure affects the poem's meaning.

3. How can nakedness (line 10) be a shield?

4. In the last stanza, to what "deed" do you think Roethke refers? Is the language of this poem "strict and pure"? If so, how?

Frau Bauman, Frau Schmidt, and Frau Schwartze

Gone the three ancient ladies
Who creaked on the greenhouse ladders,
Reaching up white strings
To wind, to wind
5   The sweet-pea tendrils,[1] the smilax,[2]

---

[1] **tendril:** a long, slender, coiling extension of a climbing plant.
[2] **smilax:** a vine with glossy foliage; used for floral decoration.

Nasturtiums, the climbing
Roses, to straighten
Carnations, red
Chrysanthemums; the stiff
10 Stems, jointed like corn,
They tied and tucked,—
These nurses of nobody else.
Quicker than birds, they dipped
Up and sifted the dirt;
15 They sprinkled and shook;
They stood astride pipes,
Their skirts billowing out wide into tents,
Their hands twinkling with wet;
Like witches they flew along rows
20 Keeping creation at ease;
With a tendril for needle
They sewed up the air with a stem;
They teased out the seed that the cold kept asleep,—
All the coils, loops, and whorls.
25 They trellised[3] the sun; they plotted for more than themselves.

I remember how they picked me up, a spindly kid,
Pinching and poking my thin ribs
Till I lay in their laps, laughing,
Weak as a whiffet;[4]
30 Now, when I'm alone and cold in my bed,
They still hover over me,
These ancient leathery crones,
With their bandannas stiffened with sweat,
And their thorn-bitten wrists,
35 And their snuff-laden breath blowing lightly over me in my first sleep.

[3] **trellised:** the act of attaching climbing plants to a supporting structure called a trellis.
[4] **whiffet:** a small dog.

COMMENTARY AND QUESTIONS

1. Roethke fills a poem with precisely recalled detail from his childhood. How does he employ the greenhouse as a symbol of life? What aspect of life does the poem suggest?

2. Describe the "three ancient ladies." Do you detect an allusion to other trios of ancient females in classic literature? If so, how does this allusion affect the poem?

3. List here the nouns and the verbs Roethke uses to name and to animate his three ladies. Now comment on this list.

4. Describe the speaker's attitude toward the ladies.

5. Discuss how the poem's last six lines clarify the theme.

My Papa's Waltz

The whiskey on your breath
Could make a small boy dizzy;
But I hung on like death:
Such waltzing was not easy.

5   We romped until the pans
Slid from the kitchen shelf;
My mother's countenance
Could not unfrown itself.

The hand that held my wrist
10 Was battered on one knuckle;
At every step you missed
My right ear scraped a buckle.

You beat time on my head
With a palm caked hard by dirt,
15 Then waltzed me off to bed
Still clinging to your shirt.

COMMENTARY AND QUESTIONS

1. What is the strongest image in this poem?

2. What is the brief plot's source of conflict? Is the conflict resolved?

3. What does the poem show us about the father? Why do you think Roethke chose to use the second person, *you*?

4. Note that Roethke, as usual, does not tell us directly what he means. Instead, he *shows* us a scene and lets us draw our own conclusions. Should Roethke tell us, for instance, how he felt at the time or how he felt about his father when he wrote the poem years later? What do you think Roethke thought of his father at the time of the poem's composition?

Elegy for Jane

My Student, Thrown by a Horse

I remember the neckcurls, limp and damp as tendrils;
And her quick look, a sidelong pickerel smile;[1]
And how, once startled into talk, the light syllables leaped for her,
And she balanced in the delight of her thought,
5 A wren,[2] happy, tail into the wind,
Her song trembling the twigs and small branches.

[1] **pickerel smile:** a pickerel is a long, thin northern game fish whose mouth extends well back along the side of its head.
[2] **wren:** a small, lively song bird whose short tail points upward, making it a brace against the wind.

The shade sang with her;
The leaves, their whispers turned to kissing;
And the mold sang in the bleached valleys under the rose.

10 Oh, when she was sad, she cast herself down into such a pure depth,
Even a father could not find her;
Scraping her cheek against straw;
Stirring the clearest water.

My sparrow, you are not here,
15 Waiting like a fern, making a spiny shadow.
The sides of wet stones cannot console me,
Nor the moss, wound with the last light.

If only I could nudge you from this sleep,
My maimed darling, my skittery pigeon.
Over this damp grave I speak the words of my love:
I, with no rights in this matter,
Neither father nor lover.

COMMENTARY AND QUESTIONS

1. List the nouns Roethke uses to name Jane herself or certain aspects of her. How do these nouns affect the poem's meaning?

2. Describe the image in lines 12 and 13. What does Jane appear to be doing? What is the physical position of her body? What mood does this position and her action of "stirring the clearest water" suggest?

3. Why should "the sides of wet stones" (line 16) and the "moss, wound with the last light" (line 17) console the speaker? What do these lines tell us about the speaker?

4. How, if at all, does line 20 help locate the images in lines 17 and 18?

5. Does this poem avoid being simply a sentimental recollection of a lost loved one? If so, how?

REVIEW

1. Describe Roethke's style.

2. Compare Roethke's use of nature imagery to that of another American poet.

3. In what sense is Roethke a confessional poet?

4. Write a poem of at least eight lines in the style of Theodore Roethke.

ELIZABETH BISHOP
1911–1979

With their precise visual descriptions and exotic airs, Elizabeth Bishop's poems reflect the influence of Marianne Moore, whom Bishop met in her last year of college. A certain tenderness, a fascination with nature, and an interest in traditional form, however, distinguish Bishop's poetry from Moore's—placing Bishop in the tradtion of Dickinson and Frost.

Elizabeth Bishop was born in Worcester, Massachusetts. But after her father's death and her mother's nervous breakdown, she lived with her grandparents in Nova Scotia until she was six and then with her Aunt in Boston. Her health was poor during these years, so she was educated at home until she was sixteen, at which time she went to Walnut Hill School in Natick, Massachusetts. In 1930 she enrolled at Vassar College a year behind the writer Mary McCarthy, who became a lifelong friend. After graduating from Vassar, Bishop traveled to Europe and North Africa, eventually settling in Key West, Florida. She moved to Brazil in 1951, residing there until 1964, when she took a teaching position at Harvard University.

Having lost her parents at a young age as well as having traveled much of her life, Elizabeth Bishop wrote poems that portrayed a sense of dislocation sometimes reminiscent of Edgar Allan Poe's poems. Bishop's friend and fellow poet Richard Wilbur observed this similarity when he wrote,

> If the world is a strange place, then it really shades into dream. So many of Elizabeth's poems take place [like Poe's] at the edge of sleep. (*Ploughshares*, vol. 6, 1980)

Although she did not write a large number of poems, Bishop has been widely praised; she received a Pulitzer Prize, a Guggenheim Fellowship, the Shelley Memorial Award, the National Book Award, and the National Book Critics Circle Award. She published four volumes of poems in her lifetime, and her *Collected Poems* appeared posthumously.

The Reprimand

If you taste tears too often, inquisitive tongue,
You'll find they've something you'd not reckoned on;
Crept childish out to touch eye's own phenomenon,
Return, into your element. Tears belong
5   To only eyes; their deepest sorrow they wrung
From water. Where wept water's gone
That residue is sorrow, salt and wan,
Your bitter enemy, who leaves the face white-strung.

Tears, taster, have dignity in display,
10   Carry an antidotal gift for drying.
Unsuited to a savoring by the way,
Salt puckers tear-drops up, ends crying.
Oh curious, cracked and chapped, now will you say,
Tongue, "Grief's not mine" and bend yourself to sighing?

COMMENTARY AND QUESTIONS

1. What does the speaker address? What is the predominant figure of speech used in the poem, and how does it affect the poem's tone?

2. Paraphrase and then discuss the sentence beginning in line 6.

3. Paraphrase and discuss the second stanza, paying particular attention to "and bend yourself to sighing?" What distinction does the speaker imply between sighing and crying?

4. Discuss the poem's theme and how the title relates to it.

Insomnia

The moon in the bureau mirror
looks out a million miles
(and perhaps with pride, at herself,
but she never, never smiles)
5   far and away beyond sleep, or
perhaps she's a daytime sleeper.

By the Universe deserted,
she'd tell it to go to hell,
and she'd find a body of water,
10   or a mirror, on which to dwell.
So wrap up care in a cobweb
and drop it down the well

into that world inverted
where left is always right,
15   where the shadows are really the body,
where we stay awake all night,
where the heavens are shallow as the sea
is now deep, and you love me.

COMMENTARY AND QUESTIONS

1. Why is the speaker experiencing insomnia? What clues does the poet give us?

2. What do we associate with the moon?

3. To what extent are the rhyme and meter of this poem regular? How does the poem's form complement the poem's meaning?

4. Note that the poem is written in three sentences. Discuss how the third sentence affects the way we read the last eight lines.

5. Describe the poem's tone, quoting two or three phrases that help set this tone.

6. Literally, what is "that world inverted" (line 13) and what does it suggest?

7. The word *So* in line 11 suggests that the speaker is beginning to conclude an idea established in the first two sentences. What is this idea, and what is the speaker's conclusion?

8. How do the last three words help us understand the poem's theme?

One Art

The art of losing isn't hard to master;
so many things seem filled with the intent
to be lost that their loss is no disaster.

Lose something every day. Accept the fluster
5   of lost door keys, the hour badly spent.
The art of losing isn't hard to master.

Then practice losing farther, losing faster:
places, and names, and where it was you meant
to travel. None of these will bring disaster.

10   I lost my mother's watch. And look! my last, or
next-to-last, of three loved houses went.
The art of losing isn't hard to master.

I lost two cities, lovely ones. And, vaster,
some realms I owned, two rivers, a continent.
15   I miss them, but it wasn't a disaster.

—Even losing you (the joking voice, a gesture
I love) I shan't have lied. It's evident
the art of losing's not too hard to master
though it may look like (*Write* it!) like disaster.

COMMENTARY AND QUESTIONS

1. Describe the poem's tone, quoting two or three phrases that help set this tone.

2. List what the speaker has lost, and examine the logic of the list's order.

3. Compare this poem to "Insomnia."

4. Discuss Bishop's use of parentheses in this poem. Is it a useful technique? Is it distracting? Would pairs of dashes work better?

5. Discuss the poem's theme.

6. This poem is written in a French form called a *villanelle*. Study the poem's stanza, rhyme, and metrical patterns; and then define a villanelle.

7. Heavily rhymed forms like the villanelle can hinder the natural flow of poems written in English, a language with fewer rhymes than French. To what extent is this villanelle an effective poem?

REVIEW

1. What appeals to you most about Elizabeth Bishop's poetry?

2. Discuss two or three of her most precise images. Do you think Bishop deserves her reputation as a poet who creates extremely precise images? Do you detect in Bishop's work the influence of Marianne Moore? If so, where? Refer specifically to Moore's poetry.

3. Compare Bishop's poems to those of another American poet.

ROBERT HAYDEN

1913–1980

Robert Hayden was born and raised in Detroit, Michigan. He attended Detroit City College, which is now Wayne State University, and later the University of Michigan. After studying at Michigan with the esteemed poet W. H. Auden, Hayden said, "I think he [Auden] showed me my strengths and weaknesses as a poet in ways no one else before had done" (from John O'Brian, *Interviews with Black Writers*, 1973). Other poets who had a significant influence on Hayden were Carl Sandburg, Langston Hughes, and Countee Cullen.

Like Cullen, Hayden wrote formal poetry and was accused by some other African American writers of following the white European literary tradition, rather than contributing to the new African American movement. Poet Michael Harper has said that Hayden was, "a man of considered reserve, with an irrepressible elegance, his bowties, watch chain, and old man's comforts giving him a glow of a courtly preacher who was summoned to give the word" ("Remembering Robert E. Hayden," *The Carleton Miscellany*, Winter 1980). His personal and artistic formality aside, Hayden wrote movingly about the African American experience in America, often employing symbols to amplify precisely rendered characters and events.

After earning a master's degree at the University of Michigan, Hayden taught at Fisk University in Nashville, Tennessee. In 1947 he won a Rosenwald Fellowship in creative writing and in 1954 to 1955, he traveled to Mexico through a grant from the Ford Foundation. He also won the grand prize for poetry at the Dakar (Senegal) World Festival of the Arts. Robert Hayden ended his teaching career at the University of Michigan. He is the author of seven books of poems.

202

Night, Death, Mississippi

I.

A quavering cry. Screech-owl?[1]
Or one of them?
The old man in his reek
and gauntness laughs—

5   One of them, I bet—
and turns out the kitchen lamp,
limping to the porch to listen
in the windowless night.

Be there with Boy and the rest
10 if I was well again.
Time was. Time was.
White robes like moonlight[2]

In the sweetgum[3] dark.
Unbucked that one then
15 and him squealing bloody Jesus
as we cut it off.

Time was. A cry?
A cry all right.
He hawks and spits,
20 fevered as by groinfire.

Have us a bottle,
Boy and me—
he's earned him a bottle—
when he gets home.

II.

25 Then we beat them, he said,
beat them till our arms was tired
and the big old chains
messy and red.

O Jesus burning on the lily cross

30 Christ, it was better
than hunting bear
which don't know why
you want him dead.

O night, rawhead and bloodybones night

---

[1] **Screech-owl:** a screech owl's song is a quavering whistle or a series of short notes.
[2] **white robes like moonlight:** a reference to the robes worn by the Ku Klux Klan during their
    night raids.
[3] **sweetgum:** a tree common in the American South.

35 You kids fetch Paw
  some water now so's he
  can wash that blood off him, she said.

  O night betrayed by darkness not its own

COMMENTARY AND QUESTIONS

1. How many speakers are there in this poem? Describe each.

2. Describe the plot and action in part I and then in part II.

3. Discuss the connotations of *"lily cross"* in line 29.

4. How does Robert Hayden, a black man, use point of view (the narrator's) to dramatize the plight of the blacks in Mississippi?

5. How, if at all, does the last line describe the poem's theme?

Tour 5

  The road winds down through autumn hills
  in blazonry of farewell scarlet
  and recessional gold,
  past cedar groves, through static villages
5 whose names are all that's left
  of Choctaw, Chickasaw.[1]

  We stop a moment in a town
  watched over by Confederate sentinels,
  buy gas and ask directions of a rawboned man
10 whose eyes revile us as the enemy.

  Shrill gorgon[2] silence breathes behind
  his taut civility
  and in the ever-tautening air,
  dark for us despite its Indian summer glow.
15 We drive on, following the route
  of highwaymen and phantoms,

  Of slaves and armies.
  Children, wordless and remote,
  wave at us from kindling porches.
20 And now the land is flat for miles,
  the landscape lush, metallic, flayed,
  its brightness harsh as bloodstained swords.

---

[1] **Choctaw** and **Chickasaw:** Indian tribes who once lived in the Mississippi and Alabama areas but who, according to the poem, survive now only as place names—such as Chickasaw, Alabama.

[2] **gorgon:** In Greek mythology Medusa, who had snakes for hair, was one of the three gorgons; a terrifying or repulsively ugly woman.

COMMENTARY AND QUESTIONS

1. How does the first stanza set a tone? What is the time of year?

2. What do lines 5–6 suggest about the speaker's attitude toward the white man's treatment of Native Americans?

3. How can a twentieth-century town be "watched over by Confederate sentinels" (line 8)?

4. Note how the sentence beginning in line 15 ends at the end of line 17, the first line of the next stanza. How does this *enjambment* (a sentence carrying over from one line to the next) from one stanza to the next affect our reading of the poem? Note that the other three stanzas end with periods.

5. How can the front porches of rural houses be described as "kindling" (line 19)?

6. Discuss the imagery in lines 20–22. How does it serve to conclude the poem?

7. Discuss the title. How is the poem a tour? Why is the tour numbered? Do you think the title is ironic? If so, explain.

Those Winter Sundays

Sundays too my father got up early
and put his clothes on in the blueblack cold,
then with cracked hands that ached
from labor in the weekday weather made
5   banked fires[1] blaze. No one ever thanked him.

I'd wake and hear the cold splintering, breaking.
When the rooms were warm, he'd call,
and slowly I would rise and dress,
fearing the chronic angers of that house,

10   Speaking indifferently to him,
who had driven out the cold
and polished my good shoes as well.
What did I know, what did I know
of love's austere and lonely offices[2]?

---

[1] **banked fires:** Banking a fire, covering it with ashes or fresh fuel, helps keep coals or a low
    flame burning throughout the night.
[2] **offices:** duties.

COMMENTARY AND QUESTIONS

1. What is this poem's source of emotional power?

2. Of how many sentences is this poem composed? How many lines end without punctuation? Discuss how some aspect of the poem's grammatical structure complements its meaning.

3. A poem regretting one's taking a parent's love for granted could easily become self-pitying and sentimental. How, if at all, does Hayden avoid self-pity and sentimentality? In your discussion, consider the poem's last two lines.

REVIEW

1. To what extent are Hayden's poem's formal? Think of Walt Whitman and William Carlos Williams as free verse poets whose subtle patterns of stressed syllables are difficult to identify, and think of Emily Dickinson and Robert Frost as formal poets whose regular rhymes and meters stand out. Remember, *formal* in this sense means working within a pattern such as a certain number of syllables in each line, a certain number of unstressed syllables between stressed syllables, a certain number of stressed syllables in each line, a certain rhyme scheme, or a certain length stanza. Nearly all poets use some kind of pattern to shape (or form) poems, but the patterns used in formal poetry are more recognizable than those employed in free verse.

2. List the subjects of Hayden's poems, and compare these subjects to those of one or two other American poets. Can one make any generalizations about the subject matter of twentieth-century African American poetry? Of twentieth-century American poetry?

3. Compare Hayden's treatment of the African American experience to that of another African American poet. Which poet is more effective? Explain why.

WILLIAM STAFFORD
1914–

"Poetry for me," William Stafford says, "is talk with some luck in it; it springs right out of the language we speak. It does ask for a certain kind of attention; you should be alert for signals of all kinds, be ready, lean into the experience" (letter to H. R., 1990).

Born in Hutchinson, Kansas, Stafford has lived most of his adult life in the Far West. He studied at the University of Kansas and, after working in labor camps as a conscientious objector during World War II, attended the writing program at the University of Iowa. Later he took a teaching position at Lewis and Clark University in Portland, Oregon. Now retired and still living in Oregon, Stafford teaches at poetry conferences, where he generously supports younger poets.

As in the poetry of Robert Frost, Stafford's deceivingly simple poems often describe characters interacting with nature. The powerful presence of the natural world in Stafford's poetry makes him—along with Whitman, Dickinson, Frost, Roethke, and others—another poet in the romantic tradition of Emerson. Unlike many modern poets who describe human behavior but do not judge it, Stafford—again in the romantic tradition—often takes a moral stance.

Although Stafford was forty-six when he published his first book, he had perfected his craft. His second book, *Traveling Through the Dark* (1962), won the National Book Award. He is the author of ten books of poems and two collections of essays.

Traveling Through the Dark

Traveling through the dark I found a deer
dead on the edge of the Wilson River road.
It is usually best to roll them into the canyon:
that road is narrow; to swerve might make more dead.

5   By glow of the tail-light I stumbled back of the car
and stood by the heap, a doe, a recent killing;
she had stiffened already, almost cold.
I dragged her off; she was large in the belly.

My fingers touching her side brought me the reason—
10   her side was warm; her fawn lay there waiting,
alive, still, never to be born.
Beside that mountain road I hesitated.

The car aimed ahead its lowered parking lights;
under the hood purred the steady engine.
15   I stood in the glare of the warm exhaust turning red;
around our group I could hear the wilderness listen.

I thought hard for us all—my only swerving—,
then pushed her over the edge into the river.

COMMENTARY AND QUESTIONS

1. Describe the action of the narrative (plot).

2. Read the following rewritten lines, compare each revision to the original, and discuss the differences. Be sure to explain why certain words should not be omitted.

line 2: dead on the edge of the river road.
line 9: When I touched its side, I knew the reason.
line 12: I stood beside the road, hesitating.
line 13: The car's parking lights were on low beam;
line 15: I stood in the glare of the headlights;
line 16: It seemed as though the wilderness listened.
line 17: I thought hard about the fawn's still being alive.

3. How does the title help us understand the poem's meaning?

Listening

My father could hear a little animal step,
or a moth in the dark against the screen,
and every far sound called the listening out
into places where the rest of us had never been.

5   More spoke to him from the soft wild night
than came to our porch for us on the wind;
we would watch him look up and his face go keen
till the walls of the world flared, widened.

My father heard so much that we still stand
10   inviting the quiet by turning the face,
waiting for a time when something in the night
will touch us too from that other place.

COMMENTARY AND QUESTIONS

1. Ernest Hemingway wrote a short story called "Fathers and Sons" about a father's exceptional sight and a son's equally exceptional sense of smell. Do you recall being close to any adults with exceptional senses? How could knowing someone like this, particularly a parent, be an important experience?

2. How has the time and situation changed in the third stanza?

3. Explain the image in line 10.

4. What do the last two words suggest about the poem's meaning?

5. Compare this poem to Robert Hayden's "Those Winter Sundays."

Adults Only

Animals own a fur world;
people own worlds that are variously, pleasingly, bare.
And the way these worlds *are* once arrived for us kids with a jolt,
that night when the wild woman danced
5   in the giant cage we found we were all in
at the state fair.

Better women exist, no doubt, than that one,
and occasions more edifying, too, I suppose.
But we have to witness for ourselves what comes for us,
10   nor be distracted by barkers[1] of irrelevant ware;
and a pretty good world, I say, arrived that night
when that woman came farming right out of her clothes,
by God,

At the state fair.

[1] **barker:** one who stands at the entrance to a show and solicits customers loudly and colorfully.

COMMENTARY AND QUESTIONS

1. Paraphrase the first stanza and explain its function in the poem.

2. Explain the statement (lines 5 and 6) "we found we were all in/at the state fair." How, if at all, does the statement enlarge the poem's meaning?

3. Cite some phrases that help the reader understand the speaker's attitude toward the woman and his experience at the state fair.

4. How do lines 9 and 10 suggest that the poem is about more than the speaker's memory of seeing a stripper?

5. Describe the tone of the last four lines and discuss how certain words help achieve that tone.

6. State and discuss the poem's meaning.

At the Bomb Testing Site

At noon in the desert a panting lizard
waited for history, its elbows tense,
watching the curve of a particular road
as if something might happen.

5   It was looking at something farther off
than people could see, an important scene
acted in stone for little selves
at the flute end of consequences.

There was just a continent without much on it
10   under a sky that never cared less.
Ready for a change, the elbows waited.
The hands gripped hard on the desert.

COMMENTARY AND QUESTIONS

1. Describe the scene.

2. Discuss the word *panting*. Do lizards pant? Why is this one panting?

3. Discuss lines 6–8. How is a bomb test "acted in stone"? Who are the "little selves," and how are they "little"? What does the speaker mean by the "flute end of consequences"?

4. Do you think the speaker is using understatement in lines 9 and 10? Discuss.

5. How does the poet use the sentence, as well as the line and the stanza, to structure his poem? Note that six of the twelve lines are not end-stopped. Discuss how the poem's form complements content.

6. Does this poem make a moral judgment? If so, what is the judgment and how is it made?

Ceremony

On the third finger of my left hand
under the bank of the Ninnescah[1]
a muskrat[2] whirled and bit to the bone.
The mangled hand made the water red.

5   That was something the ocean would remember:
I saw me in the current flowing through the land,
rolling, touching roots, the world incarnadined,[3]
and the river richer by a kind of marriage.

---

[1] **Ninnescah:** a river in south-central Kansas, near where Stafford was raised.
[2] **muskrat:** an aquatic rodent sleeker and somewhat smaller than a woodchuck, trapped for its fur.
[3] **incarnadined:** turned blood red; reddened. Shakespeare uses this word in *Macbeth* in connection with Macbeth's guilt for having murdered Duncan: "my hand will rather/the multitudinous seas incarnadine/making the green one red" (II, ii, 11.59–61).

While in the woods an owl started quavering
10 with drops like tears I raised my arm.
Under the bank a muskrat was trembling
with meaning my hand would wear forever.

In that river my blood flowed on.

COMMENTARY AND QUESTIONS

1. What would most people's reaction be if they were badly bitten by a muskrat? Discuss the speaker's reaction.

2. Discuss what important meanings would be if lines 9 and 10 were rewritten like this:

> While I was there in the woods, an owl quavered;
> and when I raised my arm, blood dropped from my finger like tears.

3. Referring to specific lines and phrases, explain how this poem demonstrates Stafford's idea of and his relationship with nature.

4. Do you like this poem? Why or why not?

REVIEW

1. Using at least two examples, show how apparently simple phrases and lines of Stafford's poetry in fact carry significant meaning. Demonstrate how Frost also used this technique.

2. Compare one of Stafford's poems that judges human behavior with another author's poem that describes human behavior without judging it.

3. What techniques does Stafford use to structure his poems? Would you call him a formalist? Discuss.

4. Write a poem of at least eight lines in the style of William Stafford.

GWENDOLYN BROOKS
1917–

Unlike Langston Hughes, whose free verse poems create the sound of African American speech, and unlike Countee Cullen and Robert Hayden, whose formal poems describe African Americans in a voice that is not distinctly African American, Gwendolyn Brooks's formal poems often employ African American dialect to treat African American themes. Although Brooks works in free verse as well as in formal verse, it is by marrying the regular rhymes and measured meters of formal poetry to the rolling cadences of African American speech that she best demonstrates the excellence of her craft.

Among her many awards are the National Institution of Arts and Letters grant in literature, 1946; Guggenheim Fellowship, 1946, 1947; the Pulitzer Prize for poetry, 1950; Poet Laureate of Illinois, 1969; the Black Academy of Arts and Letters Award, 1971; and the Shelley Memorial Award. She has received honorary degrees from thirty-eight colleges and universities, and in 1985 was the poetry consultant to the Library of Congress.

The appeal evidenced by this list of awards and other recognitions stems not only from Brooks's poetic craft but probably more from her ability to portray the local lives of African Americans in a way that somehow includes all people. As Blyden Jackson tells us, Brooks offers "a view of life in which one may see a microscopic portion of the universe intensely and yet through that microscopic portion see all the truth for the human condition" (cited in *Contemporary Authors, New Revision,* Vol. 1).

a song in the front yard

I've stayed in the front yard all my life.
I want a peek at the back
Where it's rough and untended and hungry weed grows.
A girl gets sick of a rose.

212

5   I want to go in the back yard now
And maybe down the alley,
To where the charity children play,
I want a good time today.

They do some wonderful things.
10 They have some wonderful fun.
My mother sneers, but I say it's fine
How they don't have to go in at quarter to nine.
My mother, she tells me that Johnnie Mae
Will grow up to be a bad woman.
15 That George'll be taken to Jail soon or late
(On account of last winter he sold our back gate.)

But I say it's fine. Honest, I do.
And I'd like to be a bad woman, too,
And wear the brave stockings of night-black lace
20 And strut down the streets with paint on my face.

COMMENTARY AND QUESTIONS

1. Citing significant words and phrases, describe the speaker—sex, age, background, and interests. Comment on how Brooks works this information into the poem.

2. Describe the speaker's voice and how it influences the poem. Note specific places where the voice is particularly significant.

3. Comment on the effect of each of the following words: "hungry" (line 3), "charity" (line 6), "brave" (line 19).

4. Compare and contrast the first two stanzas of "a song in the front yard" to Emily Dickinson's typical stanza form.

5. Note how Brooks alters her stanza form after the second stanza. What appears to be the purpose of these alterations and how effective are they?

6. What appeals to you most about this poem?

the independent man

Now who could take you off to tiny life
In one room or in two rooms or in three
And cork you smartly, like the flask[1] of wine
You are? Not any woman. Not a wife.
5 You'd let her twirl you, give her a good glee
Showing your leaping ruby to a friend.
Though twirling would be meek. Since not a cork
Could you allow, for being made so free.

[1] **flask:** a small container with a cap, used for wine or liquor.

A woman would be wise to think it well
10   If once a week you only rang the bell.

COMMENTARY AND QUESTIONS

1. Who appears to be addressing whom?

2. Describe the poem's tone.

3. Discuss the metaphor established in line 3. How does Brooks extend this metaphor in lines 5–8? Pay close attention to these words and phrases: "twirl" (line 5), "your leaping ruby" (line 6), "twirling would be meek" (line 7), and "not a cork / Could you allow" (lines 7–8). What does the metaphor suggest about the "independent man's" influence on women?

4. Paraphrase the poem.

5. Write your own poem that imitates this poem's tone, rhyme, and meter; that addresses someone with whom the speaker is angry; and that employs an extended metaphor.

Sadie and Maud

Maud went to college.
Sadie stayed at home.
Sadie scraped life
With a fine-tooth comb.

5   She didn't leave a tangle in.
Her comb found every strand.
Sadie was one of the livingest chits
In all the land.

Sadie bore two babies
10   Under her maiden name.
Maud and Ma and Papa
Nearly died of shame.
Every one but Sadie
Nearly died of shame.

15   When Sadie said her last so-long
Her girls struck out from home.
(Sadie had left as heritage
Her fine-tooth comb.)

Maud, who went to college,
20   Is a thin brown mouse.
She is living all alone
In this old house.

COMMENTARY AND QUESTIONS

1. Paraphrase lines 3–6.

2. Referring to significant lines and phrases, contrast Sadie and Maud.

3. Describe the poem's rhyme and meter, and explain how it contributes to the poem's effect.

4. Discuss the poem's meaning.

REVIEW

1. Judging by the poems in this book, comment on this statement by Gwendolyn Brooks:

> I think that my poetry is related to life in the broad sense of the word, even though the subject matter relates closest to the Negro. (from *Contemporary Authors, New Revision,* Vol. 1)

2. In your opinion, does Brooks's use of form inhibit her efforts to imitate African American language? In answering this question, look back at the poetry of Langston Hughes, who is known for his ability to capture the sounds and rhythms of African American English.

3. Discuss what you like about Brooks's poetry.

4. Do you think it is correct to call these poems formal? Discuss.

ROBERT
LOWELL
1917–1977

The most respected and influential poet of his generation, Robert Lowell created intense images of personal loneliness and dejection as well as themes describing the nation's spiritual decay. After winning the Pulitzer Prize in 1946 for his book *Lord Weary's Castle,* a collection of closely rhymed and metered poems, and then in 1951 winning the Harriet Monroe Prize for *The Mills of the Kavanaughs,* another collection of formal verse, Lowell became interested in William Carlos Williams's ideas about free verse. "How few modern poems," Lowell once remarked, " . . . have the distinction of good conversation." He went on to say that "literary people have less of their own to say and consequently use words with less subtlety and precision than a Maine farmer" (Steven Gould Axelrod, *Robert Lowell: Life and Art*). In his book *Life Studies,* winner of the 1959 National Book Award, Lowell employed for the first time these natural rhythms of American speech, and thereby joined the tradition first espoused by Emerson and practiced by Whitman, Williams, Frost, and others.

Born in Boston, Massachusetts, Robert Lowell was a member of the same New England family as poets Amy Lowell and James Russell Lowell and Harvard president Abbott Lawrence Lowell. After living briefly in Philadelphia and Washington—where his father, a naval officer was stationed—the family resettled in Boston when Lowell was eight. He attended local private day schools around Boston, and then entered St. Mark's, a boys' boarding school (now co-educational) in Southboro, Massachusetts. There he met and was encouraged by Richard Eberhart, a young poet who was teaching English at St. Mark's. Lowell later enrolled at Harvard, where he remained for two years before leaving for Tennessee to study with the poet Allen Tate. In the fall of 1937, he enrolled at Kenyon College, where he continued his study of poetry with the formalist poet John Crowe Ransom, and became friends with poet Randall Jarrell.

In 1942 Lowell taught briefly at Kenyon, where he had graduated with a degree in classics. Sentenced in 1943 to a year and a day for refusing to be inducted into the armed services and thus violating the Selective Service Act, Lowell served five months in the federal prison in Danbury, Connecticut, and West Street Jail in New York.

After the success of *Lord Weary's Castle* in 1946, Lowell won a Guggenheim Fellowship the following year and in 1947 to 1948 he was Poetry Consultant to the

Library of Congress. During most of his career he taught at universities such as the University of Iowa; Boston University, where he taught poets Donald Junkins, Sylvia Plath, and Anne Sexton; and Harvard. Also a playwright, Lowell taught at the Yale School of Drama.

During the 1960s Lowell's political activity made him nationally known. He supported John Kennedy's presidency in 1960. As a protest against American foreign policy, Lowell declined the invitation of President Johnson to attend the White House Festival of the Arts in 1965. In 1967 he joined an anti-Vietnam march to the Pentagon and in 1968 backed the presidential candidacy of Senator Eugene McCarthy.

Robert Lowell's life is marked by conflict: his leaving Harvard and the New England tradition it represented to attend Kenyon; his revolt against his Protestant background through his conversion to Catholicism; his rejection of formalist poetry for a more open, freer form; his refusal to join the armed services; his three often painful marriages; and his debilitating depressions. Yet from these difficult periods he built powerful collections of poems, each markedly different from the last. The personal nature of *Life Studies* and much of his later collections—such as *For the Union Dead, Notebooks 1967–1968,* and *Day by Day*—have led critics to use the term *confessional poetry,* a movement centered on Lowell as well as Sylvia Plath, Anne Sexton, John Berryman, W. D. Snodgrass, and others.

Alfred Corning Clark

(1916–1961)

You read the *New York Times*
every day at recess,
but in its dry
obituary, a list
5   of your wives, nothing is news,
except the ninety-five
thousand dollar engagement ring
you gave the sixth.
Poor rich boy,
10 you were unseasonably adult
at taking your time,
and died at forty-five.
Poor Al Clark,
behind your enlarged,
15 hardly recognizable photograph,
I feel the pain.
You were alive. You are dead.
You wore bow-ties and dark
blue coats, and sucked
20 wintergreen or cinnamon lifesavers
to sweeten your breath.

There must be something—
some one to praise
your triumphant diffidence,
25   your refusal of exertion,
the intelligence
that pulsed in the sensitive,
pale concavities of your forehead.
You never worked,
30   and were third in the form.[1]
I owe you something—
I was befogged,
and you were too bored,
quick and cool to laugh.
35   You are dear to me, Alfred;
our reluctant souls united
in our unconventional
illegal games of chess
on the St. Mark's[2] quadrangle.
40   You usually won—
motionless
as a lizard in the sun.

[1] **form:** a class or grade in school.
[2] **St. Mark's:** the boarding school that Robert Lowell attended from 1930–1935.

COMMENTARY AND QUESTIONS

1. Describe Al Clark, noting significant facts and images.

2. By quoting significant words and phrases, describe the attitude of the speaker toward Al Clark.

3. Discuss the poem's form, keeping in mind that Lowell's early collections of poems were tightly rhymed and metered. Do you find this poem too proselike to be called poetry? What aspects of form does it possess?

For the Union Dead

"Relinquunt Omnia Servare Rem Publicam."[1]

This poem describes a Civil War memorial located in the Boston Common. The monument portrays Colonel Robert Shaw leading the 54th Massachusetts regiment's attack on Fort Wagner, where he and 40 percent of his men were killed. The

[1] **"Relinquunt Omnia Servare Rem Publicam":** "They leave everything to save their republic." This is a slight alteration of the epigram inscribed on the statue.

Confederates buried Shaw with his men in a ditch. The film *Glory* is based on the story of Colonel Shaw, a white man, and the first black regiment to enter combat in the Civil War.

The old South Boston Aquarium stands
in a Sahara of snow now. Its broken windows are boarded.
The bronze weathervane cod has lost half its scales.
The airy tanks are dry.

5   Once my nose crawled like a snail on the glass;
my hand tingled
to burst the bubbles
drifting from the noses of the cowed, compliant fish.

My hand draws back. I often sigh still
10 for the dark downward and vegetating kingdom
of the fish and reptile. One morning last March,
I pressed against the new barbed and galvanized

fence on the Boston Common. Behind their cage,
yellow dinosaur steamshovels were grunting
15 as they cropped up tons of mush and grass
to gouge their underworld garage.

Parking spaces luxuriate like civic
sandpiles in the heart of Boston.
A girdle of orange, Puritan-pumpkin colored girders
20 braces the tingling Statehouse,

shaking over the excavations, as it faces Colonel Shaw
and his bell-cheeked Negro infantry
on St. Gaudens' shaking Civil War relief,[2]
propped by a plank splint against the garage's earthquake.

25 Two months after marching through Boston,
half the regiment was dead;
at the dedication,
William James[3] could almost hear the bronze Negroes breathe.

Their monument sticks like a fishbone
30 in the city's throat.
Its Colonel is as lean
as a compass-needle.

---

[2] **St. Gaudens' shaking Civil War relief:** Augustus St. Gaudens cast his monument in bronze. A relief is an art form that projects figures or forms from a flat background.
[3] **William James:** (1842–1910) American psychologist and philosopher; brother of novelist Henry James (1843–1916).

He has an angry wrenlike vigilance,
a greyhound's gentle tautness;
35   he seems to wince at pleasure,
and suffocate for privacy.

He is out of bounds now. He rejoices in man's lovely,
peculiar power to choose life and die—
when he leads his black soldiers to death,
40   he cannot bend his back.

On a thousand small town New England greens,
the old white churches hold their air
of sparse, sincere rebellion, frayed flags
quilt the graveyards of the Grand Army of the Republic.

45   The stone statues of the abstract Union Soldier
grow slimmer and younger each year—
wasp-waisted, they doze over muskets
and muse through their sideburns . . .

Shaw's father[4] wanted no monument
50   except the ditch,
where his son's body was thrown
and lost with his "niggers."

The ditch is nearer.
There are no statues for the last war[5] here;
55   on Boylston Street, a commercial photograph
shows Hiroshima boiling

over a Mosler Safe,[6] the "Rock of Ages"
that survived the blast. Space is nearer.
When I crouch to my television set,
60   the drained faces of Negro school-children rise like balloons.

Colonel Shaw
is riding on his bubble,
he waits
for the blessèd break.

65   The Aquarium is gone. Everywhere,
giant finned cars nose forward like fish;
a savage servility
slides by on grease.

---

[4] **Shaw's father:** a well-known abolitionist of his day.
[5] **the last war:** World War II.
[6] **Mosler Safe:** a popular safe used in many banks, is advertised as the "Rock of Ages," the
    name of a famous spiritual.

COMMENTARY AND QUESTIONS

1. Discuss the content and purpose of the first eleven lines. Why could the poem not begin with "One morning last March"?

2. How does the poet connect his childhood memories of the Aquarium to the new parking garage?

3. What is suggested by the State House "shaking over the excavations, as it faces Colonel Shaw / and his bell-cheeked Negro infantry" (lines 21–22)? How does the rest of stanza 6 extend this idea? Note words such as "propped," "splint," and "earthquake."

4. Why is it that the "monument sticks like a fishbone / in the city's throat" (lines 29–30)? How are the "old white churches" (line 42) symbols of rebellion? What rebellion do they symbolize? What rebellion do the "frayed flags" (line 44) represent? What seems to be the purpose of stanza 12? Of stanza 13?

5. Why is the "ditch" (line 53) where Shaw was buried with his troops "nearer"?

6. Discuss the irony in lines 54–58.

7. How in the poem's last ten lines does Lowell draw together the parts of his poem and make a conclusion? What is the effect of our last seeing the speaker "crouched to [his] television set"? Why does Colonel Shaw want his bubble to break (line 64)?

8. Noting particularly the last stanza, discuss how the poem expands the idea of servitude beyond the Civil War issue of slavery.

9. What does the poem say about modern America? Make specific reference to lines and phrases.

For Sale

Poor sheepish plaything,
organized with prodigal animosity,
lived in just a year—
my Father's cottage at Beverly Farms[1]
5   was on the market the month he died.
Empty, open, intimate,
its town-house furniture
had an on tiptoe air
of waiting for the mover
10   on the heels of the undertaker.
Ready, afraid
of living alone till eighty,
Mother mooned in a window,
as if she had stayed on a train
15   one stop past her destination.

---

[1] **Beverly Farms:** an affluent community north of Boston.

COMMENTARY AND QUESTIONS

1. What does the poem (lines 1–10) tell us about the speaker, his parents, and how the three characters relate? Note critical lines and phrases. As you answer this question, you may want to explain how the house helps us understand the characters.

2. Discuss the image in lines 13–15. What emotion does it convey? How?

3. Describe the poem's tone and tell how it affects the poem's meaning.

REVIEW

1. Some have noted that Lowell uses more adjectives than most modern poets, that his verbs are strong and his images powerful, that he often addresses his subject in the second person "you," and that his line-breaks are rough. Discuss to what extent you observe these characteristics in these poems. How do these characteristics and others you have noted affect Lowell's style?

2. To what extent do these poems share a common voice? Describe that voice or voices.

3. Does the personal element of these poems prevent them from being universal? Discuss the personal or "confessional" side of the poems. What seems to be the purpose of the confessional poem? Do you like this kind of poetry?

4. Write a poem in the style of Robert Lowell.

JAMES DICKEY
1923–

James Dickey was born in Buckhead, Georgia, not far from Atlanta. After graduating from North Fulton High School, he entered Clemson A&M College, where he played football. In 1942 he left college to join the Army Air Corps. Serving with the 418th Night Fighter Squadron, Dickey flew over one hundred bombing missions in the Pacific. He tells a story that it was through the love letters he sent home during the war that he discovered his talent for writing. Whether or not this tale is true, when the war was over he did not return to Clemson. Instead, he chose to complete his bachelor's degree and then earn his master's degree at Vanderbilt University—whose English department, through John Crowe Ransom and others, had gaind a strong reputation. After publishing a few early poems and teaching briefly, Dickey joined the Air Force to fight in Korea. He later returned to college teaching, continued writing, and won a *Sewanee Review* fellowship, which enabled him to live and write for a year in Europe.

In 1956 Dickey left college teaching to work as a copywriter and executive for advertising firms in New York City and Atlanta. During the late 1950s and the 1960s he won a Guggenheim Fellowship, the National Book Award, several other awards, and in 1968 was appointed consultant in poetry for the Library of Congress. The author of several books of poems, Dickey has also written two novels, a collection of critical essays, television and movie scripts, and children's books. His novel *Deliverance* was made into a movie that won several nominations for an academy award.

Although primarily a poet, Dickey writes in the generous, rich narrative tradition of Southern fiction writer William Faulkner. Critics of Dickey complain that his descriptions can be too generous, too long, and ponderous. As you read the poems, you will sense an openness—both in the imagery and in the structure of the poems—that sets Dickey in sharp contrast with formalist John Crowe Ransom. You will also note that Robert Lowell's work, even his free verse collected in this text, seems much more crafted and precise than Dickey's poetry. On the other hand, Dickey, who called the confessional poetry of Robert Lowell, Sylvia Plath, and Anne Sexton "the poetry of personal complaint," might argue that Lowell's poems are too finely tuned and too personal to sufficiently move the reader. As you read Dickey's flowing lines,

223

you may also be reminded of Whitman's long, open lines, and at times you may even
recall the flowing melodies of Dickey's fellow Georgian Sidney Lanier.

The Leap

The only thing I have of Jane MacNaughton
Is one instant of a dancing-class dance.
She was the fastest runner in the seventh grade,
My scrapbook says, even when boys were beginning
5   To be as big as the girls,
But I do not have her running in my mind,
Though Frances Lane is there, Agnes Fraser,
Fat Betty Lou Black in the boys-against-girls
Relays we ran at recess: she must have run

10   Like the other girls, with her skirts tucked up
So they would be like bloomers,
But I cannot tell; that part of her is gone.
What I do have is when she came,
With the hem of her skirt where it should be
15   For a young lady, into the annual dance
Of the dancing class we all hated, and with a light
Grave leap, jumped up and touched the end
Of one of the paper-ring decorations

To see if she could reach it. She could,
20   And reached me now as well, hanging in my mind
From a brown chain of brittle paper, thin
And muscular, wide-mouthed, eager to prove
Whatever it proves when you leap
In a new dress, a new womanhood, among the boys
25   Whom you easily left in the dust
Of the passionless playground. If I said I saw
In the paper where Jane MacNaughton Hill,

Mother of four, leapt to her death from a window
Of a downtown hotel, and that her body crushed-in
30   The top of a parked taxi, and that I held
Without trembling a picture of her lying cradled
In that papery steel as though lying in the grass,
One shoe idly off, arms folded across her breast,
I would not believe myself. I would say
35   The convenient thing, that it was a bad dream
Of maturity, to see that eternal process

37   Most obsessively wrong with the world
Come out of her light, earth-spurning feet
Grown heavy: would say that in the dusty heels
40   Of the playground some boy who did not depend
On speed of foot, caught and betrayed her.
Jane, stay where you are in my first mind:
It was odd in that school, at that dance.
I and the other slow-footed yokels sat in corners
45   Cutting rings out of drawing paper

Before you leapt in your new dress
And touched the end of something I began,
Above the couples struggling on the floor,
New men and women clutching at each other
50   And prancing foolishly as bears: hold on
To that ring I made for you, Jane—
My feet are nailed to the ground
By dust I swallowed thirty years ago—
While I examine my hands.

COMMENTARY AND QUESTIONS

1. Describe the speaker's first memories of Jane MacNaughton. In particular, what details seem most significant and why?

2. What is the "convenient thing" (line 35) and why is it "convenient"? Does the speaker ever say more than the "convenient thing"? Discuss.

3. Why was it "odd in that school" (line 43)?

4. How and to what purpose does Dickey employ the image of leaping?

5. Who is the poem's central character?

A Screened Porch in the Country

All of them are sitting
Inside a lamp of coarse wire
And being in all directions
Shed upon darkness,
5   Their bodies softening to shadow, until
They come to rest out in the yard
In a kind of blurred golden country
In which they more deeply lie
Than if they were being created
10   Of Heavenly light.

Where they are floating beyond
Themselves, in peace,
Where they have laid down
Their souls and not known it,
15   The smallest creatures,
As every night they do,
Come to the edge of them
And sing, if they can,
Or, if they can't, simply shine
20   Their eyes back, sitting on haunches,

Pulsating and thinking of music.
Occasionally, something weightless
Touches the screen
With its body, dies,
25   Or is unmurmuringly hurt,
But mainly nothing happens
Except that a family continues
To be laid down
In the midst of its nightly creatures,
30   Not one of which openly comes

Into the golden shadow
Where the people are lying,
Emitted by their own house
So humanly that they become
35   More than human, and enter the place
Of small, blindly singing things,
Seeming to rejoice
Perpetually, without effort,
Without knowing why
40   Or how they do it.

COMMENTARY AND QUESTIONS

1. Paraphrase the first stanza, paying particular attention to lines 2 and 7.

2. What does the speaker mean by "more than human" (line 35)?

3. Discuss the relationship between the family and the creatures beyond the screen?

4. Beyond setting, can one make any useful comparisons between this poem and William Stafford's "Listening"?

The Heaven of Animals

Here they are. The soft eyes open.
If they have lived in a wood
It is a wood.
If they have lived on plains
5   It is grass rolling
Under their feet forever.

Having no souls, they have come,
Anyway, beyond their knowing.
Their instincts wholly bloom
10   And they rise.
The soft eyes open.

To match them, the landscape flowers,
Outdoing, desperately
Outdoing what is required:
15   The richest wood,
The deepest field.

For some of these,
It could not be the place
It is, without blood.
20   These hunt, as they have done,
But with claws and teeth grown perfect,

More deadly than they can believe.
They stalk more silently,
And crouch on the limbs of trees,
25   And their descent
Upon the bright backs of their prey

May take years
In a sovereign floating of joy.
And those that are hunted
30   Know this as their life,
Their reward: to walk

Under such trees in full knowledge
Of what is in glory above them,
And to feel no fear,
35   But acceptance, compliance.
Fulfilling themselves without pain

At the cycle's center,
They tremble, they walk
Under the tree,
40   They fall, they are torn,
They rise, they walk again.

COMMENTARY AND QUESTIONS

1. Describe this heaven of animals.

2. What do you think of Dickey's vision of a heaven of animals? What are its moral implications?

3. How, if at all, could humans fit into this vision? Judging from this poem, how would Dickey envision a human heaven?

REVIEW

1. "The Leap" is taken from a collection of poems called *Falling*, and employs images of rising and falling. Examine how these images help make meaning in the poem.

2. How do these poems depict nature and man's relationship to nature?

3. Discuss Dickey's use of form: his stanzas, line breaks, line lengths, sentences as they relate to lines, repetitions of words, and other devices he uses (and does not use) to form his poems. To what extent are these poems formal? Compare to another poet's use of form.

4. Which of these three poems do you like the best? Discuss your reasons.

5. Write a poem in the style of James Dickey.

RICHARD WILBUR
1921–

The son of an artist and the grandson of a newspaper editor, Richard Wilbur was born in New York City. When he was two years old his parents moved to a farm in rural New Jersey, where Wilbur gained an enduring affection for rural life. In 1938 he entered Amherst College, edited the college newspaper, and in the summers traveled the country in freight-cars. After graduating from Amherst in 1942, he married and then entered the army, serving with the 38th Infantry Division. Like James Dickey's, his experience in the war helped focus his interest in writing poetry.

After the war Wilbur earned a master's degree at Harvard, and in 1947 he received high praise for *Beautiful Changes,* his first book. Since then Wilbur has published eleven books of poems, several translations, song lyrics, and essays. He has taught at Harvard, Wellesley, Wesleyan, and Smith.

In an interview with the *New York Quarterly* magazine, Richard Wilbur remarked, "I agree with Emerson that it's not the meter but meter-making argument that's important." In other words, Wilbur, a formalist, believes that the form of a poem—its rhyme, meter, stanza pattern—should grow naturally out of its content or, to use Emerson's word, its argument. Like coaches who wait to see what kinds of players they have before deciding on formations (the formal structure of a team's play), formal poets like Wilbur let their ideas and feelings determine the forms their poems will take.

Wilbur's poetry celebrates the beauty of everyday life—revealing, in the Emersonian tradition, the spirit that unites and elevates the mundane "things of this world." Much honored, he has received, among other awards, two Guggenheim fellowships, a Prix de Rome, a Pulitzer Prize, the National Book Award, and a Bollingen Prize. Recently, he has served as America's Poet Laureate in the Library of Congress.

The Writer

In her room at the prow of the house
Where light breaks, and the windows are tossed with linden,[1]
My daughter is writing a story.

I pause in the stairwell, hearing
5 From her shut door a commotion of typewriter-keys
Like a chain hauled over a gunwale.

Young as she is, the stuff
Of her life is a great cargo, and some of it heavy:
I wish her a lucky passage.

10 But now it is she who pauses,
As if to reject my thought and its easy figure.
A stillness greatens, in which

The whole house seems to be thinking,
And then she is at it again with a bunched clamor
15 Of strokes, and again is silent.

I remember the dazed starling
Which was trapped in that very room, two years ago;
How we stole in, lifted a sash

And retreated, not to affright it;
20 And how for a helpless hour, through the crack of the door,
We watched the sleek, wild, dark

And iridescent creature
Batter against the brilliance, drop like a glove
To the hard floor, or the desk-top,

25 And wait then, humped and bloody,
For the wits to try it again; and how our spirits
Rose when, suddenly sure,

It lifted off from a chair-back,
Beating a smooth course for the right window
30 And clearing the sill of the world.

It is always a matter, my darling,
Of life or death, as I had forgotten. I wish
What I wished you before, but harder.

[1] **linden:** a beautiful, spreading tree with fragrant blossoms.

COMMENTARY AND QUESTIONS

1. In line 11 the speaker refers to the "easy figure" of the thought—that is, the metaphor developed in the first three stanzas. Describe this metaphor and explain how it is extended through nine lines. Why should it be regarded as easy?

2. How does the poet use the starling to add meaning to the poem?

3. Explain how the last stanza clarifies the poem's theme.

A Plain Song for Comadre[1]

Though the unseen may vanish, though insight fails
And doubter and downcast saint
Join in the same complaint,
What holy things were ever frightened off
5   By a fly's buzz, or itches, or a cough?
Harder than nails

They are, more warmly constant than the sun,
At whose continual sign
The dimly prompted vine
10 Upbraids itself to a green excellence.
What evening, when the slow and forced expense
Of sweat is done,

Does not the dark come flooding the straight furrow
Or filling the well-made bowl?
15 What night will not the whole
Sky with its clear studs and steady spheres
Turn on a sound chimney? It is seventeen years
Come tomorrow

That Bruna Sandoval has kept the church
20 Of San Ysidro, sweeping
And scrubbing the aisles, keeping
The candlesticks and the plaster faces bright,
And seen no visions but the thing done right
From the clay porch

25 To the white altar. For love and in all weathers
This is what she has done.
Sometimes the early sun
Shines as she flings the scrubwater out, with a crash
Of grimy rainbows, and the stained suds flash
30 Like angel-feathers.

[1] **Comadre:** One applies this Spanish term to a woman for whom one feels a close bond, such as a sister.

COMMENTARY AND QUESTIONS

1. Explain the paradox in line 1. What "holy things" (line 4) does the speaker mention specifically in stanza 4?

2. Paraphrase the first two sentences, noting particularly "upbraids" (line 10).

3. Explain "studs" and "spheres" in line 16. How in line 17 does the sky "Turn on a sound [well-constructed] chimney"?

4. How do lines 6–17 develop the idea established in the first sentence?

5. Why does the speaker admire Bruna Sandoval?

6. How do the last four lines conclude the poem?

7. Describe and comment on the poem's form.

8. Compare the theme of this poem to that of Robert Frost's "Mowing."

The Pardon

My dog lay dead five days without a grave
In the thick of summer, hid in a clump of pine
And a jungle of grass and honeysuckle-vine.
I who had loved him while he kept alive

5 Went only close enough to where he was
To sniff the heavy honeysuckle-smell
Twined with another odor heavier still
And hear the flies' intolerable buzz.

Well, I was ten and very much afraid.
10 In my kind world the dead were out of range
And I could not forgive the sad or strange
In beast or man. My father took the spade

And buried him. Last night I saw the grass
Slowly divide (it was the same scene
15 But now it glowed a fierce and mortal green)
And saw the dog emerging. I confess

I felt afraid again, but still he came
In the carnal sun, clothed in a hymn of flies,
And death was breeding in his lively eyes.
20 I started in to cry and call his name,

Asking forgiveness of his tongueless head.
. . . I dreamt the past was never past redeeming:
But whether this was false or honest dreaming
I beg death's pardon now. And mourn the dead.

COMMENTARY AND QUESTIONS

1. Paraphrase the sentence beginning in line 10.

2. What happened in the speaker's dream?

3. How is the sun "carnal" (line 18)?

4. For what in his dream did the speaker ask "forgiveness" (line 21)?

5. Why does the speaker "beg death's pardon" (line 24)?

To an American Poet Just Dead

In the *Boston Sunday Herald* just three lines
Of no-point[1] type for you who used to sing
The praises of imaginary wines,
And died, or so I'm told, of the real thing.

5   Also gone, but a lot less forgotten,
Are an eminent cut-rate druggist, a lover of Giving,
A lender, and various brokers: gone from this rotten
Taxable world to a higher standard of living.

It is out in the comfy suburbs I read you are dead,
10   And the soupy summer is settling, full of the yawns
Of Sunday fathers loitering late in bed,
And the ssshh of sprays on all the little lawns.

Will the sprays weep wide for you their chaplet[2] tears?
For you will the deep-freeze units melt and mourn?
15   For you will Studebakers[3] shred their gears
And sound from each garage a muted horn?

They won't. In summer sunk and stupefied
The suburbs deepen in their sleep of death.
And though they sleep the sounder since you died.
20   It's just as well that now you save your breath.

---

[1] **point:** a unit of type size about 1/72 of an inch. The word is normally preceded by a number, such as *ten-point type.*
[2] **chaplet:** a string of beads.
[3] **Studebaker:** an American automobile no longer manufactured.

COMMENTARY AND QUESTIONS

1. Considering footnote one, what does the speaker mean by "no-point" type (line 2)?

2. Is stanza 2 necessary to the poem's final meaning? Why or why not?

3. How do stanzas 3 and 4 characterize the suburbs?

4. Explain the suburbs' "sleep of death." Why do the suburbs "sleep the sounder" (line 19) since the poet's death?

5. Discuss the meaning of the last line in particular and of the poem in general. From your experience, do middle-class Americans and American poets have a relationship like the one described in the poem? Discuss the place of poetry in American society.

REVIEW

1. Using examples from at least two poems, show how Wilbur makes physical objects suggest the spiritual.

2. Describe and discuss Wilbur's use of form. How well does he use his meters, rhyme schemes, stanzas, and line breaks to enhance his poem's meanings? Use specific examples.

3. Tell which of these poems you like the best and why, or tell which you like the least and why.

JOHN HAINES
1924–

Unlike most of the poets we have studied who make the natural world a subject of their poetry, John Haines seems to write *from* nature rather than about it. In an essay called "The Writer as Alaskan: Beginnings and Reflections" published in *Cutbank* magazine (1976), Haines tells us that his poetry grew from his interaction with a certain place, Richardson Hill, Alaska, where he lived, "for the better part of twenty-two years." From this homestead, where Haines learned to survive on the arctic tundra by gardening, foraging, hunting, and trapping, he could walk all the way to the Arctic Ocean "and never cross a road nor encounter a village." Haines goes on to say, "As a poet I was born. . . . Such a purity of feeling, of joy and of being in the right place, I have not felt since." For Haines, Richardson Hill was a real location—a "dream place," as he called it—that somehow mirrored Haines's interior self. He goes on to explain that in the solitude of the Alaskan wilderness he "learned to listen to [his] own voice" and thus to be able to write poems that were not imitations of other poets' work, but truly his own.

Born in Norfolk, Virginia, Haines attended the National Art School and American University. Later he studied at the Hans Hoffman School of Fine Arts in New York. After serving in the U.S. Navy from 1943 to 1946, he homesteaded in Alaska for two years, left, and returned in 1954 to remain until 1969.

Since 1969, Haines has lived in California, Montana, and Alaska, where he has taught and continued writing poems, fiction, and essays. Among other honors, he has received the Jenny Tane Award for poetry, two Guggenheim fellowships, a National Endowment for the Arts grant, and recently the Western States Book Award.

Poem of the Forgotten

I came to this place,
a young man green and lonely.

Well quit of the world,
I framed a house of moss and timber,
5 called it a home,
and sat in the warm evenings
singing to myself as a man sings
when he knows there is
no one to hear.

10 I made my bed under the shadow
of leaves, and awoke
in the first snow of autumn,
filled with silence.

COMMENTARY AND QUESTIONS

1. How do the physical objects in this poem contribute to the poem's impact?

2. Describe the poem's tone. How does Haines achieve that tone?

3. How, if at all, does the title contribute to the poem's meaning?

4. Note the relationship between sentences and stanzas, and comment on how this relationship affects the poem.

5. Recall that a poem may or may not have a theme, but that all poems convey meaning—their impact or effect on the reader. For instance, the poems included in this text by Richard Wilbur have themes, whereas imagistic poems like Williams's "The Red Wheelbarrow" and Pound's "In a Station of the Metro" convey meaning without having definite themes. Does "Poem of the Forgotten" have a theme, a central point or idea? If so, explain it. If not, explain the poem's meaning.

If the Owl Calls Again

at dusk
from the island in the river,
and it's not too cold,

I'll wait for the moon
5 to rise,
then take wing and glide
to meet him.

We will not speak,
but hooded against the frost
10 soar above
the alder[1] flats, searching
with tawny eyes.

---

[1] **alder:** a tree or shrub that grows in cool, moist climates.

And then we'll sit
in the shadowy spruce and
15   pick the bones
of careless mice,

while the long moon drifts
toward Asia
and the river mutters
20   in its icy bed.

And when morning climbs
the limbs
we'll part without a sound,

fulfilled, floating
25   homeward as
the cold world awakens.

COMMENTARY AND QUESTIONS

1. Describe the poem's plot. Explain in what sense the action takes place.

2. What images are particularly effective and why?

3. What do we learn about the speaker? Describe his relationship with nature.

4. In what way does the poem's tone contribute to meaning?

5. Explain and comment on the grammatical relationship between the title and the poem's first sentence. Then discuss the relationship between sentences and stanzas. To what extent is this free verse poem structured?

6. Compare this poem to Bryant's "To a Waterfowl," paying particular attention the poet's relationship to nature.

And When the Green Man Comes

The man is clothed
in birchbark,
small birds cling to his limbs
and one builds
5   a nest in his ear.

The clamor of bedlam
infests his hair, a wind
blowing in his head
shakes down
10   a thought that turns
to moss and lichen[1]
at his feet.

[1] **lichen:** a scaly, or branching fungus that grows on tree trunks and rocks.

His eyes are blind
with April,
15 his breath distilled
of butterflies
and bees, and in his beard
the maggot sings.

He comes again
20 with litter of chips[2]
and empty cans,
his shoes full of mud and dung;

an army of shedding dogs
attends him,
25 the valley shudders where
he stands,
            redolent of roses,
exalted in
the streaming rain.

[2] **litter of chips:** The snow's spring melt exposes wood chips left on the ground from months cutting firewood.

COMMENTARY AND QUESTIONS

1. What does this poem describe?
2. Is the title effective? What if it were simply "Spring"?
3. List the concrete nouns and verbs in this poem, and discuss their effect.
4. Discuss the source of this poem's power.

REVIEW

1. How does Haines structure these three free verse poems?
2. Describe and discuss Haines's poetic voice.
3. How do these poems present nature?
4. Does Haines's training as an artist appear to influence his poetry?
5. Note that with the exception of "the green man," there are no characters in these poems besides the speaker. Do you think the absence or presence of characters is significant in understanding a poem or a poet? Discuss.
6. What is your opinion of these poems by John Haines?

GALWAY KINNELL
1927–

By just glancing at the Kinnell poems collected in this book, one can see that the poet writes long, Whitmanesque lines as well as shorter, more measured lines. Unlike Richard Wilbur—who presents his poems as complete, polished, and often contained within an established poetic form—Galway Kinnell seems to pour forth his longer poems in powerful rushes of feeling. This strong emotion, usually colored by a sense of human mortality, is more evident in "Fergus Falling" than in the other poems collected here and characterizes most of Kinnell's well-known, longer poems, such as "The Avenue Bearing the Initial of Christ into the New World," "Freedom, New Hampshire," and "The Bear." Through his mastery of free verse and his ability to evoke powerful feeling, Kinnell has become a highly respected American poet. "For me," says Kinnell, "poetry is an attempt to understand something that you have not understood before. Whatever discovery you come to in writing about it—whether wonderful or horrible—the thrill of poetry is to say it with intensity and absolute truthfulness" (letter to H. R., 1991).

Born in Providence, Rhode Island, he attended Wilbraham Academy (now Wilbraham-Munson), in Wilbraham, Massachusetts, and Princeton University. In the 1960s he participated in poetry readings protesting the Vietnam War. An effective reader who said once that a poet's words must sound as if they have come from God, Kinnell has fascinated, charmed, informed, and powerfully moved thousands of listeners throughout the country. As a poet-in-residence at the University of California at Irvine, Columbia, Sarah Lawrence, Brandeis, Princeton, and other colleges and universities, he has also influenced a multitude of young poets.

Among many other honors, Kinnell has won the American Book Award and the Pulitzer Prize for poetry. He currently lives in New York City.

Crying

Crying only a little bit
is no use. You must cry
until your pillow is soaked!
Then you can get up and laugh.
5   Then you can jump in the shower
and splash-splash-splash!
Then you can throw open your window
and, "Ha ha! ha ha!"
And if people say, "Hey,
10   what's going on up there?"
"Ha ha!" sing back, "Happiness
was hiding in the last tear!
I wept it! Ha ha!"

COMMENTARY AND QUESTIONS

1. Describe the poem's voice and discuss how Kinnell achieves this voice.

2. What, if anything, appeals to you about this poem?

3. Explain how Kinnell uses repetition of sounds and rhythms to intensify the poem.

Duck-Chasing

I spied a very small brown duck
Riding the swells. "Little duck!"
I cried. It paddled away,
I paddled after it. When it dived,
5   Down I dived too: too smokey was the sea,
We were lost. It surfaced
In the west, I swam west
And when it dived I dived,
And we were lost and lost and lost
10   In the slant smoke of the sea.
When I came floating up on it
From the side, like a deadman,
And yelled suddenly, it took off,
It skimmed the swells as it ascended,
15   Brown wings burning and flashing
In the sun as the sea it rose over
Burned and flashed underneath it.
I did not see the little duck again.
Duck-chasing is a game like any game.
20   When it is over it is all over.

COMMENTARY AND QUESTIONS

1. Describe the poem's action.

2. What does the poem seem to be about beyond duck-chasing? What specific parts of the poem lead the reader to look beyond the literal action? Of what mythological creature do lines 14–17 remind you? How, if at all, does this creature's behavior inform (expand or illuminate) the poem's meaning?

3. Discuss how Kinnell uses the length of sentences to help achieve a vital voice. Describe the poem's voice.

4. Count the syllables in each line and mark the accented syllables. Discuss the effect of any patterns you may detect.

5. Note and discuss the effect of repeated sounds.

6. If this poem were written out as a paragraph, how would its meaning change? Be specific in your discussion.

Fergus Falling

He climbed to the top
of one of those million white pines
set out across the emptying pastures
of the fifties—some program to enrich the rich
5   and rebuke the forefathers
who cleared it all once with ox and axe—
climbed to the top, probably to get out
of the shadow
not of those forefathers but of this father,
10   and saw for the first time,
down in its valley, Bruce Pond, giving off
its little steam in the afternoon,

pond where Clarence Akley came on Sunday mornings to cut down the
    cedars around the shore, I'd sometimes hear the slow spondees[1] of
    his work, he's gone,
where Milton Norway came up behind me while I was fishing and
    stood awhile before I knew he was there, he's the one who put the
    cedar shingles on the house, some have curled or split, a few have
    blown off, he's gone,
15   where Gus Newland logged in the cold snap of '58, the only man
    willing to go into those woods that never got warmer than ten
    below, he's gone,
pond where two wards of the state wandered on Halloween, the
    National Guard searched for them in November, in vain, the next
    fall a hunter found their skeletons huddled together, in vain,
    they're gone,
pond where an old fisherman in a rowboat sits, drowning hooked
    worms, when he goes he's replaced and is never gone,

---

[1] **spondee:** a metrical foot containing two stresses, as in *stáircáse.*

and when Fergus
saw the pond for the first time
20   in the clear evening, saw its oldness down there
in its old place in the valley, he became heavier suddenly
in his bones
the way fledglings do just before they fly,
and the soft pine cracked . . .

25   I would not have heard his cry
if my electric saw had been working,
its carbide teeth speeding through the bland spruce of our time, or
        burning
black arcs into some scavenged hemlock plank,
like dark circles under eyes
30   when the brain thinks too close to the skin,
but I was sawing by hand and I heard that cry
as though he were attacked; we ran out,
when we bent over him he said, "Galway, Inés, I saw a pond!"
His face went gray, his eyes fluttered closed a frightening moment . . .

35   Yes—a pond
that lets off its mist
on clear afternoons of August, in that valley
to which many have come, for their reasons,
from which many have gone, a few for their reasons, most not,
40   where even now an old fisherman only the pinetops can see
sits in the dry gray wood of his rowboat, waiting for pickerel.

COMMENTARY AND QUESTIONS

1. Describe the poem's action.

2. What does stanza 2 add to the poem? How does it contribute to the impact of the last stanza?

3. In what sense is this poem about human mortality?

4. Reread the last stanza and replace the last word, "pickerel" with "death." Does "death" fit? If so, why do you think Kinnell used "pickerel"? Which is better and why?

5. Look at the poem's physical shape. Note the absence of periods in the poem's interior, and note other poetic devices. Now discuss how the poem's form influences its meaning.

REVIEW

1. Describe and discuss the effectiveness of one poetic technique used by Kinnell in these poems.

2. Which poem do you like the most and why?

3. Compare "Duck-Chasing" to "Fergus Falling."

JAMES WRIGHT
1927–1980

Born in Martin's Ferry, Ohio, the son of a glass factory worker, Wright wrote of the hard lives of blue-collar workers as well as of the powerful beauty of the natural world. He earned his bachelor's degree from Kenyon College, where he studied with John Crowe Ransom, and his doctorate from the University of Washington, where he studied with Theodore Roethke.

Wright has said that as a young poet he was strongly attracted to the styles of Edwin Arlington Robinson and Robert Frost. We can also see in the formal rhyme and meter of his early poems that Wright was influenced by John Crowe Ransom. Like Lowell, who you will recall was also a student of John Crowe Ransom's, Wright later moved away from formal verse to a more free and open style.

Learning from Robert Bly, his friend and fellow poet, Wright used the image as his primary tool to convey strong emotion. Recall Walt Whitman's use of imagery in his short poem "A Farm Picture" and then his lists of images in "Song of Myself." Think also of the imagist poems by Pound, H. D., Williams, and others. Like Pound, Wright read and was influenced by Chinese poetry, particularly its spareness and simple but powerful imagery. Looking backward from Wright to Whitman, one could argue that the image has become the primary tool in American poetry.

In 1957 Wright won the Yale Younger Poets Award for his first book and the Pulitzer Prize for poetry in 1972. At the time of his death he was teaching at Hunter College in New York City.

In Ohio

White mares lashed to the sulky carriages[1]
Trot softly
Around the dismantled fairgrounds
Near Buckeye Lake.[2]

[1] **sulky carriages:** light, two-wheeled vehicles drawn by one horse, still used in trotting races.
[2] **Buckeye Lake:** about fifteen miles east of Columbus, Ohio.

243

5   The sandstone blocks of a wellspring
     Cool dark green moss.

     The sun floats down, a small golden lemon dissolves
     In the water.
     I dream, as I lean over the edge, of a crawdad's mouth.[3]

10   The cellars of haunted houses are like ancient cities,
     Fallen behind a big heap of apples.

     A widow on a front porch puckers her lips
     And whispers.

[3] **crawdad's mouth:** the mouth of a crayfish, a freshwater crustacean.

COMMENTARY AND QUESTIONS

1. "In Ohio" characterizes the poet's later style, for which he has become well-known and well-respected. How is this poem organized? How, if at all, are its stanza's related?

2. Which image do you find the strongest? Why?

3. Discuss the significance of the poem's title.

Depressed by a Book of Bad Poetry, I Walk Toward an Unused Pasture and Invite the Insects to Join Me

     Relieved, I let the book fall behind a stone.
     I climb a slight rise of grass.
     I do not want to disturb the ants
     Who are walking single file up the fence post,
5   Carrying small white petals,
     Casting shadows so frail that I can see through them.
     I close my eyes for a moment, and listen.
     The old grasshoppers
     Are tired, they leap heavily now,
10   Their thighs are burdened.
     I want to hear them, they have clear sounds to make.
     Then lovely, far off, a dark cricket begins
     In the maple trees.

COMMENTARY AND QUESTIONS

1. Explain how Wright relates poetry to insects and thus to nature.

2. Compare this poem to another modern poem that has praised the inspirational power of nature.

3. How does line 11 make the reader recall the title?

4. Some would say that long, explanatory titles do some of the poem's work and thus violate the assumption that titles should simply name poems, not be part of the poem itself. What is your opinion? What other poems have we read where the titles have seemed to merge with the poem?

5. Compare the organization of this poem to "In Ohio." Which poem do you like better? Why?

Lying in a Hammock at William Duffy's Farm in Pine Island, Minnesota

Over my head, I see the bronze butterfly,
Asleep on the black trunk,
Blowing like a leaf in green shadow.
Down the ravine behind the empty house,
5   The cowbells follow one another
Into the distances of the afternoon.
To my right,
In a field of sunlight between two pines,
The droppings of last year's horses
10   Blaze up into golden stones.
I lean back, as the evening darkens and comes on.
A chicken hawk floats over, looking for home.
I have wasted my life.

COMMENTARY AND QUESTIONS

1. This is another of Wright's poems that uses strong images to carry emotion. What images are particularly surprising and how do they affect the poem?

2. How do lines 11–12 begin to conclude the poem?

3. Discuss the last line. How is its language different from the previous twelve lines? What if the line were omitted?

Outside Fargo, North Dakota

Along the sprawled body of the derailed
   Great Northern[1] freight car,
I strike a match slowly and lift it slowly.
No wind.

---

[1] **Great Northern:** a railroad company.

5   Beyond town, three heavy white horses
      Wade all the way to their shoulders
      In a silo shadow.

      Suddenly the freight car lurches.
      The door slams back, a man with a flashlight
10   Calls me good evening.
      I nod as I write good evening, lonely
      And sick for home.

COMMENTARY AND QUESTIONS

1. Discuss the following rewrite of stanza 2:

> Outside of the town, three heavy horses
> Walk up to their shoulders
> Into the shadow of a silo.

Be specific in your explanation of how certain new words and certain original words affect the poem.

2. Read through the poem marking repeated sounds. Then comment on the effect of some of these repetitions.

3. List the poem's verbs. What do they suggest about the poem?

4. Emily Dickinson's poems have often been praised for their compression—their spare, almost immaculate quality, where no word seems unnecessary or out of place. On the other hand, most of Walt Whitman's longer poems seem to take life from the poet's long exhalations of song. In this poem we can see that Wright compresses in the phrase "Beyond town" (line 5), whereas the rewritten phrase "Outside of the town" uses extra words that seem to dilute. Can we say that from this and other examples that this is a compressed poem in the tradition of Dickinson? Or do you detect the influence of Whitman? Something in between, or something altogether different? Discuss.

5. Compare the last two lines of this poem to the last line of "Lying in a Hammock. . . ." To what extent are the endings effective?

REVIEW

1. Describe the two styles exhibited in these five poems, and compare the style of the last four poems to that of another modern poet.

2. Give specific examples of earlier poets and poems that you think may have influenced Wright.

3. Do you like Wright's poetry? Why or why not?

4. Write a poem in the style of James Wright.

5. Identify any lines or passages that you think reflect the influence of Chinese poetry. You may first want to review the Chinese influence in Ezra Pound's poetry.

ROBERT
BLY
1926–

In a letter to poet Donald Hall, Robert Bly defines poetry's purpose:

> That the poems are useful to other people, that they are bread, that they can be
> eaten, and strengthen strangers, that is precisely our goal, our reward, and our
> vocation. (Donald Hall, *The Weather for Poetry,* 1982)

Toward that purpose, Bly uses common language and straightforward syntax to
present images that he allows to speak for themselves. The power of his poems is
rarely in their exotic subject matter, for many of Bly's best poems depict moments in
everyday life. Instead, in their understated simplicity combined with their surprising,
illuminating metaphors, they suggest that these everyday moments, if seen clearly,
can connect us to a larger existence—to what Emerson called that Unity, that
Oneness.

Orginally from Madison, Minnesota, Robert Bly served in the U.S. Navy during
World War II. After the war he attended St. Olaf's College in Minnesota, and then
transferred to Harvard, graduating in 1950. He studied in Norway on a Fulbright
Fellowship, later lived in New York, and finally moved with his family to a farm in
Minnesota. Bly's return to rural Minnesota, like novelist William Faulkner's return to
Mississippi, reflects Bly's belief that the place of his childhood would be the best
nourishment for his art.

Despite his attachment to rural life, Bly has remained thoroughly in touch with
the world. A respected translator of European and third-world poets; an activist
against the Veitnam War; the editor of *The Sixties,* an important literary magazine; a
compelling reader and speaker; and an open, generous-spirited person—Bly may
well be the most influential American poet of his generation.

247

Watering the Horse

How strange to think of giving up all ambition!
Suddenly I see with such clear eyes
The white flake of snow
That has just fallen on the horse's mane!

COMMENTARY AND QUESTIONS

1. How does "giving up all ambition" relate to the last three lines?

2. Do you sense in this poem an Oriental influence? Discuss.

3. Compare this poem to Ezra Pound's "In a Station of the Metro" and Williams's "The Red Wheelbarrow."

Poem in Three Parts

I

Oh, on an early morning I think I shall live forever!
I am wrapped in my joyful flesh,
As the grass is wrapped in its clouds of green.

II

Rising from a bed, where I dreamt
5   Of long rides past castles, and hot coals,
The sun lies happily on my knees;
I have suffered and survived the night
Bathed in dark water, like any blade of grass.

III

The strong leaves of the box elder tree,
10   Plunging in the wind, call us to disappear
Into the wilds of the universe,
Where we shall sit at the foot of a plant,
And live forever, like the dust.

COMMENTARY AND QUESTIONS

1. Explain the simile in lines 2 and 3.

2. What is the figure of speech in line 6, and how does it affect the meaning of part II of the poem?

3. Explain the figurative language of part III.

4. How does the poem show the connection between individual human lives and the rest of existence?

5. Do you detect echoes of Walt Whitman? If so, how do they affect the poem?

Waking from Sleep

Inside the veins there are navies setting forth,
Tiny explosions at the waterlines,
And seagulls weaving in the wind of the salty blood.

It is the morning. The country has slept the whole winter.
5 Window seats were covered with fur skins, the yard was full
Of stiff dogs, and hands that clumsily held heavy books.

Now we wake, and rise from bed, and eat breakfast!
Shouts rise from the harbor of the blood,
Mist, and masts rising, the knock of wooden tackle in the sunlight.

10 Now we sing, and do tiny dances on the kitchen floor.
Our whole body is like a harbor at dawn;
We know that our master has left us for the day.

COMMENTARY AND QUESTIONS

1. State the poem's central metaphor, and explain how it contributes to the poem's meaning.

2. Does the image of "hands that clumsily held heavy books" (line 6) make sense rationally, as does, for instance, the image of dogs stiff from the cold? How does the image of the hands make meaning in the poem?

3. Who is the "master" in the last line, and how does this line conclude the poem?

My Father at Eighty-five

His large ears
hear everything.
A hermit wakes
and sleeps in a hut
5 underneath
his gaunt cheeks.
His eyes blue,
alert, dis-
appointed and suspicious
10 complain
I do not bring him
the same sort of jokes
the nurses do. He
is a small bird
15 waiting to be fed,
mostly beak,
and eagle, or a vulture, or
the Pharoah's servant
just before death.

20 My arm on the bedrail
  rests there, relaxed,
  with new love.
  All I know of the Troubadours[1]
  I bring
25 to this bed.
  I do not want
  or need
  to be shamed
  by him
30 any longer.
  The general of shame
  has discharged
  him and left him in this
  small provincial
35 Egyptian town.
  If I do not wish
  to shame him, then
  why not
  love him?
40 His long hands,
  large, veined, capable,
  can still retain
  hold of what
  he wanted.
45 But is that
  what he desired?
  Some powerful
  river of desire
  goes on flowing
50 through him.
  He never phrased
  what he desired,
  and I am
  his son.

[1] **Troubadours:** 12th- and 13th-century poets of France and Italy, who also composed songs. Traveling minstrels. A kind of modern troubadour himself, Robert Bly travels widely, performing his poems to music.

COMMENTARY AND QUESTIONS

1. How do the images in the sentence beginning in line 13 and ending in line 19 evoke the image of an old man in a hospital bed?

2. Lines 26 to 54 allude to but do not directly state the source of some "shame." Should the poet have been more specific? Discuss.

3. What is "this / small provincial / Egyptian town?" How, if at all, is the image appropriate?

4. How does the poem distinguish between want (line 44) and desire (line 46)?

5. How does the poem's last sentence suggest how Bly may view his role as a poet?

6. Describe the poet's feeling for his father.

7. How does the shape of this poem complement its meaning? What if the lines were longer? Comment on the effectiveness of two or more line breaks.

REVIEW

1. Using two poems for your examples, discuss how Robert Bly connects the individual's existence with all existence.

2. We know that James Wright and Robert Bly admired and influenced each other's poetry. Compare a James Wright poem to a Robert Bly poem.

3. Write a poem in the style of Robert Bly.

ROBERT CREELEY
1926–

Robert Creeley said in a *New York Quarterly* interview that he rarely revises poems dramatically. When a poem is not working, he begins again. In other words, when his poems are working, words that do not contribute to the feeling he wants to communicate do not find their way to the paper. Unlike writers who revise until they have discovered the heart of their poem, Robert Creeley writes, so to speak, from his poem rather than toward it. In the tradition of Emily Dickinson, who also revised relatively little, Robert Creeley writes poems whose almost stumbling rhythms keep readers off balance yet attentive to each step the poem takes. We are also reminded in these short, well-wrought, surprising poems of Ezra Pound's attention to craft and to William Carlos William's brevity and vitality.

Robert Creeley was born in Arlington, Massachusetts. He attended Holderness School in Plymouth, New Hampshire, where in his last year he became interested in writing. He then attended Harvard and left one term before taking a degree. After living in India, Burma, New Hampshire, Cape Cod, and Majorca, he taught at Black Mountain College in North Carolina, an experimental college devoted to the arts. At Black Mountain he was influenced by the poet Charles Olson's idea that a poem must be structurally "open," not hampered by imposed forms like, for instance, the sonnet. We see the influence of Olson in Robert Creeley's famous satement about how a poem's content dictates its form: "Form is never more than an extension of content."

Leaving Black Mountain in 1956, Creeley taught in New Mexico and received a master's degree from the University of New Mexico. Since 1966 he has taught at the State University of New York at Buffalo. He is the author of twelve books of poetry, and in 1989 was named New York State Poet.

I Know a Man

As I sd to my
friend, because I am
always talking,—John, I

252

sd, which was not his
5 name, the darkness sur-
rounds us, what

can we do against
it, or else, shall we &
why not, buy a goddamn big car,

10 drive, he sd, for
christ's sake, look
out where yr going.

COMMENTARY AND QUESTIONS

1. Note the places in the poem where the grammar, diction, punctuation, or rhythm surprises you. Discuss two examples.

2. Are "sd" and "&" effective and legitimate devices? Discuss. What other poet(s) used similar devices?

3. How does the last stanza clarify and conclude the poem?

Naughty Boy

When he brings home a whale,
she laughs and says, that's not for real.

And if he won the Irish sweepstakes,
she would say, where were you last night?

5 Where are you now, for that matter? Am
I always (she says) to be looking

at you? She says,
if I thought it would get any better I

would shoot you, you
10 nut, you. Then pats her hair

into place, and waits
for Uncle Jim's deep-fired, all-fat, real gone

whale steaks.

COMMENTARY AND QUESTIONS

1. Describe the relationship between "he" and "she" in the first ten lines.

2. What do the last three lines reveal?

Like They Say

Underneath the tree on some
soft grass I sat, I

watched two happy
woodpeckers be dis-

5   turbed by my presence. And
why not, I thought to

myself, why
not.

COMMENTARY AND QUESTIONS

1. Describe the poem's voice.

2. How does the title inform (add meaning to) the poem?

3. Respond to this statement: " 'Like they Say' is funny in its flippancy and insensitivity to nature (the woodpeckers), but at heart it predicts the inevitability of man's destruction of the world. By saying "why not" to disturbing nature, the speaker arrogantly admits that of course the environment will have to be disturbed, for humanity will always prevail over nature."

The Flower

I think I grow tensions
like flowers
in a wood where
nobody goes.

5   Each wound is perfect,
encloses itself in a tiny
imperceptible blossom,
making pain.

Pain is a flower like that one,
10   like this one,
like that one,
like this one.

COMMENTARY AND QUESTIONS

1. Explain the poem's central metaphor.

2. How does the poem extend the denotative meaning of *flower*?

3. How do the last three lines affect the poem's tone and meaning?

REVIEW

1. To what extent do the poems here prove Robert Creeley's statement that the content of a poem determines its structure? Offer specific examples.

2. Discuss in some detail the relationship Creeley tries to create between his speaker and the reader?

3. Respond to this statement: "Robert Creeley does not write *about* experiences; he *writes* experiences." Could this statement be made about all poets?

4. Write a poem in Robert Creeley's style.

LAWRENCE FERLINGHETTI
1919–

One of the most widely read members of the Beat movement, Lawrence Ferlinghetti writes poems that celebrate love, art, and everyday life as well as confront political, religious, and moral issues. It is this mixture of radical, prophet, and lover of life that makes Ferlinghetti both delightful and provocative.

Born in Yonkers, New York, Ferlinghetti was raised by a relative after his father's death and his mother's mental breakdown. Later when his guardian also suffered a mental breakdown, he was taken care of by a family named Lawrence. Ferlinghetti attended the University of North Carolina, where he received his bachelor's degree. When World War II began, he joined the Navy, doing duty in France and Norway, and rising to the rank of lieutenant commander. After the war he attended Columbia University for his master's degree and the Sorbonne for a Doctorate de l'University, which he received in 1951. It was in France that Ferlinghetti began painting. Although he is much better known as a poet and a promoter of Beat poetry than as a painter, Ferlinghetti has painted since the 1940s, shown his work on the West Coast, and written art criticism. His most recent book, *When I Look at Pictures*, published in 1990, is an illustrated collection of poems he has written about famous paintings.

After returning from France, he settled in San Francisco and co-founded City Lights Books, the country's first all paperback bookstore. In 1955 Ferlinghetti began publishing his now-famous City Lights Pocket Series, which included titles by other Beat authors such a Jack Kerouac, Allen Ginsberg, and Gregory Corso. Since then Ferlinghetti has published many books of poems and one novel. *Endless Life: Selected Poems*, published in 1981, includes most of his famous work.

The Pennycandystore Beyond The El[1] . . .

The pennycandystore beyond the El
is where I first
           fell in love
                  with unreality
5   Jellybeans glowed in the semi-gloom
of that september afternoon
A cat upon the counter moved among
                 the licorice sticks
       and tootsie rolls
10   and Oh Boy Gum

Outside the leaves were falling as they died

A wind had blown away the sun

A girl ran in
Her hair was rainy
15 Her breasts were breathless in the little room

Outside the leaves were falling
        and they cried
           Too soon! too soon!

[1] **El:** an abbreviated term for the elevated subway, thus suggesting an urban scene.

COMMENTARY AND QUESTIONS

1. Describe the poem's setting. Discuss how certain images help convey the atmosphere of the setting.

2. Although the rhythms in this poem vary, there is one primary rhythm. By marking the stressed syllables, note the poem's primary meter and the impact of this meter on the poem's meaning. It may be helpful to read the poem aloud several times, stressing the accented syllables.

3. Discuss the possible meanings of the last line.

4. Describe the poem's tone.

5. To what extent is this poem realistic?

Baseball Canto[1]

Watching baseball
sitting in the sun
eating popcorn
reading Ezra Pound

[1] **Canto:** a section of a long poem. Ezra Pound, referred to in line 4, wrote a long, difficult poem called "The Cantos."

5   and wishing Juan Marichal[2]
would hit a hole right through
the Anglo-Saxon tradition
in the First Canto
and demolish the barbarian invaders

10   When the San Francisco Giants take the field
and everybody stands up to the National Anthem
with some Irish tenor's voice
piped over the loudspeakers
with all the players struck dead in their places
15   and the white umpires like Irish cops
in their black suits and little black caps
pressed over their hearts
standing straight and still
like at some funeral of a blarney[3] bartender
20   and all facing East
as if expecting some Great White Hope
or the Founding Fathers
to appear on the horizon
like 1066 or 1776 or all that

25   But Willie Mays[4] appears instead
in the bottom of the first
and a roar goes up
        as he clouts the first one into the sun
        and takes off
30   like a footrunner from Thebes
      The ball is lost in the sun
        and maidens wail after him
          but he keeps running
            through the Anglo-Saxon epic

35   And Tito Fuentes[5] comes up
      looking like a bullfighter
      in his tight pants and small pointed shoes

   And the rightfield bleachers go mad
      with chicanos & blacks & Brooklyn beerdrinkers
40   "Sweet Tito! Sock it to heem, Sweet Tito!"
And Sweet Tito puts his foot in the bucket
      and smacks one that don't come back at all

---

[2] **Juan Marichal:** pitcher for the San Francisco Giants for fourteen years. He logged 243 wins and 142 losses.

[3] **Blarney:** an Irish expression for flattering talk.

[4] **Willie Mays:** One of baseball's great players, he played first with the New York Giants from 1951 to 1957, then with the San Francisco Giants from 1958 to 1972. Twice the National League's Most Valuable Player, Mays earned a career batting average of .302.

[5] **Tito Fuentes:** played with the San Francisco Giants from 1965 to 1974. His career batting average was .268.

and flees around the bases
like he's escaping from the United Fruit Company[6]
45   as the gringo dollar beats out the Pound
and Sweet Tito beats it out
like he's beating out usury
not to mention fascism and anti-semitism
And Juan Marichal comes up
50   and the chicano bleachers go loco again
as Juan belts the first fast ball
out of sight
and rounds first and keeps going
and rounds second and rounds third
55   and keeps going
and hits pay-dirt
to the roars of the grungy populace
As some nut presses the backstage panic bottom
for the tape-recorded National Anthem again
60   to save the situation

but it don't stop nobody this time
in their revolution round the loaded white bases
in this last of the great Anglo-Saxon epics
in the *Territorio Libre*[7] of baseball

[6] **United Fruit Company:** an allusion to conflicts between fruit growers and migrant laborers,
     many of whom were Hispanics.
[7] *Territorio Libre:* Spanish for the free land.

COMMENTARY AND QUESTIONS

1. Describe this poem's tone, quoting lines and phrases that seem particularly illustrative of this tone.

2. Who were the Angles and the Saxons, and what is the Anglo-Saxon tradition?

3. Discuss the significance of specific allusions to race and national origin.

4. How do the last four lines conclude the poem?

5. Discuss the poem's form—particularly line breaks, stanzas, and indentations. How does the poem's form affect its meaning?

REVIEW

1. Using specific examples, discuss Ferlinghetti's style. What earlier American poems appear to have influenced him. Identify these influences as specifically as possible.

2. Do you like Ferlinghetti's poems? Discuss.

3. Write a poem in the style of Ferlinghetti.

ALLEN GINSBERG
1926–

In his introduction to "Howl," Ginsberg's most famous poem, William Carlos Williams tells us that he knew Allen Ginsberg as a boy "always on the point of going away." The young poet seemed much disturbed by both his personal life and American life, thus Williams thought that Ginsberg would "never . . . grow up and write a book of poems. His ability to survive, travel, and go on writing astonishes me. That he has gone on developing and perfecting his art is no less amazing" (from the introduction to *Howl and Other Poems*). To a large measure Ginsberg's poetry projects the vitality of a human spirit that has endured what Ginsberg sees as a misguided, corrupt world.

Growing up in Newark, New Jersey—his father a teacher and poet and his mother a political activist who also suffered from mental illness—Ginsberg began writing formal verse as a boy. Dickinson and Poe were early influences, as were English poets Wordsworth and Shelley. After graduating from Columbia University, he went to San Francisco, where he became associated with novelists Jack Kerouac and William Burroughs, poets Lawrence Ferlinghetti and Gregory Corso, and other members of the Beat movement. Ferlinghetti published *Howl and Other Poems* as well as other Ginsberg books through his company, City Lights Books.

During the 1960s Ginsberg became a spokesman for the counterculture, gay rights, and antiwar movements. Traveling around the country to speak on political issues and to give powerful readings of his passionate, often obscene poems, he became a national figure. Today he is considered the best poet of the Beat movement.

A Supermarket in California

What thoughts I have of you tonight, Walt Whitman, for I walked
down the sidestreets under the trees with a headache self-conscious
looking at the full moon.

In my hungry fatigue, and shopping for images, I went into the neon fruit supermarket, dreaming of your enumerations!

What peaches and what penumbras! Whole families shopping at night! Aisles full of husbands! Wives in the avocados, babies in the tomatoes! and you, Garcia Lorca,[1] what were you doing down by the watermelons?

I saw you, Walt Whitman, childless, lonely old grubber, poking among the meats in the refrigerator and eyeing the grocery boys.

5   I heard you asking questions of each: Who killed the pork chops? What price bananas? Are you my Angel?

I wandered in and out of the brilliant stacks of cans following you, and followed in my imagination by the store detective.

We strode down the open corridors together in our solitary fancy tasting artichokes, possessing every frozen delicacy, and never passing the cashier.

Where are we going, Walt Whitman? The doors close in an hour. Which way does your beard point tonight?

(I touch your book and dream of our odyssey in the supermarket and feel absurd.)

10   Will we walk all night through solitary streets? The trees add shade to shade, lights out in the houses, we'll both be lonely.

Will we stroll dreaming of the lost America of love past blue automobiles in driveways, home to our silent cottage?

Ah, dear father, graybeard, lonely old courage-teacher, what America did you have when Charon[2] quit poling his ferry and you got out on a smoking bank and stood watching the boat disappear on the black waters of Lethe?

[1] **Garcia Lorca:** Federico Garcia Lorca (1898–1936), a Spanish poet and playwright who wrote *Ode to Walt Whitman.*
[2] **Charon:** In Greek mythology Charon ferried the dead across the river Lethe to Hades.

COMMENTARY AND QUESTIONS

1. In what ways does this poem reflect Whitman's influence on Ginsberg? How was Whitman a "courage-teacher"?

2. Compare this poem to any of Ferlinghetti's poems. In what sense do the two poems qualify as Beat poems? Consider form, tone, humor, and theme.

3. Like Whitman's, Ginsberg's poetry has been criticized as too loosely structured. Do you agree? Discuss.

REVIEW

Write a poem in the style of "A Supermarket in California."

GARY SNYDER
1930–

Born in San Francisco, Gary Snyder grew up on small farms in Washington and Oregon. At Reed College he majored in literature and anthropology. Balancing his academic life with a more embracive view of education, Snyder has worked as a seaman, a logger, a fire look-out, and a forest service trail worker. From 1953 to 1956 he studied Oriental languages at Berkeley, and during those years he became associated with the Beat movement. His interest in Oriental culture led him to Japan, where he has lived and studied Zen Buddhism.

The influence of the Western landscape and of Oriental philosophy and literature characterizes Snyder's poetry, and the latter influence connects his work with other American poets such as Ralph Waldo Emerson, Ezra Pound, Robert Bly, and James Wright. In an essay published in *The Sixties,* a literary magazine edited by Robert Bly, James Wright describes Snyder's poems as "powerfully located—sown, rooted—in the landscape of the far Western states." Wright goes on to say that Gary Snyder's poems resemble Chinese poems in that "both are formed out of images whose sensory force strikes the mind directly, not as an abstract substitute for an experience, but as an original experience in itself" (from "The Work of Gary Snyder," *The Sixties,* Spring 1962). This immediacy creates a freshness of vision that distinguishes Snyder's poetry.

After returning to the United States in 1964, Snyder taught at the University of California at Berkeley. Now, after another stay in Japan, he lives in the Sierra Nevada Mountains, teaches at the University of California at Davis, and is actively involved in environmental issues. The author of eleven books of poems and two books of essays, Gary Snyder won the Pulitzer Prize in 1974.

Mid-August at Sourdough Mountain[1] Lookout

Down valley a smoke haze
Three days heat, after five days rain
Pitch glows on the fir-cones
Across rocks and meadows
5   Swarms of new flies.

I cannot remember things I once read
A few friends, but they are in cities.
Drinking cold snow-water from a tin cup
Looking down for miles
10   Through high still air.

[1] **Sourdough Mountain:** This and the other poems collected here are set in the Pacific Northwest.

COMMENTARY AND QUESTIONS

1. List the most noticeable words in the poem.

2. What is the primary poetic device used in this poem, and how does Snyder employ it?

3. Describe the poem's mood and discuss how Snyder creates that mood.

Above Pate Valley

We finished clearing the last
Section of trail by noon,
High on the ridge-side
Two thousand feet above the creek
5   Reached the pass, went on
Beyond the white pine groves,
Granite shoulders, to a small
Green meadow watered by the snow,
Edged with Aspen—sun
10   Straight high and blazing
But the air was cool.
Ate a cold fried trout in the
Trembling shadows. I spied
A glitter, and found a flake
15   Black volcanic glass—obsidian—
By a flower. Hands and knees

Pushing the Bear grass, thousands
of arrowhead leavings over a
Hundred yards. Not one good
20 Head, just razor flakes
On a hill snowed all but summer,
A land of fat summer deer,
They came to camp. On their
Own trails. I followed my own
25 Trail here. Picked up the cold-drill,
Pick, singlejack,[1] and sack
Of dynamite.
Ten thousand years.

[1] **cold-drill, pick, singlejack:** tools used to drill holes in rock to insert dynamite.

COMMENTARY AND QUESTIONS

1. How does the last line affect the poem's meaning?

2. Paraphrase the poem in clear prose, and then comment on how the list of tools (lines 25 and 26) and the dynamite contribute to the poem's economy.

Water

Pressure of sun on the rockslide
Whirled me in a dizzy hop-and-step descent,
Pool of pebbles buzzed in a Juniper shadow,
Tiny tongue of a this-year rattlesnake flicked,
5 I leaped, laughing for little boulder-color coil—
Pounded by heat raced down the slabs to the creek
Deep tumbling under arching walls and stuck
Whole head and shoulders in the water:
Stretched full on cobble—ears roaring
10 Eyes open aching from the cold and faced a trout.

COMMENTARY AND QUESTIONS

1. Compare the last line of this poem to the last line of "Above Pate Valley."

2. Comment on how well the line-by-line development of this poem fits the poem's content.

3. Have you ever had an experience similar to this? If so, explain.

Hay for the Horses

He h...
From ...en half the night
Through... San Joaquin
Dangerou...a, up the
5 And pulled...
With his big ...n roads,
With winch an... a.m.
We stacked the ...f hay behind the barn.
To splintery redw... hooks
10 High in the dark, fl...
Whirling through sh...
Itch of haydust in the ...
At lunchtime under Bla...
Out in the hot corral,
15 —The old mare nosing lun...ght,
Grasshoppers crackling in t...hoes.
"I'm sixty-eight" he said,
"I first bucked hay when I was
I thought, that day I started,
20 I sure would hate to do this all n...
And dammit, that's just what
I've gone and done."

COMMENTARY AND QUESTIONS

1. Judging from its context, what do you t...

2. How do the structures of the first two sent...
person hard at work?

3. Is this a sentimental poem—drawing, in...
sympathy for the stereotypic hardworking old

...ion of a

...ral

All through the rains

That mare stood in the field—
A big pine tree and a shed,
But she stayed in the open
Ass to the wind, splash wet.
5 I tried to catch her April
For a bareback ride,
She kicked and bolted
Later grazing fresh shoots
In the shade of the down
10 Eucalyptus on the hill.

266

COMMENTARY AND QUESTIONS

1. Note the poem's strongest images.
2. Comment on how, if at all, the poem's shape (number ... of lines) fits its content.
3. Respond to this statement: " 'All Through th... brief prose description posing as a poem."

August on Sourd... a Visit
from Dick Brew...

...sco

You hitched a thou... side   a mil... eaks.

Hiked up the ... e room—
The little cab... walled in ... ht;
...snowfields, ...ain rain.

5   Meadow... ur sleeping bags
     We la... talki...
     w... in the guy-cables ... oss the shale—
10   Next morning I went w... nd
     Loaned you my po... the clouds
     You down the sn...
     ...rk;

     Waving a last ...r, west.
15   To go on hit...

     Me back t...

"Separation on the River Kiang." Both are ...ems of leave-taking. Which poem do you

COMM... formal, possess rhythm, the poet Robert Hass
... poem for its beautifully arranged groupings of
1. ... poem, do you sense that one group of words
... Mark the stressed syllables and comment on

REVIEW

1. How does the inclusion of actual place names affect these poems?
2. Describe Gary Snyder's style. Does it remind you at all of Ferlinghetti's, Ginsberg's, Bly's, or Wright's style? Discuss.
3. Write a poem in the style of Gary Snyder.

DONALD HALL
1928–

Donald Hall has written that most Americans live in a "panic-present of continual speed," traveling here and there, always wanting to be where they are not. Much of his recent poetry is an antidote to what he sees as our frantic daily lives, for it looks backward, anchoring the present to the past.

Born in Hamden, Connecticut, Don Hall began writing poetry when he was twelve. During the summers he visited his grandparents' farm in Danbury, New Hampshire, where he acquired an enduring love of nature and rural life. After attending Phillips Exeter Academy in Exeter, New Hampshire, he took his undergraduate degree in 1951 from Harvard College, where he knew Robert Bly and Adrienne Rich, who was a student in the same class at Radcliffe. Later Hall studied at Oxford University and Stanford University.

Like other poets of his generation, Donald Hall began by writing formal poetry, publishing his first book, *Exiles and Marriages*, in 1956. While he was teaching English in the 1960s at the University of Michigan, his work became less formal and more surreal, relying on incongruously juxtaposed images to express unconscious feelings.

In 1976 Hall left the University of Michigan to move to his grandparents' New Hampshire farmhouse, which he had recently inherited. Here his poetry began to explore the past, using simple language, a quiet voice, and clear, powerful images. Although Donald Hall is well-known for his prose works about everything from baseball to country life to the work and lives of poets, he is best known as a poet.

Old Roses

White roses, tiny and old, hover among thorns
by the barn door.
              For a hundred years
under the June elm, under the gaze
of seven generations,

268

they floated briefly,
5 like this, in the moment of roses,
                               by the fields
stout with corn, or with clover and timothy
making sweet hay,
                      grown over, now,
with milkweed, sumac, paintbrush. . . .
                                    Old
roses survive
10 winter drifts, the melt in April, August
parch,
         and men and women
who sniffed roses in spring and called them pretty
as we call them now,
                      strolling beside the barn
on a day that perishes. . . .

COMMENTARY AND QUESTIONS

1. Written not long after Donald Hall moved to his grandparents' farmhouse in New Hampshire, this poem reflects this return to a childhood place. What is the poem's theme and what specific words and phrases help establish this theme?

2. List the physical objects in the poem, know what each looks like, and then discuss how certain objects contribute to the poem's meaning.

3. Discuss how Hall's placement of certain words within lines helps convey meaning.

Names of Horses

All winter your brute shoulders strained against collars, padding
and steerhide over the ash hames,[1] to haul
sledges of cordwood for drying through spring and summer,
for the Glenwood stove next winter, and for the simmering range.

5 In April you pulled cartloads of manure to spread on the fields,
dark manure of Holsteins, and knobs of your own clustered with oats.
All summer you mowed the grass in meadow and hayfield, the mowing
         machine
clacketing beside you, while the sun walked high in the morning;

and after noon's heat, you pulled a clawed rake through the same acres,
10 gathering stacks, and dragged the wagon from stack to stack,
and the built hayrack back, uphill to the chaffy barn,
three loads of hay a day from standing grass in the morning.

---

[1] **hames:** the curved wooden or metal pieces that fit around the neck of a draft horse.

Sundays you trotted the two miles to church with the light load
of a leather quartertop buggy, and grazed in the sound of hymns.
15 Generation on generation, your neck rubbed the windowsill
of the stall, smoothing the wood as the sea smooths glass.

When you were old and lame, when your shoulders hurt bending to
     graze,
one October the man, who fed you and kept you, and harnessed you
     every morning,
led you through corn stubble to sandy ground above Eagle Pond,
20 and dug a hole beside you where you stood shuddering in your skin,

and lay the shotgun's muzzle in the boneless hollow behind your ear,
and fired the slug into your brain, and felled you into your grave,
shoveling sand to cover you, setting goldenrod upright above you,
where by next summer a dent in the ground made your monument.

25 For a hundred and fifty years, in the pasture of dead horses,
roots of pine trees pushed through the pale curves of your ribs,
yellow blossoms flourished above you in autumn, and in winter
frost heaved your bones in the ground—old toilers, soil makers:

O Roger, Mackerel, Riley, Ned, Nellie, Chester, Lady Ghost.

COMMENTARY AND QUESTIONS

1. Describe the poem's tone.

2. Note the poem's grammar and its relationship to each of the poem's lines and
sections. How does the poem's grammar complement the poem's meaning?

3. What does the poet achieve by naming horses in the last line?

4. Is the technique of listing names effective as a conclusion? Discuss.

5. State and discuss the poem's theme.

6. After noting alliteration, assonance, and consonance, discuss the poem's musi-
cal qualities.

The Impossible Marriage

The bride disappears. After twenty minutes of searching
we discover her in the cellar, vanishing against a pillar
in her white gown and her skin's original pallor.
When we guide her back to the altar, we find the groom
5 in his slouch hat, open shirt, and untended beard
withdrawn to the belltower with the healthy young sexton
from whose comradeship we detach him with difficulty.
O never in all the cathedrals and academies
of compulsory Democracy and free-thinking Calvinism
10 will these poets marry!—O pale, passionate
anchoret of Amherst! O reticent kosmos of Brooklyn!

COMMENTARY AND QUESTIONS

1. What two American poets are the subject of this poem? What clues help us discover the poets' identities?

2. What does the poem conclude in the last four lines? Do you agree with this conclusion? What exactly does the speaker mean by *marry*? What would this marriage mean to American poetry? Using examples from poems in this book, discuss the poem's conclusion.

3. By which of the two poets alluded to in "The Impossible Marriage" does Donald Hall appear to be more influenced? Discuss.

Scenic View

Every year the mountains
get paler and more distant—
trees less green, rock piles
disappearing—as emulsion
5 from a billion Kodaks
sucks color out.
In fifteen years
Monadnock and Kearsarge,[1]
the Green Mountains
10 and the White[2] will turn
invisible, all
tint removed
atom by atom to albums
in Medford and Greenwich,[3]
15 while over the valleys
the still intractable granite
rears with unseeable peaks
fatal to airplanes.

[1] **Monadnock and Kearsarge:** New Hampshire mountains.
[2] **Green Mountains and the White:** the primary mountain ranges of Vermont and New Hampshire, respectively.
[3] **Medford and Greenwich:** suburban towns in Massachusetts and Connecticut, respectively.

COMMENTARY AND QUESTIONS

1. According to the poem, what is happening to the scenic mountain landscape of New England and why?

2. Describe the poem's tone, quoting passages that best illustrate this tone.

3. Discuss three interesting line breaks.

4. State and discuss the poem's theme.

REVIEW

1. Reread the poetry by Robert Frost, James Wright, and John Haines; then compare their poems to these by Donald Hall.

2. Discuss Donald Hall's treatment of the past in "Old Roses" and "Names of Horses." Is it simply a way of escaping the present through nostalgia, or does it present a way of using the past to help deal with the present?

3. Cite and explain any connections you see between the poetry of Robert Lowell and Donald Hall.

4. Donald Hall is one of the few contemporary American poets who proclaims an enduring respect for the poetry of John Greenleaf Whittier. What, if anything, does their work share?

ADRIENNE RICH
1929–

Like Robert Lowell, James Wright, and others, Adrienne Rich began writing formal poems and moved to a freer, less formal style. Her first book, *The Change of World,* published when she was in college, won the Yale Younger Poets Award. Today, having become the best known poet of the woman's movement, Adrienne Rich has achieved a powerful national reputation. Her poetry not only portrays the concerns of women but, as she tells us, attempts to create for women "a common language."

Born in Baltimore, Adrienne Rich attended Radcliffe College in the class of 1951, where she knew then Harvard students and poets Donald Hall and Robert Bly. She married in her twenties, had three children, and in 1955 published her second book, *Diamond Cutters and Other Poems.* Like other important poets of her generation Rich has read her work across the country and has taught at several colleges and universities, including Swathmore College, Columbia University, City University of New York, and Brandeis University. She has won two Guggenheim fellowships and, in 1973, the National Book Award. Author of thirteen books of poems and three books of prose, Adrienne Rich "will be remembered," as critic Helen Vendler has put it, "in literary history as one of the first American women to claim a public voice" through poetry (review of *The Fact of a Doorframe,* cited in *Contemporary Literary Criticism,* vol. 36).

Holiday

Summer was another country, where the birds
Woke us at dawn among the dripping leaves
And lent to all our fêtes[1] their sweet approval.
The touch of air on flesh was lighter, keener,
5   The senses flourished like a laden tree

[1] **fêtes:** feasts or elaborate parties.

Whose every gesture finishes in a flower.
In those unwardened provinces we dined
From wicker baskets by a green canal,
Staining our lips with peach and nectarine,
10   Slapping at golden wasps. And when we kissed,
Tasting that sunlit juice, the landscape folded
Into our clasp, and not a breath recalled
The long walk back to winter, leagues away.

COMMENTARY AND QUESTIONS

1. Respond to the following statement: "Although 'Holiday' portrays the pleasures of summer love, the poem's tone is melancholy, perhaps even despairing." Quote passages that support your opinion of this statement.

2. In what sense is this a formal poem?

Moving in Winter

Their life, collapsed like unplayed cards,
is carried piecemeal through the snow:
Headboard and footboard now, the bed
where she has lain desiring him
5   where overhead his sleep will build
its canopy to smother her once more;
their table, by four elbows worn
evening after evening while the wax runs down;
mirrors grey with reflecting them,
10   bureaus coffining from the cold
things that can shuffle in a drawer,
carpets rolled up around those echoes
which, shaken out, take wing and breed
new altercations, the old silences.

COMMENTARY AND QUESTIONS

1. List the physical objects in this poem and discuss their effect on the poem. Discuss two or three objects specifically, showing how they help convey feeling.

2. Show how Adrienne Rich uses grammar (this fourteen-line poem is built out of only one sentence) working with and against line length to extend the poem's meaning. Note particularly the extra syllables in lines 6, 8, and 14.

3. Identify and discuss the poem's theme.

4. Is winter the appropriate season for this poem to be set? What if the title were simply "Moving"?

"I Am in Danger—Sir—"[1]

"Half-cracked" to Higginson, living,
afterward famous in garbled versions,
your hoard of dazzling scraps a battlefield,
now your old snood[2]

5   mothballed at Harvard
and you in your variorum monument
equivocal to the end—
who are you?

Gardening the day-lily,
10   wiping the wine-glass stems,
your thought pulsed on behind
a forehead battered paper-thin,

you, woman, masculine
in single-mindedness,
15   for whom the word was more
than a symptom—

a condition of being.
Till the air buzzing with spoiled language
sang in your ears
20   of Perjury

and in your half-cracked way you chose
silence for entertainment,
chose to have it out at last
on your own premises.

---

[1] **"I Am in Danger—Sir—"**: Emily Dickinson's equivocal response in a letter dated June 8,
1862, to her mentor Thomas Wentworth Higginson, who had suggested her rhymes were
too irregular.
[2] **snood:** a woman's netlike cap to keep hair in place.

COMMENTARY AND QUESTIONS

1. What is the speaker's suggestion about Thomas Wentworth Higginson's appreciation of Emily Dickinson's poetry, and how does the poem establish Dickinson's present fame?

2. In what sense, according to the poem, was Emily Dickinson masculine?

3. Working from your knowledge of Emily Dickinson's life and work, discuss the poem's last seven lines.

4. Discuss the poem's purpose.

The Observer

Completely protected on all sides
by volcanoes
a woman,[1] darkhaired, in stained jeans
sleeps in central Africa.
5   In her dreams, her notebooks, still
private as maiden diaries,
the mountain gorillas move through their life term;
their gentleness survives
observation. Six bands of them
10   inhabit, with her, the wooded highland.
When I lay me down to sleep
unsheltered by any natural guardians
from the panicky life-cycle of my tribe
I wake in the old cellblock
15   observing the daily executions,
rehearsing the laws
I cannot subscribe to,
envying the pale gorilla-scented dawn
she wakes into, the stream where she washes her hair,
20   the camera-flash of her quiet
eye.

[1] **woman:** Dian Fossey, who from 1967 to 1985 studied and protected the endangered mountain gorilla of east central Africa, was found slain, probably by poachers. "The Observer" was written when Dian Fossey first began her studies.

COMMENTARY AND QUESTIONS

1. Noting that the poem divides into two ten-line parts, summarize each part and discuss the poem's structure.

2. Relate the poem's title to the last two lines.

3. Contrast the form of this poem to any of the others by Adrienne Rich.

REVIEW

1. According to " 'I Am in Danger—Sir—' " and "The Observer," what qualities do Emily Dickinson and Dian Fossey share? Why do you think that Rich is interested in this quality?

2. What technique do both Robert Lowell's "Alfred Corning Clark" and " 'I Am in Danger—Sir—' " employ? Do you see any other similarities between Lowell's and Rich's poetry? Discuss.

ANNE SEXTON
1928–1974

More than Robert Lowell, Sylvia Plath, or other poets associated with the confessional movement, Anne Sexton introduced into her work subjects that had been previously considered too personal to be included in poems. Powerful and extremely readable, these poems won her considerable honor during her lifetime. She was, for instance, elected to be a fellow in the Royal Society of Literature and was awarded the Pulitizer Prize in 1966.

Born in Newton, Massachusetts, Anne Sexton grew up in Wellesley and spent one year at Garland Junior College. In 1948 she was married and lived with her husband in Baltimore and San Francisco before returning to Massachusetts. Suffering throughout her life from depression, Anne Sexton used the composition of poems as a way of clarifying and objectifying her problems. In writing workshops with Robert Lowell and other respected poets who were also working in the confessional mode, Anne Sexton quickly perfected her craft, placing poems in *The New Yorker, Harper's Magazine,* and the *Saturday Review.* Her first three books—*To Bedlam and Part Way Back* (1960), *All My Pretty Ones* (1962), and *Live or Die* (1966)—established her place in contemporary American poetry. She eventually published eleven books of poetry.

When Anne Sexton took her life in 1974, the public's curiosity increased her readership and raised the question of whether her poems are read for their artistic merit or simply for their treatment of what people have called private matters. There is no question, however, that, as the poet Maxine Kumin has said, "Women poets in particular owe a debt to Anne Sexton, who broke new ground, shattered taboos, and endured a barrage of attacks along the way" (introduction to Sexton's *Collected Poems*).

Housewife

Some women marry houses.
It's another kind of skin; it has a heart,
a mouth, a liver and bowel movements.
The walls are permanent and pink.
5   See how she sits on her knees all day,
faithfully washing herself down.
Men enter by force, drawn back like Jonah
into their fleshy mothers.
A woman *is* her mother.
10   That's the main thing.

COMMENTARY AND QUESTIONS

1. What is the poem's central metaphor and how does the poet extend it? What is the purpose of this metaphor?

2. Describe the poem's tone and discuss some passages that illustrate this tone.

3. Who was Jonah, and how does the allusion to him inform (increase the meaning of) the poem?

4. Do you think that the final line succeeds as a conclusion? Discuss.

5. How does the poem characterize men, women, and the relationship between the sexes?

The Abortion

Somebody who should have been born
is gone.

Just as the earth puckered its mouth,
each bud puffing out from its knot,
I changed my shoes, and then drove south.

5   Up past the Blue Mountains, where
Pennsylvania humps on endlessly,
wearing, like a crayoned cat, its green hair,

its roads sunken in like a gray washboard;
where, in truth, the ground cracks evilly,
10   a dark socket from which the coal has poured,

Somebody who should have been born
is gone.

the grass as bristly and stout as chives,
and me wondering when the ground would break,
and me wondering how anything fragile survives;

15 up in Pennsylvania, I met a little man,
not Rumpelstiltskin, at all, at all . . .
he took the fullness that love began.

Returning north, even the sky grew thin
like a high window looking nowhere.
20 The road was as flat as a sheet of tin.

Somebody who should have been born
is gone.

Yes, woman, such logic will lead
to loss without death. Or say what you meant,
you coward . . . this baby that I bleed.

COMMENTARY AND QUESTIONS

1. Why has the speaker driven south through Pennsylvania?

2. Cite passages that suggest the season, and tell why this season is appropriate to the poem?

3. Who was the "little man" and why does Anne Sexton allude to Rumpelstiltskin?

4. Cite and discuss the effect of three unexpected images.

5. How does the refrain (the repetition of a line) effect the poem?

6. Explain what you feel is the source of this poem's power.

Young

A thousand doors ago
when I was a lonely kid
in a big house with four
garages and it was summer
5 as long as I could remember,
I lay on the lawn at night,
clover wrinkling under me,
the wise stars bedding over me,
my mother's window a funnel
10 of yellow heat running out,
my father's window, half shut,
an eye where sleepers pass,
and the boards of the house
were smooth and white as wax
15 and probably a million leaves
sailed on their strange stalks
as the crickets ticked together
and I, in my brand new body,
which was not a woman's yet,

20 told the stars my questions
and thought God could really see
the heat and the painted light,
elbows, knees, dreams, goodnight.

COMMENTARY AND QUESTIONS

1. What do the images in lines 9–12 suggest?

2. Discuss how two or three other unexpected images give meaning to the poem.

3. How does the poem's grammar affect the way one reads and understands the poem?

4. What statement does this poem make about the speaker's youth and perhaps youth in general?

REVIEW

1. Anne Sexton is noted for using startling images and unusual associations to depict real-life situations. Find and discuss some examples of these techniques.

2. Critics have said that Anne Sexton's poems are too much like prose, and they lack the intensity that should characterize poetry. Do you agree with this criticism? Use examples to defend your position. You may want to use examples of poems by other poets.

SYLVIA PLATH
1932–1963

Born in Boston, Massachusetts, Sylvia Plath lived in the seaside town of Winthrop for six years before moving at the age of ten to Wellesley. The Massachusetts coast and the death of her father in 1940 powerfully influenced the imagery and themes of Plath's extremely personal poetry.

An excellent student, Plath received a scholarship to Smith College. In the summer of 1953 she was, along with women from other colleges, a guest editor at *Mademoiselle* magazine, where as managing editor she interviewed Richard Wilbur and other poets and writers. Feeling disoriented by her experience in New York and feeling she was not living up to her high standards, she unsuccessfully attempted to take her life. Plath tells the story of her attempted suicide and the events surrounding it in her autobiographical novel, *The Bell Jar.*

After graduating from Smith in 1955, Sylvia Plath won a Fulbright Fellowship to attend Cambridge University, England. The next year she married Ted Hughes, a young English poet who is currently England's Poet Laureate. Back in the United States for two years, she taught at Smith College and in 1958 attended Robert Lowell's poetry workshop at Boston University. After returning to England, she published in 1960 her first book, *Colossus and Other Poems.*

In 1963 after having two children, separating from her husband, and moving from the couple's country house in Devon to London, Sylvia Plath published *The Bell Jar* under a pseudonym. Still suffering from the mental disturbances that had troubled her in college and being further depressed by her failing marriage and ill health, she took her life February 11, 1963. Three years later *The Bell Jar* was published under the poet's own name; during the next nine years three more books of poems were published posthumously.

Due to the personal nature of her poetry and her association with Robert Lowell and Anne Sexton, Sylvia Plath is called a confessional poet. Although sometimes a useful term, it tends (like the name of any literary movement) to focus and consequently limit our observations. What is more important than knowing the school of poetry with which she has been associated is to appreciate the skill, intensity, and power of her craft; in the years since her death Sylvia Plath has become one of the most respected and widely read American poets since World War II.

Mirror

I am silver and exact. I have no preconceptions.
Whatever I see I swallow immediately
Just as it is, unmisted by love or dislike.
I am not cruel, only truthful—
5   The eye of a little god, four-cornered.
Most of the time I meditate on the opposite wall.
It is pink, with speckles. I have looked at it so long
I think it is a part of my heart. But it flickers.
Faces and darkness separate us over and over.

10   Now I am a lake. A woman bends over me,
Searching my reaches for what she really is.
Then she turns to those liars, the candles or the moon.
I see her back, and reflect it faithfully.
She rewards me with tears and an agitation of hands.
15   I am important to her. She comes and goes.
Each morning it is her face that replaces the darkness.
In me she has drowned a young girl, and in me an old woman
Rises toward her day after day, like a terrible fish.

COMMENTARY AND QUESTIONS

1. Who or what is the speaker in the first stanza? In the second? Are there one or two speakers? Discuss.

2. Explain the last two lines, paying particular attention to the final simile.

Blackberrying

Nobody in the lane, and nothing, nothing but blackberries,
Blackberries on either side, though on the right mainly,
A blackberry alley, going down in hooks, and a sea
Somewhere at the end of it, heaving. Blackberries
5   Big as the ball of my thumb, and dumb as eyes
Ebon in the hedges, fat
With blue-red juices. These they squander on my fingers.
I had not asked for such a blood sisterhood; they must love me.
They accommodate themselves to my milkbottle, flattening their sides.

10 Overhead go the choughs[1] in black, cacophonous flocks—
Bits of burnt paper wheeling in a blown sky.
Theirs is the only voice, protesting, protesting.
I do not think the sea will appear at all.
The high, green meadows are glowing, as if lit from within.
15 I come to one bush of berries so ripe it is a bush of flies.
Hanging their blue-green bellies and their wing panes in a Chinese
screen.
The honey-feast of the berries has stunned them; they believe in
heaven.
One more hook, and the berries and bushes end.

The only thing to come now is the sea.
20 From between two hills a sudden wind funnels at me,
Slapping its phantom laundry in my face.
These hills are too green and sweet to have tasted salt.
I follow the sheep path between them. A last hook brings me
To the hills' northern face, and the face is orange rock
25 That looks out on nothing, nothing but a great space
Of white and pewter lights, and a din like silversmiths
Beating and beating at an intractable metal.

[1] **choughs:** crowlike birds.

COMMENTARY AND QUESTIONS

1. This poem contains the powerful imagery and intensity of feeling characteristic of Sylvia Plath's most well-known poems. After noting the poem's action, list images that you find particularly powerful.

2. How do the images of blackberries in lines 5–9 contribute to the poem's meaning? List all the images of blackness in the poem and discuss their effect.

3. In lines 15 and 16, how do flies look like a Chinese screen?

4. Summarize how the poem's three-part structure develops.

5. How does Plath use the words *hook* and *nothing* to unify and clarify?

6. How does the speaker feel about finally reaching the sea? Why do you suppose the poem is named "Blackberrying" and not the "The Sea"? How, if at all, is the sea a clue to understanding the feelings that generate this poem?

Crossing the Water

Black lake, black boat, two black, cut-paper people.
Where do the black trees go that drink here?
Their shadows must cover Canada.

A little light is filtering from the water flowers.
5 Their leaves do not wish us to hurry:
They are round and flat and full of dark advice.

Cold worlds shake from the oar.
The spirit of blackness is in us, it is in the fishes.
A snag is lifting a valedictory, pale hand;

10 Stars open among the lilies.
Are you not blinded by such expressionless sirens[1]?
This is the silence of astounded souls.

[1] **sirens:** sea nymphs whose beautiful songs lured sailors to their deaths.

COMMENTARY AND QUESTIONS

1. In line 2, how do trees "drink"? Explain the hyperbole in line 3.
2. Identify and explain three examples of personification.
3. Discuss the effect of the figurative language in this poem.
4. How do the two interrogative sentences affect the poem?
5. Are there any other allusions to Greek mythology besides the sirens?
6. Is the last line a succesful conclusion to the poem? Explain.

Sheep in Fog

The hills step off into whiteness.
People or stars
Regard me sadly, I disappoint them.

The train leaves a line of breath.
5 O slow
Horse the colour of rust,

Hooves, dolorous bells—
All morning the
Morning has been blackening,

10 A flower left out.
My bones hold a stillness, the far
Fields melt my heart.

They threaten
To let me through to a heaven
15 Starless and fatherless, a dark water.

COMMENTARY AND QUESTIONS

1. List the objects in this poem. What is the "horse" (line 6)?

2. In line 10 what is "a flower left out?"

3. As in "Blackberrying," Plath uses images, primarily of nature, to objectify a strong feeling. What is the feeling that generates these images? As you answer this question, refer to specific lines to support your insights.

REVIEW

1. What images, other poetic devices, and themes characterize these poems?

2. Compare one of these poems to a similar one by Emily Dickinson and draw some interesting, useful conclusions.

3. Write a poem that uses images to convey an unstated feeling.

DONALD JUNKINS
1931–

The *New York Times* reviewed Donald Junkins's *Crossing By Ferry: Poems New and Selected* as "carefully, even lovingly written" and went on to say,

> History, especially his own family history, is Mr. Junkins's presiding theme. He moves from present to past with a liquid ease. . . . In our bureaucratic and myth-free world, the self and its roots in a cherished past seem to have taken on an especially tender and vulnerable significance. (*Sunday Book Review*, 31 December 1978)

By focusing on his own life in the light of his family roots, Junkins, like Donald Hall in *Kicking the Leaves* and Robert Lowell in *Life Studies,* treads vulnerable ground indeed; for beginning with Emerson's demand for an American poetry "of insight and not of tradition," the main currents of modern American poetry have flowed away from the predictable, easily sentimentalized past toward the stark, surprising future. Junkins's poetry, however, by recording early memories, family histories, and the events and places of childhood with an almost historical authenticity, validates the part of us we cannot know without looking backward.

Donald Junkins was born in Saugus, Massachusetts, in 1931. He attended the University of Massachusetts, where he played football and still holds the record for the most passes intercepted in one season. During the late 1950s, he attended, with Anne Sexton and other now well-known poets, Robert Lowell's poetry workshops at Boston University. Earning his doctorate from that institution in 1963, he taught for three years at California State University at Chico and then from 1966 to present at the University of Massachusetts, where he headed the Graduate Writing Program for ten years. A winner of the John Masefield Memorial Award, the Jenny Tane Award, and two National Endowment for the Arts fellowships, Donald Junkins is the author of nine books of poems.

Uncle Harry: Splitting Oak
before Pickerel Fishing, 1942

                    the way he said
            it moving his thumb just
            enough before the axe

                    tossing both
  5   pieces at the pile:
                            I heard they was a fire
            in the bed this morning
            then he left it alone and kept on
            with the wood
  10   in one hand, the axe in
            the other, cracking it apart, now
            and then smelling the grain
                            (that morning
            I had wet the bed, and skipped
  15   breakfast)
                            when they yelled over did I want
            anything to eat he had two or three days
            fall burning in the pile

            out on the water he talked low:
  20   just skip the belly along
            like this
                    now   one's got it
            see there?   we'll just sit and wait
            till he chews it. You've got
  25   to let them chew it. See his jaws
            working? Pretty soon the belly'll be
            gone. He'll have the whole thing
            in his mouth. Then you can set
            the hook. It just takes time.

COMMENTARY AND QUESTIONS

1. Write this poem as prose, filling it out by adding a few words for clarification and the appropriate puncuation marks and capital letters. Now comment on the effectiveness of the poem's ecomomy and its line breaks.

2. Explain how the poem's first eighteen lines inform the last eleven lines.

3. Describe the relationship between the uncle and the speaker. Have you had or known of such a relationship? If so, discuss.

Playing Glassies with Dickie Mallar, 1943

Alone in the garage, I worked my hand
through the floppy topcloth of my marble
bag and squeezed whole handsfull of little glass
balls, dribbling them on the pile
5   in the metallic dark. I knew the crystal balls
by heart, swirls of cream and raspberries,
here a wine red, here a buttercup yellow streaked
with devil's grass. May: the marble season. I

carried the sugar bag around
10   the neighborhood after school, plopping
it in backyards, calling for takers. We
gouged holes with our heels in lawns,
driveways, sidewalks, earth gutters, We
scooped fistsfull of dirt with our hands,
15   patted the edges of our holes with our finger-
tips. Closest to the hole shot first. Tucking
my thumb against my curved forefinger
I nubbed the sweet rolling glassies
into the hole, every one. I never lost, I
20   was Midas Junkins the glassy king. One

day, Dickie Mallar walked up from Blue
Ridge Road and stood in the street outside
my house: "You got any
glassies?"
25   "Sure."
"You want to play?"
                        He dug ten giant purees
out of his pocket: he'd roll against everything
in my bag. One by one he fingered them
30   in the late afternoon sun: blue bachelor-
buttons, orange poppies, copper-green lily
pads—the colors were so rich my belly
churned with a lover's passion. Mallar
kept throwing them: candlewax
35   black, burnt-pumpkin-belly
black, the black eyes of the new girl
on her back in the field, staring
sideways—Mallar rolled them all
and lost every one.
40   When it was over, his risky
debonair ways puzzled me. "What's

a glassy?" he said, and walked
home in the dusk. I felt cheated. I
had everthing in the bag.
45   I stashed
my glassies in the garage. Behind
closed doors I fingered them
in the dark.

COMMENTARY AND QUESTIONS

1. Why does the speaker like to play marbles?

2. Note some of the crucial images that convey the poem's mood.

3. Discuss two or three line breaks that you feel are unusual.

4. Is there any justification in the poem for Dickie Mallar's sense of superiority when he says, "What's a glassie" (lines 41, 42) and the speaker's feeling "cheated" (line 43)? Discuss.

REVIEW

1. Compare either of these poems to one of Robert Lowell's poems about his family or friends.

2. Donald Junkins has said that a poet must come to the line of sentimentality without crossing it. Do either of these poems become sentimental? Discuss why or why not. In your discussion, you may wish to compare one or more of Junkins's poems to Snyder's "Hay for the Horses."

3. Write a poem about a childhood experience that you understand better now than you did when it happened. Like Junkins, do not interpret the experience. Instead, tell your story in a way that will let the reader learn from it what you have learned.

MICHAEL HARPER
1938–

Michael Harper was born in Brooklyn, New York, where jazz and blues music were among his earliest influences. When he was thirteen, his parents moved to Los Angeles. After high school he attended California State College in Los Angeles and the University of Iowa, where he was enrolled in the Writers' Workshop. He has worked as a postal distributor, lifeguard, counselor, teacher of functional writing, and professional football player.

Harper began writing poetry when he was in college and published his first poems in the late 1960s. He has said that during those years his travels to Mexico and Europe

> broadened my scope and interest in poetry and culture of other countries while I searched my own family and racial history for folklore, history, and myths for themes that would give my writing the tradition and context where I could find my own voice.

Rooted strongly in the history of the African American people, Michael Harper's poetry, like that of Langston Hughes, employs more often the rhythms of blues and jazz than the traditional European poetic forms. A superb reader of his own work, he has read his poems widely.

Harper has taught at California State College in Hayward, Lewis and Clark College, Reed College, Contra Costa College, and is currently on the faculty at Brown University. The author of seven books of poems, he has won awards from the National Institute of Arts and Letters and the Black Academy of Arts and Letters.

Martin's[1] Blues

He came apart in the open,
the slow motion cameras
falling quickly
neither alive nor kicking;
5   stone blind dead
on the balcony
that old melody
etched his black lips
in a pruned echo:
10   *We shall overcome*
some day—
Yes we did!
Yes we did!

[1] **Martin's:** Martin Luther King, Jr. (1929–1968), American civil rights leader and Nobel Prize
winner, was assassinated on a motel balcony in Memphis, Tennessee.

COMMENTARY AND QUESTIONS

1. How do the words of the famous civil rights anthem "We shall Overcome" affect
the poem's meaning?

2. Discuss the strongest image in this poem.

3. Discuss the source of the poem's power.

American History

Those four black girls blown up
in that Alabama church
remind me of five hundred
middle passage blacks,
5   in a net, under water
in Charleston harbor
so *redcoats* wouldn't find them.
Can't find what you can't see
can you?

COMMENTARY AND QUESTIONS

1. What does this comparison between events two hundred years apart suggest
about America's history?

2. What is the tone of the last line and how does the line affect the poem's
meaning?

Last Affair: Bessie's[1] Blues Song

Disarticulated[2]
arm torn out,
large veins cross
her shoulder intact,
5   her tourniquet
her blood in all-white big bands:

Can't you see
what love and heartache's done to me
I'm not the same as I used to be
10   *this is my last affair*

Mail truck or parked car
in the fast lane,
afloat at forty-three
on a Mississippi road,
15   Two-hundred-pound muscle on her ham bone,
'nother nigger dead 'fore noon:

Can't you see
what love and heartache's done to me
I'm not the same as I used to be
20   *this is my last affair*

Fifty-dollar record
cut the vein in her neck,
fool about her money
toll her black train wreck,
25   white press missed her fun'ral
in the same stacked deck:

Can't you see
what love and heartache's done to me
I'm not the same as I used to be
30   *this is my last affair*

Loved a little blackbird
heard she could sing,
Martha in her vineyard
pestle[3] in her spring,
35   Bessie had a bad mouth
made my chimes ring:

[1] **Bessie's:** Bessie Smith (1894?–1937), a famous American blues singer of the 1920s and 1930s. Michael Harper has said that Bessie Smith played the piano at his family's house in Brooklyn, New York. After being badly injured in an automobile accident in Mississippi, Bessie Smith was taken to a hospital, where her arm was amputated. She died hours later.
[2] **disarticulated:** separated at the joints, disjointed.
[3] **pestle:** a hand tool for mashing or grinding.

Can't you see
what love and heartache's done to me
I'm not the same as I used to be
40   *this is my last affair*

COMMENTARY AND QUESTIONS

1. How is the first word of the poem ironic?

2. How does the refrain, which is composed of lyrics from Bessie Smith's song "Last Affair," intensify the poem's meaning?

3. Note and discuss specific lines that express strong emotion.

REVIEW

1. Make some interesting and useful comparisons between one or two of Michael Harper's poems and one or two of Langston Hughes's poems.

2. Write a short poem in the style of Michael Harper about a current historical event.

SIMON ORTIZ
1941–

Originally from Acoma Pueblo in rural central New Mexico, Simon Ortiz has lived in Arizona, California, Colorado, Iowa, South Dakota, and Oregon. A storyteller, television script writer, essayist, and short story writer, as well as a poet, Ortiz says this of the creative process:

> I let myself feel or try to. Thinking gets in the way too often. Being critically involved in and committed to the process of "coming into being" confirms existence and relationships to ideas, places, people, the "Creative Source," everything. I don't know how well I do in confirming existence and relationships but I feel I'm like everyone else: I try. From that struggle I derive the "meaning" of poetry, that is, the poetics language shares with me. (letter to H. R., 1991)

The last sentence of Simon Ortiz's statement implies what is central to his writing: Language for him is not just a tool but rather a living entity that "shares" with the poet the power to name "into being" whatever the poet wishes to bring forth.

Ortiz's writing embraces aspects of the traditional Acoma Pueblo Indian culture as well as events of contemporary life. For instance, his book *From Sand Creek: Rising in This Heart Which Is Our America* recounts Ortiz's experiences as a patient in a Veterans Administration Hospital, and *Fight Back: For the Sake of The People, For the Sake of the Land* describes the lives of uranium mine workers in New Mexico.

Currently Simon Ortiz lives on the Acoma Pueblo, where he is completing two poetry-prose collections.

The Creation, According to Coyote[1]

"First of all, it's all true."
Coyote, he says this, this way,
humble yourself, motioning and meaning
what he says.

5   You were born when you came
from that body, the earth;
your black head burst from granite,
the ashes cooling,

until it began to rain.
10   It turned muddy then,
and then green and brown things
came without legs.

They looked strange.
Everything was strange.
15   There was nothing to know then,

until later, Coyote told me this,
and he was b.s.-ing probably,
two sons were born,
Uyuyayeh and Masaweh.

20   They were young then,
and then later on they were older.

And then the people were wondering
what was above.
They had heard rumors.

25   But, you know, Coyote,
he was mainly bragging
when he said (I think),
"My brothers, the Twins then said,
'Let's lead these poor creatures
30   and save them.' "

And later on, they came to light
after many exciting and colorful
and tragic things of adventure;
and this is the life, all these, all these.

---

[1] **Coyote:** a Native American mythic character, a culture hero. Ortiz says of him, "Because Coyote is mythic, he is story, storyteller, and story being created (coming into being)."

35 My uncle told me all this, that time.
Coyote told me too, but you know
how he is, always talking to the gods,
the mountains, the stone all around.

And you know, I believe him.

COMMENTARY AND QUESTIONS

1. What aspects of this poem reflect the New Mexico environment?

2. Compare and contrast the source of the speaker's knowledge of creation to the source of your knowledge of creation, and then note ways in which you might see yourself in relationship to the universe differently than does the speaker.

3. Describe the speaker's voice. What seems to be his attitude toward the story he is telling? Toward his audience?

4. What, if anything appeals to you about Coyote's story of creation?

5. Discuss the importance of the last line. Could the poem stand without it? Why or why not?

My Father's Song

Wanting to say things,
I miss my father tonight.
His voice, the slight catch,
the depth from his thin chest,
5 the tremble of emotion
in something he has just said
to his son, his song:

We planted corn one Spring at Acu—
we planted several times
10 but this one particular time
I remember the soft damp sand
in my hand.

My father had stopped at one point
to show me an overturned furrow;
15 the plowshare had unearthed
the burrow nest of a mouse
in the soft moist sand.

Very gently, he scooped tiny pink animals
into the palm of his hand
20 and told me to touch them.
We took them to the edge
of the field and put them in the shade
of a sand moist clod.

I remember the very softness
25   of cool and warm sand and tiny alive mice
and my father saying things.

COMMENTARY AND QUESTIONS

1. According to this poem, what is a song? How would Walt Whitman have defined a song? What, if anything, do the two definitions have in common?

2. How might Simon Ortiz respond to the composer Charles Ives's statement, "I found my music in the ground"?

3. Discuss the relationship in the poem between father and son.

4. Describe the relationship between humankind and nature as depicted in this poem.

Making an Acquaintance

I walk outside without my shoes
on searing hot asphalt front yard.
Howard, my new landlord, says,
"It's gonna be a bitch of a Summer."
5   Strange, I think, what words mean.
He has a tanned middle-aged face,
used to be in real estate in Ohio,
sold his business and moved West.
We get acquainted by talking
10   about the coming Summer.
"Yeah," I agree with him,
"it's gonna be a bitch."
My feet are burning for coolness.

COMMENTARY AND QUESTIONS

1. What do we know about each speaker?

2. How well does the last line conclude the poem?

3. In what sense is this a poem about language?

4. What does this poem show about how people relate?

A Patience Poem for the Child That Is Me

Be patient child,
be patient, quiet.
The rivers run into the center
of the earth
5   and around

revolve all things
and flow
into the center.
Be patient, child,
10 quiet.

COMMENTARY AND QUESTIONS

1. Explain how lines 2–7 justify being patient.
2. Discuss the title.
3. How well does the last line conclude the poem?

REVIEW

1. Describe the relationship between man and nature in two or three of these poems.

2. Compare Ortiz's view of nature in one of these poems to the view in two other American poems—one from the nineteenth century and one from the twentieth century.

3. Where and how, if at all, does Ortiz echo these passages from Ralph Waldo Emerson's essay "The Poet"?

   "Words are also actions and actions are kinds of words."

   "For poetry was all written before time was, and whenever we are so finely organized that we can penetrate into that region where the air is music, we hear those primal warblings and attempt to write them down."

SHARON OLDS
1942–

The energy, accessibiltiy, and the sexual nature of much of Sharon Olds's poetry reminds one at times of passages from Walt Whitman's "Song of Myself," an association that becomes explicit in poems like "The Language of Brag," where Olds proclaims: "I have done what you wanted to do, Walt Whitman . . . I am putting my proud American boast / right here with the others." However, Olds's poems about her personal relationships with her parents also remind readers of Lowell, Plath, Sexton, and other so-called confessional poets. Yet in Sharon Olds's poems, even those that recount painful memories, an essential sense of physical and mental robustness remains, connecting her initially personal themes with all humanity and reminding us again of the tradition of Emerson, Whitman, Dickinson, Williams, and Roethke.

Born in San Francisco, Sharon Olds attended Stanford University for her bachelor's degree and Columbia University for her doctorate. She has taught at New York University, Sarah Lawrence College, Columbia University, and the State University of New York at Purchase. The author of three books of poems, she was the Lamont Poetry Selection for the Academy of American Poets and is the winner of many other awards and grants, including the National Book Critics Circle Award. Currently she directs the creative writing program at New York University.

Quake Theory

When two plates of earth scrape along each other
like a mother and daughter
it is called a fault.

There are faults that slip smoothly past each other
5   an inch a year, with just a faint rasp
like a man running his hand over his chin,
that man between us,

and there are faults that get stuck at a bend for twenty years.
The ridge bulges up like a father's sarcastic forehead
10 and the whole thing freezes in place, the man between us.

When this happens, there will be heavy damage
to industrial areas and leisure residence
when the deep plates
finally jerk past
15 the terrible pressure of their contact.

                                    The earth cracks
and innocent people slip gently in like swimmers.

COMMENTARY AND QUESTIONS

1. What part does the word *fault* play in the poem's central metaphor?
2. Explain line 7.
3. Respond to this statement: "This poem gains its power from its calm, descriptive, almost scientific tone."
4. Discuss the effect of the last word.
5. Discuss this mother and daughter relationship. Is it typical?

Primitive

I have heard about the civilized,
the marriages run on talk, elegant and
honest, rational. But you and I are
savages. You come in with a bag,
5 hold it out to me in silence.
I know Moo Shu Pork when I smell it
and understand the message: I have
pleased you greatly last night. We sit
quietly, side by side, to eat,
10 the long pancakes dangling and spilling,
fragrant sauce dripping out,
and glance at each other askance, wordless,
the corners of our eyes clear as spear points
laid along the sill to show
15 a friend sits with a friend here.

COMMENTARY AND QUESTIONS

1. In what sense are "you and I . . . savages" (lines 3 and 4)?
2. How would the following replacement of the last line change the poem: "these lovers are well protected"?

Young Mothers IV

The look on the face of the young mother
at the coffeehouse, looking down. No one
is looking at her. Everyone is looking at her
looking at the young child tottering
5 like a lunatic, who might do anything next.

We watch that mother.
The toddler approaches
a big poinsettia like a blood bomb gone off,
and looks at the mother. We look at the mother.
10 She holds up a cookie. Our mouths water.

Suddenly I think she will scream,
this watched woman, this marked woman,
stared at like the women with shaved heads
in Germany in 44. I think she will
15 turn to us all and shriek, her face
swelling dark as a heart. But she cannot. The child
watches her, the small face
unmarked by anything, mad with curiosity,
bearded with crumbs, the child sees her rise and
20 ease her big belly a moment before she walks.

COMMENTARY AND QUESTIONS

1. Why does the poet include "Our mouths water"?
2. Explain the allusion in line 14, and discuss how it extends the poem's meaning.
3. Should the poem end with the word *crumbs* in line 19? Why or why not?

The Unjustly Punished Child

The child screams in his room. Rage
heats his head.
He is going through changes like metal under deep
pressure at high temperatures.

5 When he cools off and comes out of that door
he will not be the same child who ran in
and slammed it. An alloy has been added. Now he will
crack along different lines when tapped.

He is stronger. The long impurification
10 has begun this morning.

COMMENTARY AND QUESTIONS

1. How does the metaphor beginning in line 3 clarify the change in the child?
2. Explain how the child will be stronger, yet less pure (line 9)? Is this a paradox?

REVIEW

1. Using examples from three poems, discuss how Sharon Olds breaks her lines in ways that amplify and emphasize the meanings of words.
2. Show how in two poems Olds employs central metaphors. How successful are these metaphors and why?
3. Write a poem that uses a strong, surprising central metaphor to convey its theme.

MOLLY PEACOCK
1947–

Molly Peacock has said of herself and her work,

> I was the caretaker of our family, coming home from high school and fixing dinner for my younger sister and my father, who was an alcoholic, and verbally abusive to us both. What does this have to do with writing poetry? Everything, because I began to write to go to a safe place inside my mind, a healthy place, to escape the insanity around me. I also began to create something verbally beautiful, instead of brutal. People say you have to be crazy to make art, but I feel art comes from whatever inside us struggles to be whole and strives for health. (letter to H. R., 1990)

As she wrote about what was inside her, Molly Peacock eventually found that poetic forms, such as the sonnet, helped clarify her poems. Form was not, as she had thought, a container that shapes and limits one's imagination but rather "more like a skeleton, providing flexible bone structure for feelings and thoughts."

Born in Buffalo, New York, Molly Peacock was educated at the State University of New York at Binghamton and at the Johns Hopkins University Writing Seminars. She is a member of the Friends Seminary faculty in New York City and a learning specialist in private practice. She also teaches as a writer-in-residence at various colleges and universities such as Barnard College, the University of Southern Maine, and Hofstra University. The author of three books of poetry, Peacock has been the recipient of two Ingram Merrill Foundation Awards and three fellowships from the New York Foundation for the Arts. Currently she serves as president of the Poetry Society of America.

The Lull

The possum lay on the tracks fully dead.
I'm the kind of person who stops to look.
It was big and white with flies on its head,
a thick healthy hairless tail, and strong, hooked
5 nails on its racoon-like feet. It was a full-
grown possum. It was sturdy and adult.
Only its head was smashed. In the lull
that it took to look, you took the time to insult
the corpse, the flies, the world, the fact that we were
10 traipsing in our dress shoes down the railroad tracks.
"That's disgusting." You said that. Dreams, brains, fur
and guts: what we are. That's my bargain, the Pax[1]
Peacock, with the world. Look hard, life's soft. Life's cache
is flesh, flesh, and flesh.

[1] **Pax:** Latin for Peace. The phrase "Pax / Peacock" reminds one of the *Pax Romana*, the peace terms that ancient Rome imposed on its dominions.

COMMENTARY AND QUESTIONS

1. Contrast the points of view of the narrator and the character addressed as "you." With which point of view do you agree and why?

2. When you first read this poem, did you notice the rhymes? How are they disguised?

3. Note that line 14 of this sonnet is a half line with only five syllables. Comment on its effect.

Our Room

I tell the children in school sometimes
why I hate alcoholics: my father was one.
"Alcohol" and "disease" I use, and shun
the word "drunk" or even "drinking," since one time
5 the kids burst out laughing when I told them.
I felt as though they were laughing at me.
I waited for them, wounded, remem-
bering how I imagined they'd howl at me
when I was in grade 5. Acting drunk
10 is a guaranteed screamer, especially
for boys. I'm quiet when I sort the junk
of my childhood for them, quiet so we
will all be quiet, and they can ask what
questions they have to and tell about what
15 happened to them, too. The classroom becomes
oddly lonely when we talk about our homes.

COMMENTARY AND QUESTIONS

1. What if the title of this poem were "Our Home"? What would this title suggest? Discuss the significance of the title "Our Room."

2. Discuss any images or ideas in this poem that strike you as particularly true.

3. How does the last sentence affect the poem's meaning?

4. Respond to this statement: "This poem begins with the ABBA of an Italian sonnet, then changes to the ABAB of an English sonnet, then adds an extra couplet, making the poem two lines too long to be any kind of a sonnet. A sonnet is a sonnet is a sonnet, and a poet should not pervert its traditional form."

Good Girl

Hold up the universe, good girl. Hold up
the tent that is the sky of your world at which
you are the narrow center pole, good girl. Rup-
ture is the enemy. Keep all whole, The itch
5   to be yourself, plump and bending, below a sky
unending, held up by God forever
is denied by you as Central Control. Sever
yourself, poor false Atlas, poor "Atlesse," lie
recumbent below the sky. Nothing falls down,
10   except you, luscious and limited on the ground.
Holding everything up, always on your own,
creates a loneliness so profound
you are nothing but a column, good girl,
a temple ruin against a sky held up
15   by forces beyond you. Let yourself curl
up: a fleshy fetal figure cupped
about its own vibrant soul. You are
the universe about its pole. God's not far.

COMMENTARY AND QUESTIONS

1. Paraphrase the sentence that begins in line 4 with "The itch."

2. How does the "good girl" see herself, and how does the speaker want the girl to see herself? What kind of person is the "good girl"? Do you know people like her? Discuss.

3. Compared to your first reading of the other poems by Peacock, to what extent were you aware of rhyme as you first read "Good Girl"? How does rhyme pattern affect the poem's tone?

4. Focusing on the last three sentences, discuss this poem as a piece of advice.

REVIEW

1. Molly Peacock has said that when a poem that began to take shape as a sonnet wants to go on farther than fourteen lines, she lets it. Discuss this approach, using Peacock's poems as examples.

2. Make an interesting and useful comparison between one of these poems and one by another poet.

3. Write a poem that comes as close to being a sonnet as possible, without bending the shape that the poem wants to take.

BRUCE WEIGL
1949–

Bruce Weigl was born and grew up in Lorain, Ohio. After graduation from high school, he joined the army and served with the First Air Cavalry in Vietnam. After his discharge he received his bachelor's degree from Oberlin College in 1974, his master's degree from the University of New Hampshire in 1975, and his doctorate from the University of Utah in 1979. Weigl has taught at the University of Arkansas, Old Dominion University, and currently teaches in the writing program at Pennsylvania State University.

More than any of the war veterans we have read, Bruce Weigl has written extensively and powerfully about war experiences. His book of poems entitled *Song of Napalm* recounts not only memories of battle and the American soldier's life amongst the Vietnamese people but also the impact of the war on the veteran, his family, and American society. Novelist Russell Banks has said that *Song of Napalm* may be "the best novel so far about the Vietnam War" (jacket copy, *Song of Napalm*).

The author of five books of poetry, Weigl has received a National Endowment for the Arts grant for creative writing, a Pennsylvania Arts Council grant, the Academy of American Poets Prize, and an award from the Vietnam War Veterans of America for "contributions to American culture." Reading his apparently autobiographical poems about Vietnam, one admires Weigl's steady courage to recount lucidly and honestly his gruesome, often embarrassing, and sometimes humorous memories.

The Sharing

I have not ridden a horse much,
two, maybe three times,
a broken gray mare my cousin called Ghost,
then only in the fall
5   through the flat pastures of Ohio,
that's not much.

But I watched two Chinese tanks
roll out of the jungle side by side,
their turret guns feeling before them
10   like a man walking through his dream,
their tracks slapping the bamboo like hooves.

I can't name the gaits of a horse
except the canter
and that rocks you to the withers,
15   but I saw those arms,
those guns and did not know for a moment
what they were, but knew they were not horses
as they pulled themselves deep
into the jungle
20   until there was only the dull rattle of their track
and a boy on a gray horse
flying through the opening fields.

COMMENTARY AND QUESTIONS

1. Discuss how the poem connects the image of "a broken gray mare my cousin called Ghost" (line 3) to "two Chinese tanks" (line 7). How does this metaphor create meaning in the poem?

2. Explain the title's significance.

3. Describe the speaker's voice. How does it contribute to the poem's power?

Snowy Egret[1]

My neighbor's boy has lifted his father's shotgun and stolen
down to the backwaters of the Elizabeth
and in the moon he's blasted a snowy egret
from the shallows it stalked for small fish.

5   Midnight. My wife wakes me. He's in the backyard
with a shovel so I go down half drunk with pills
that let me sleep to see what I can see and if it's safe.
The boy doesn't hear me come across the dewy grass.
He says through tears he has to bury it,
10   he says his father will kill him
and he digs until the hole is deep enough and gathers
the egret carefully into his arms
as if not to harm the blood-splattered wings
gleaming in the flashlight beam.

---

[1] **Snowy Egret:** a snow white heronlike wading bird with long legs and a long beak for catching fish; it is twenty inches long with a thirty-eight-inch wingspead.

15 His man's muscled shoulders
   shake with the weight of what he can't set right no matter what,
   but one last time he tries to stay a child, sobbing
   please don't tell. . . .
   He says he only meant to flush it from the shadows,
20 he only meant to watch it fly
   but the shot spread too far
   ripping into the white wings
   spanned awkwardly for a moment
   until it glided into brackish death.

25 I want to grab his shoulders,
   shake the lies loose from his lips but he hurts enough,
   he burns with shame for what he's done.
   with fear for his hard father's
   fists I've seen crash down on him for so much less.
30 I don't know what to do but hold him.
   If I let go he'll fly to pieces before me.
   What a time we share, that can make a good boy steal away
   wiping out from the blue face of the pond
   what he hadn't even known he loved, blasting
35 such beauty into nothing.

COMMENTARY AND QUESTIONS

1. Explain the narrative.

2. Describe the narrator's reaction to the boy's action. How, if at all, is the boy lying?

3. Explain how the line break at the end of line 1 helps extend the meaning of *stolen*.

4. Is the conclusion satisfactory? Is Weigl explaining his poem when, more effectively, he could end with line 31?

The Last Lie

Some guy in the miserable convoy
raised up in the back of our open truck
and threw a can of C rations at a child
who called into the rumble for food.
5 He didn't toss the can, he wound up and hung it
on the child's forehead and she was stunned
backwards into the dust of our trucks.

Across the sudden angle of the road's curving
I could still see her when she rose,
10   waving one hand across her swollen, bleeding head,
wildly swinging her other hand
at the children who mobbed her,
who tried to take her food.

I grit my teeth to myself to remember that girl
15   smiling as she fought off her brothers and sisters.
She laughed
as if she thought it were a joke
and the guy with me laughed
and fingered the edge of another can
30   like it was the seam of a baseball
until his rage ripped
again into the faces of children
who called to us for food.

COMMENTARY AND QUESTIONS

1. What is the speaker's attitude toward the "guy" who threw the can of rations at the child? Note "until his rage ripped / again." What rage? How well do you think the narrator understands that "rage"?

2. Explain the significance of the title.

REVIEW

1. Compare "The Last Lie" to Countee Cullen's "Incident" and Robert Hayden's "Night, Death, Mississippi."

2. How, if at all, does Weigl avoid romanticizing the war memories in "The Sharing" and "The Last Lie"?

3. Discuss the place of "Snowy Egret" in a book about the Vietnam War. Would it be possible to argue that boys killed beautiful, wild creatures long before the Vietnam War?

RITA DOVE
1952–

When Rita Dove won the Pulitzer Prize for Poetry in 1987, she was one of the youngest recipients and its second African American recipient (the first was Gwendolyn Brooks). In defining the beauty of Dove's poems, the highly regarded critic Helen Vendler has written,

> New forms of beauty declare themselves only gradually. It seems to me now that a rapid succession of dramatic "takes" is Dove's perfected form. She almost always refuses editorializing, musing, and "leading" the reader. Her brilliance lies in her arrangement of content. ("In the Zoo of the New," *New York Review of Books,* 23 October 1986)

As you read the following poems, you will notice not only their powerful dramatic moments, which the poet will not interpret for you, but also their striking, unexpected images and moments of extraordinary lyricism. Like other African American poets in this book, Rita Dove often writes about the history of African Americans in America; but, in a way that distinguishes her work, she interweaves her own life and her family's with the larger currents of history, showing the reader how the racial degradations of the past bear on us today.

Born in Akron, Ohio, Rita Dove completed high school as a Presidential Scholar, graduated from Miami University of Ohio and received a Fulbright Scholarship to study in Germany. She has published four books of poems, a collection of short stories, and currently is teaching at the University of Virginia and writing a novel.

311

The Snow King

In a far far land where men are men
And women are sun and sky,
The snow king paces. And light throws
A gold patina[1] on the white spaces
5   Where sparrows lie frozen in hallways.

And he weeps for the sparrows, their clumped feathers:
Where is the summer that lasts forever,
The night as soft as antelope eyes?
The snow king roams the lime-filled spaces,
10   His cracked heart a slow fire, a garnet.[2]

[1] **patina:** a sheen produced on an antique surface by age and use.
[2] **garnet:** used as a gemstone, often dark red.

COMMENTARY AND QUESTIONS

1. How does the poem characterize women? Men? Refer to specific lines.

2. Examine the phrase "lime-filled spaces" (line 9). What does lime look like; what are its properties; and what are its uses? How does its presence affect the poem?

3. Describe the conflict, and explain how the last line climaxes and concludes the poem.

4. How, if it all, could this poem be seen as a vision of the modern world?

Nigger Song: An Odyssey

We six pile in, the engine churning ink:
We ride into the night.
Past factories, past graveyards
And the broken eyes of windows, we ride
5   Into the gray-green nigger night.

We sweep past excavation sites; the pits
Of gravel gleam like mounds of ice.
Weeds clutch at the wheels;
We laugh and swerve away, veering
10   Into the black entrails of the earth,
The green smoke sizzling on our tongues . . .

In the nigger night, thick with the smell of cabbages,
Nothing can catch us.
Laughter spills like gin from glasses,
15   And "yeah" we whisper, "yeah"
We croon, "yeah."

COMMENTARY AND QUESTIONS

1. How, if at all, does the allusion to Homer's *Odyssey* inform the poem?
2. Contrast this poem to "The Snow King." How, if at all, do they complement one another?

The House Slave

The first horn lifts its arm over the dew-lit grass
and in the slave quarters there is a rustling—
children are bundled into aprons, cornbread

and water gourds grabbed, a salt pork breakfast taken.
5   I watch them driven into the vague before-dawn
while their mistress sleeps like an ivory toothpick

and Massa dreams of asses, rum and slave-funk.[1]
I cannot fall asleep again. At the second horn,
the whip curls across the backs of the laggards—

10   sometimes my sister's voice, unmistaken, among them.
"Oh! pray," she cries. "Oh! pray!" Those days
I lie on my cot, shivering in the early heat,

and as the fields unfold to whiteness,
and they spill like bees among the fat flowers,
15   I weep. It is not yet daylight.

[1] **funk:** an earthly quality sometimes associated with the blues.

COMMENTARY AND QUESTIONS

1. How was a house slave's life different from that of a field slave?
2. How does the speaker characterize the "massa," or master, and his wife?
3. Explain the apparent paradox in the last stanza that the "fields unfold to whiteness" but it "is not yet daylight."
4. Why does the speaker weep?

Adolescence—I

In water-heavy nights behind grandmother's porch
We knelt in the tickling grasses and whispered:
Linda's face hung before us, pale as a pecan,
And it grew wise as she said:
5   "A boy's lips are soft,
     As soft as baby's skin."

The air closed over her words.
A firefly whirred near my ear, and in the distance
I could hear streetlamps ping
10 Into miniature suns
Against a feathery sky.

COMMENTARY AND QUESTIONS

1. In what sense is this poem a dramatic "take" or scene?

2. Respond to this statement: "The poem should have ended with 'ear' in line 8. After that point it becomes unrealistic, confusing the reader and losing the effect so carefully created in the first eight lines."

First Kiss

And it was almost a boy who undid
the double sadness I'd sealed away.
He built a house in a meadow
no one stopped to admire,

5   and wore wrong clothes. Nothing
seemed to get in his way.
I promised him anything
if he would go. He smiled

and left. How
10 to re-create his motives,
irretrievable

as a gasp? Where else
to find him, counter-rising
in me, almost a boy. . . .

COMMENTARY AND QUESTIONS

1. What does "almost a boy" mean? Why is it repeated? What do we know about this character?

2. How, if at all, are lines 3 and 4 a metaphor?

3. Why is the image of a gasp appropriate?

4. What do the last two stanzas tell us about the speaker's present attitude toward the person who gave her her first kiss?

Then Came Flowers

I should have known if you gave me flowers
They would be chrysanthemums.
The white spikes singed my fingers.
I cried out; they spilled from the green tissue
5   And spread at my feet in a pool of soft fire.

If I begged you to stay, what good would it do me?
In the bed, you would lay the flowers between us.
I will pick them up later, arrange them with pincers.
All night from the bureau they'll watch me, their
10 Plumage as proud, as cocky as firecrackers.

COMMENTARY AND QUESTIONS

1. Describe the relationship between the speaker and the person who sent the flowers? Note particularly lines 3–5 and 7–10.

2. Why are chrysanthemums appropriate to help express this relationship?

3. What is the implied metaphor in the last two lines and how does it help conclude the poem?

REVIEW

1. Identify and discuss two particularly musical passages from two of Rita Dove's poems. Explain how and why the music is effective.

2. We have noted that Rita Dove presents her dramatic scenes without explaining what these scenes mean. Using one or two poems as examples, comment on the effectiveness of her showing scenes without telling us that to think of them.

3. Write in the style of Rita Dove a poem that captures a moving scene with which most people will identify.

Review of Part Three

1. Identify the influence of each of the following poets on one or more of the poets in Part III: Ralph Waldo Emerson, Walt Whitman, Emily Dickinson, Robert Frost, Wallace Stevens, Ezra Pound, William Carlos Williams, and Langston Hughes.

2. Discuss the similarities between the work of Robert Bly, James Wright, and John Haines.

3. Compare the work of Robert Lowell, Anne Sexton, and Sylvia Plath. Do you think that it is accurate and useful to refer to these poets as confessional poets? Where, if at all, do you detect their influence on other poets?

4. Discuss some ways that American poetry has developed since the first half of this century.

5. Trace views of nature as developed by two or more of the poets in Part III back through Part II to Part I.

6. Supporting your argument with examples from poems by at least three poets from Part III, respond to this statement: "By the second half of the twentieth century, free verse dominated American poetry; and virtually no formal poems of literary merit were written."

7. Write out three of your favorite lines or passages from this book, and explain why they appeal to you.

8. Discuss in some detail your favorite poet in Part III. Then write a poem of eight or more lines in the style of this poet.

A Glossary
of Literary
and Poetic Terms

Glossary terms appearing in definitions are in **bold** type.

Accented (or **Stressed**) **Syllable.** A syllable that is stressed more than its adjacent syllables (see **Meter** for further discussion).

Alliteration. The repetition of identical initial consonant sounds within words that are in close proximity (e.g., Sarah slung the stone).

Allusion. A reference to an earlier literary work or to an historical event.

Anapest (Anapestic). See **Meter.**

Assonance. The repetition of identical vowel sounds within words (e.g., the child is mine).

Ballad. A songlike narrative poem. Originating from the oral tradition, ballads often employ a **refrain** (e.g., E. A. Robinson's "John Evereldown").

Blank Verse. Unrhymed **iambic pentameter** (e.g., Robert Frost's "Home Burial").

Caesura. A pause, usually marked by punctuation, within a poetic line.

Conceit. A surprising, very clever, and elaborately extended metaphor (e.g., Edward Taylor's "Huswifery").

Confessionalism. A term describing the poetry of Robert Lowell, Anne Sexton, Sylvia Plath, and other poets who portray apparently undisguised events and feelings from their private lives.

Connotation. The implied meaning of a word, as opposed to its **denotative** or literal meaning. For instance, the word *chair* can *connote* rest or leisure, while it *denotes* a surface, elevated on legs, on which one can sit.

Consonance. The repetition of final consonant sounds with different final vowel sounds (e.g., fallen upon).

Couplet. A pair of rhyming lines.

Craft. The process that translates feeling, thought, and inspiration into poetry.

Dactyl (Dactyllic). See **Meter.**

Denotation. The literal meaning of a word (see **connotation** for a fuller explanation).

Elegy. A poem that mourns a death (e.g., Roethke's "Elegy for Jane").

End-stop (End-stopped line). To end a line with a punctuation mark, thus calling attention to the line as a structure within the poem.

Enjamb (Enjambment). To carry a thought from one line to the next without the interruption of punctuation, thus making the poem sound more proselike than if the lines were **end-stopped.**

End rhyme. Rhyme coming at the end of lines.

317

Figure of speech (Figurative language). Words that are in some way true, although not literally. To say, "Let's touch base" does not literally mean to touch a base but rather to be sure to remain in communication or in touch. Some common figures of speech are **metaphor, simile, personification, irony, hyperbole, understatement, and paradox.**

Foot. A repeated unit of sound in a poem; the basic element of regular rhythm (see **Meter** for further discussion).

Form. The structure of a poem formed from elements such as **line, foot, rhythm, rhyme,** and **stanza.** Although the word suggests traditional patterns of rhyme and stanzas, all poems possess form. Free verse tends to derive its form from the rhythms of natural speech or patterns of thought.

Formalism (Formal, Formalist). The adherence to traditional poetic forms and conventions.

Half line. A line half the length of adjacent lines.

Heroic couplet. A rhyming **iambic pentameter** couplet (e.g., Bradstreet's "To My Dear and Loving Husband").

Hyperbole (Hyperbolic). A figure of speech that exaggerates what is true (e.g., "You've been on the phone for years!").

Iamb (Iambic). See **Meter.**

Image (Imagery). A description of a sensory impression—a sight, sound, smell, taste, or touch. Note that while **image** normally refers to something visual, in literary terms the word refers to impressions gathered by all five senses.

Imagism (Imagist). Begun by Ezra Pound and then carried on by Amy Lowell and others, this important literary movement emphasized the power of the image or "thing" to convey feeling; economy of language (nothing wordy or flowery); and natural rhythms as opposed to regular patterns (e.g., Ezra Pound's "In a Station of the Metro").

Internal rhyme. Occurs when one or both of the rhyming words comes within the line.

Irony. A figure of speech where what is said or what occurs is the opposite of what is meant or expected. If a family from Georgia plans a summer vacation in Alaska to escape the heat, and the temperature during their visit there never goes below 88 degrees, the effect is ironic. (For another example, see Robert Frost's "Design").

Line. After the word, the poetic line is usually the basic unit of poetry. For centuries poets measured their lines or verses—the traditional term that reminds us of poetry's origins in song—with metrical patterns. In this century poets writing free verse have used other criteria, i.e. the visual effect of the the line's shape on the page or the normal length of a breath. In most cases, however, the line has remained an important element of poetry. Note, for instance, that when poetic lines are too long for the width of the page, the poet usually indents the extra words, showing that the poetic line continues even though the visual line does not (Walt Whitman does this frequently in "Song of Myself").

Line break. The point at which one line ends and the next begins.

Lyric (Lyric poem). A short poem where the speaker expresses his or her feelings or thoughts. It is to be distinguished from the **Narrative poem,** which is longer and tells a story. Originally sung, the lyric poem was accompanied by a lyre, thus its name.

Metaphor. This figure of speech compares dissimilar things directly. When we say, "New York City is the Big Apple," we speak metaphorically. One of the poet's primary tools, metaphor makes the abstract tangible (e.g., Emily Dickinson's " 'Hope' is a thing with feathers").

Meter (Metrical). Meter measures the regular patterns of rhythm, called metrical feet, which are created by the degree to which we accent each syllable. The **iambic foot** (˘ /) is natural to the English language and, therefore, the most common. The following are some other common metrical feet:

		˘ / ˘ / ˘ / ˘ /
iamb (iambic) ˘ /		oc•cur, ho•tel, la•crosse, sin•cere
		˘ ˘ / ˘ ˘ / ˘ ˘ /
anapest (anapestic) ˘ ˘ /		in Ju•ly, on the hill, and a child
		/ ˘ / ˘ / ˘ / ˘
trochee (trochaic) / ˘		bul•let, soc•cer, en•gine, o•pen
		/ ˘ ˘ / ˘ ˘ / ˘ ˘
dactyl (dactyllic) / ˘ ˘		re•cent•ly, love•li•est, in•dus•try
		/ / / / / /
spondee (spondaic) / /		stair•case, hot•head, fence post

The following terms are used to describe the number of feet in a line: monometer (one foot), dimeter (two feet), trimeter (three feet), tetrameter (four feet), pentameter (five feet), hexameter (six feet), heptameter (seven feet), and octameter (eight feet). Thus a line of five iambic feet is called iambic pentameter, three trochaic feet is trochaic trimeter, and so forth.

Note that although the above symbols for accented and unaccented syllables suggest that syllables are either stressed (accented) or not, in fact there are many possible levels of stress. For instance, the *ly* in *recently* is stressed a bit more than the *cent* but less than *re*, and the *est* in *loveliest* is stressed more than the *li* but less than the *love*. The degree of accent, particularly in monosyllabic words, is usually relative to the accent of adjacent syllables. The following line from E. A. Robinson's "Cliff Klingenhagen" is composed in iambic pentameter:

˘ / ˘ / ˘ / ˘ / ˘ /
And when I asked him what the duece he meant

The strongest accents fall, however, on *asked*, *deuce*, and *meant*, while *when* and *what* are accented just enough to continue the poem's iambic rhythm. Poets use the subtle differences in accent to vary rhythms while still keeping to a certain metrical pattern.

Metrical foot. See **Meter** and **Foot.**

Narrative. A story or plotline.

Narrative poem. A long poem that tells a story. To be distinguished from the short lyric poem which expresses the feelings or thoughts of the speaker.

Off rhyme. A rhyme where the final vowel or consonant sounds are not identical (e.g., *stone* and *comb*, *piece* and *race*).

Octave. A stanza containing eight lines.

Onomatopoeia. The technique of using words that sound like their meaning, i.e. thwack, thunk, and pow. Robert Frost employs onomatopoeia in "Mowing," with the use of S's and W's that mimic the sound of a scythe slicing quietly through high grass: "And that was my long scythe whispering to the ground./What was it it whispered? I knew not well myself."

Pentameter. See **Meter.**

Paradox. A figure of speech that makes an apparently contradictory statement that is in some way true. For instance, it is paradoxical to say that the harder one works the less one accomplishes (e.g., line 1 of Richard Wilbur's "A Plain Song for Comadre").

Personification. A figure of speech that gives the qualities of a human to that which is non-human (e.g., the rock laughed, freedom wept).

Quatrain. A stanza containing four lines.

Refrain. A repeated phrase or line (e.g., "Quoth the raven, 'Nevermore' " from Edgar Allan Poe's "The Raven").

Rhyme. Rhymes occur between words when their final vowel sounds and any following consonant sounds are identical (e.g., go and *snow*, *singer* and *ringer*).

Romantic. For our purposes, the word suggests excess, unusual setting and circumstances, often idealized characters and situations that may be exaggerated or idealized, strong emotions, and sometimes adventure.

Sentimental (Sentimentality, Sentimentalism). In this text the word describes a poem that conveys an easily felt emotion, one that moves the reader without extending the reader's understanding of himself and/or of the human condition (e.g., Sidney Lanier's "The Dying Words of Stonewall Jackson").

Sestet. A stanza composed of six lines.

Simile. A figure of speech that compares dissimilar things, usually using *like* or *as* (e.g., His will is like a rotting fence).

Sponde. (Spondaic). See **Meter.**

Sonnet. Originally an Italian form, the sonnet is a fourteen-line poem written in iambic pentameter. The Italian or Petrarchan sonnet contains an octave, which is rhymed a b b a a b b a and followed by a sestet, which is usually rhymed c d c d c d or c d e c d e (e.g., E. A. Robinson's "Reuben Bright"). The English or Shakespearean sonnet contains three **quatrains** and a final couplet, and rhymes as follows: a b a b, c d c d, e f e f, g g. (e.g., Edgar Allan Poe's "Sonnet: To Science). In this century some poets have broadened the definition of the sonnet to simply a fourteen line, unrhymed poem.

Stanza. A unit within a poem, composed of a group of lines which unusally contains a pattern such as the same number of lines and a certain rhyme scheme.

Surreal (Surrealism). The expression of the unconscious in art or poetry through images that alter or distort physical reality (e.g., "The droppings of horses/blaze up into golden stones," from James Wright's "Lying in a Hammock at William Duffy's Farm in Pine Island, Minnesota").

Tercet. A stanza composed of three lines.

Tetrameter. See **Meter.**

Theme. A literary work's central idea.

Tone (Tone of voice, Voice). The tone is not only the attitude of a speaker's voice as it is perceived by the reader but is also the quality that makes a poem sound true, that makes a poem, to use Emily Dickinson's word, "breathe."

Trimeter. See **Meter.**

Trochee (Trochaic). See **Meter.**

Understatement. A figure of speech that represents less than the actual case or circumstance (e.g., The Beatles were somewhat popular.)

Villanelle. A nineteen-line poem written in iambic pentameter and composed of five **tercets** and one ending **quatrain.** Its rhyme scheme is a b a, a b a, a b a, a b a, a b a, a b a a. Th villanelle repeats line 1 in lines 6, 12, and 18, and repeats line 3 in lines 9, 15, and 19 (e.g., Elizabeth Bishop's "One Art").

Voice. See **Tone.**

Index of Poets and Poems

Credits

About the Author

While teaching English at Tower Hill School from 1972 to 1985, Hilary Russell lived in Chester County, Pennsylvania, where he founded the Outland Press, a small press devoted to poetry. During these years he wrote poems that appeared in *Ploughshares*, *The Country Journal*, the *Beloit Poetry Journal*, *Poet Lore*, *The Graham House Review*, and many other magazines and journals. He has read his work at schools, universities, and poetry centers throughout the Northeast. In 1985, after serving for four years as Tower Hill School's English Department Head, Russell joined the faculty at Berkshire School, where he heads the English Department, coaches, and co-edits the *Undermountain Review*, the school's faculty journal. As well as publishing poems and essays, he is the author of *The Portable Writer*, a high school writing text.

Hilary Russell lives in Sheffield, Massachusetts, with his wife, Jenny, and his daughters, Lydia and Caitlin.